SCARS OF WAR

RESEARCH IN POLITICAL SOCIOLOGY

Series Editor: Barbara Wejnert

Recent Volumes:

RESEARCH IN POLITICAL SOCIOLOGY   VOLUME 30

SCARS OF WAR: MIGRATION, SECURITY AND SUSTAINABLE FUTURE

EDITED BY

MARIA ANITA STEFANELLI
Roma Tre University, Italy

AND

IZABELA SKÓRZYŃSKA
Adam Mickiewicz University, Poznań, Poland

United Kingdom – North America – Japan
India – Malaysia – China

Emerald Publishing Limited
Emerald Publishing, Floor 5, Northspring, 21-23 Wellington Street, Leeds LS1 4DL

First edition 2025

Editorial matter and selection © 2025 Maria Anita Stefanelli and Izabela Skórzyńska.
Individual chapters © 2025 The authors.
Published under exclusive licence by Emerald Publishing Limited.

Reprints and permissions service
Contact: www.copyright.com

British Library Cataloguing in Publication Data
A catalogue record for this book is available from the British Library

ISBN: 978-1-83608-509-6 (Print)
ISBN: 978-1-83608-508-9 (Online)
ISBN: 978-1-83608-510-2 (Epub)

ISSN: 0895-9935 (Series)

Printed and bound by CPI Group (UK) Ltd, Croydon, CR0 4YY

INVESTOR IN PEOPLE

CONTENTS

ABOUT THE EDITORS

Maria Anita Stefanelli, a graduate of Ca' Foscari University (Venice, Italy), PhD, University of Edinburgh (UK), former Chair Professor of Anglo-American Literature at Roma Tre University (Italy), Visiting Fellow, Trinity College Dublin (Ireland). She is the Vice President, "World Center for Women's Studies," and served on the bi-national Fulbright Commission for Cultural Exchanges in Rome for nearly 10 years. She has published on twentieth-century modernist American poetry, American Drama, performance theory, cinema. She has authored, in Italy and abroad, essays on gender study: Emily Dickinson (*Women's Studies*, 2002/2011), Anne Waldman (*Donne d'America*, Palermo-São Paolo, 2003), Margaret Fuller (Wisconsin, 2007), Erin Shields (Emerald, 2014), Sofia Coppola (*RSA Journal*, 26/2015), Judith Thompson-Julie Maroh (Mimesis International, Milan, 2017), Maria Edgeworth (Florence, 2019), Marisa Labozzetta (*Marriage and Family Review*, 2021), and Cheril Dunye (*Women on Women*, Milan, 2021). Her publications as a curator-author are *Performing Gender and Violence in Contemporary Transnational Context* (LED, Milan, 2016) and *Bob Dylan and the Arts* (ESL, Rome, 2020).

Izabela Skórzyńska, Associate Professor at the Faculty of History at Adam Mickiewicz University, postdoctoral fellowship at the University of Laval (Quebec, Canada), Vice-President of the World Center for Women's Studies (2024–2025). Author and co-author with C-F. Dobre, A. Wachowiak, B. Jonda, I. Chmura-Rutkowska, E. Głowacka – Sobiech, A. Chwieduk of research projects on the performative memory and didactics of history and the history and memory of women during communism in the light of autobiographical narratives "(Re)gaining the future by (re)building the past: women's narratives of life under communism in Poland, Romania and the former East Germany"; also the place and role of women in the school textbook narratives to history in Poland (women history/gender history).

ABOUT THE CONTRIBUTORS

Liliosa Azara, PhD, teaches Contemporary History and Women's History at the Department of Education, Roma Tre University. Her scientific interests focus on the critical reconstruction of the history of the evolution of sexual habits and prostitution in XX century Italy; her research stands out for a political-institutional approach, as well as a specifically ideological and cultural orientation. On these themes, she has published extensively, including contributions in volumes and scientific journals. Among her latest works: *L'uso "politico" del corpo femminile. La legge Merlin tra nostalgia, moralismo ed emancipazione* (2017) and *I sensi e il pudore. L'Italia e la rivoluzione dei costumi* (1958–1968) (2018). She is now working on the institution of the female police in Italy.

Xingyu Chen, PhD Candidate in Global Gender Studies at the University at Buffalo. Her research focuses on women's health during wars and conflicts in Asia, examining the impacts of military conflicts on maternal health outcomes among Asian countries. She assesses the severity and duration of conflicts in Asia from 1950 to 2010 and analyzes their effects on maternal health indicators. In addition to her research, Xingyu teaches a course on the environmental impact of war, exploring the intersections of women's health, conflict, and environmental issues.

Agnieszka Chwieduk, Associate Professor at the Adam Mickiewicz University, PhD, Philologist (French and Romanian), and Social Anthropologist, works at the Institute of Anthropology and Ethnology of Adam Mickiewicz University in Poznań. She develops her scientific and research interests in three areas: medical/psychiatric anthropology, migration studies, locality and processualism in didactics and qualitative research: performativity, participation, Emic Evaluation Approach, dialogue/negotiation in situations of difficult access to groups (totalizing spaces, small communities). The most recent exploratory experience concerns migration/detention in Guarded Centres for Foreigners in Poland (2018–2019), as part of the project "Spaces of detention: formal, organizational and socio-cultural aspects," while the previous ones were related to the issues of ethnicity, identity, and locality in a unifying Europe, including from the areas of Romania (Maramures), France (Alsace), and Poland. Author and co-author of monographs, numerous articles and review articles, and co-editor of the LUD journal, a leading Polish periodical in the field of ethnology and anthropology.

Cecilia Cinti, an independent scholar, is a graduate in Chinese Language at Oriental Languages and Literature Department, Ca' Foscari, University of Venice, Italy (1996). She holds a Teacher Training Diploma from the Capital

Normal University in Beijing, China (1997), and a certificate of linguistic–cultural mediator (2004). She has competence in language teaching, Italian as a second language, the use of new technologies in language learning, intercultural education, and cultural tourism. Since 2001, she teaches "English language" in a primary school (Comacchio Comprehensive School, Italian Department of Education) and writes periodically in the diocesan weekly "La Voce di Ferrara-Comacchio" on environmental issues, climate change, and the 2030 Agenda Sustainable Development Global Goals.

Weronika Halaburda, Master of Arts, graduate of the Humanities in School at the Faculty of History and Faculty of Polish and Classical Philology at Adam Mickiewicz University in Poznań, teacher of Polish and history at the Social Waldorf School and the Social High School in Wiry; her research interests are emancipatory context, the history of women of "Solidarity" as well as independent education in the broadest sense, including primarily Waldorf pedagogy.

Raffaella Leproni, PhD, English Language and Translation Professor at Roma Tre University, Department of Education. Her didactic activity, held in different curricular and postgraduate courses, develops around storytelling and authentic materials in socio-pedagogic and educational areas dealt with in CLIL perspective. Her research activity focuses on English for Specific Purposes in HR and Social Sciences, teachers' self-assessment and on the analysis of the role of language in the participated construction of intercultural social identity, with a particular attention to Special Education Needs, to stereotypes and bullyism, and to the redefinition of gender perspectives in disciplinary studies. Among her latest publications, *Women on Women. De-gendering perspectives* (FrancoAngeli, 2021), followed by *Men on Women. A collection of thought-provoking perspectives* (FrancoAngeli, 2024), "Still Blundering into Sense." *Maria Edgeworth, her context, her legacy* (R. Leproni, F. Fantaccini eds., FUP 2019).

Muthukuda Arachchige Dona Shiroma Jeeva Shirajanie Niriella, Professor in the Department of Law, Faculty of Law University of Colombo; she serves as the Dean of the Faculty of Criminal Justice at General Sir John Kotelawala Defence University (KDU) in Sri Lanka, holds an LLB with honors, and an MPhil in Law and Criminal Justice from Colombo University. She qualified as an attorney-at-law in 1997; she pioneered the introduction of Criminology and Criminal Justice courses at the postgraduate level in leading Sri Lankan universities, including the Faculty of Law, University of Colombo, Open University, and General Sir John Kotelawala Defence University (KDU) Sri Lanka. She established the first-ever Faculty of Criminal Justice at KDU; she published numerous publications with renowned publishers such as Springer and Routledge-Taylor & Francis, internationally, among other activities and honors; she is the Vice President of the Asian Criminological Society and World Center for Women's Studies.

Jasbir Singh, Professor of Economics in the University of Jammu, Jammu, India. He is currently the Chairperson, Department of Philosophy, at the University of Jammu. He is the Vice President and an Executive Committee Member of the

World-CWS. He has completed eight national projects and has six books and 45 research papers published in national and international journals and edited volumes.

Anupama Vohra, Professor of English in the Directorate of Distance and Online Education, University of Jammu, Jammu, India, and, during 2012–2014, Fellow at Indian Institute of Advanced Study Rashtrapati Niwas Shimla where she worked on Kashmiri Testimonial Literature. Her research areas are Testimonios Literature, Indian Women's Writing in English, Gender Studies, Kashmir/Conflict Literature. She has participated and presented papers at national and international conferences and seminars. She has published three books and 40 papers in reputed journals.

Barbara Wejnert, Professor in the Department of Environment and Sustainability and also a faculty member at the Jaeckel Center for Law, Democracy, and Governing at the University at Buffalo. She is the author or editor of several books, including a book published by Cambridge University Press on *Diffusion of Democracy* (2014). She is an award-winning author of research papers specializing in democracy, politics and energy security, political sociology, environmental sustainability, and gender. Her interdisciplinary, transnational research focuses on the worldwide diffusion of democracy, the rise of autocracy, and the effects of these changes on energy democracy, environmental sustainability, and gender equity.

Soe Win, PhD in Global Gender and Sexuality Studies at the University at Buffalo, The State University of New York. This chapter is an expansion of her dissertation titled, "Women's Participation in the Spring Revolution: Resistance, Resilience, and Solidarity." She considers herself as both an academic scholar and an activist. Her research interests include gender-based violence, women's movement, and women's rights under authoritarian regimes in developing countries, especially in Burma (Myanmar).

Katarzyna Witek-Dryjańska, student at the Doctoral School of Humanities at Adam Mickiewicz University in Poznań; her interests include history of education, intercultural cemeteries as places of memory, and the history of education as the crisis of materiality after World War II in Poland.

FOREWORD

Maria Anita Stefanelli and Izabela Skórzyńska

The history of wars, just like contemporary armed conflicts in Syria, Ukraine, Congo, Haiti, Palestine, and other places in the world (Comfort & Atwood, 2024), is arranged, in the post-Anthropocene era, in many different, sometimes contradictory or ambivalent but also full of hope, narratives (Szerszeń, 2024).

That is because they are characterized by a wealth of theoretical, ethical, and aesthetic approaches thanks to which ancient and contemporary wars are understood in terms of not only generalized politics, military violence, and diplomacy but also social and climatic injustices seen from the perspective of failed and/or unfinished great modernization projects, including decolonization and emancipation of women and children, migrants and refugees, inhabitants of Central and Eastern Europe in relation to the former USSR, and the global South in relation to the global North.

The pressing problems of the present and expectations for the future, as perfectly expressed in the title of this volume *Scars of War: Migration, Security and Sustainable Future*, concern what people have actually been experiencing for decades that were affected by wars, rebellions, uprisings, and coups. And everything took place, I must add, under the increasingly scorching sun of an overheated planet impoverished by war and tormented by the excessive consumerism of some against the poverty of others.

In November 2022, a few months after the Russian attack on Ukraine, a report was prepared on the "Climate costs of the Russian invasion" (Lipiński, 2022) with an indication of CO_2 emissions related to the concentration, movement, and maintenance of Russian armed forces, as a result of the destruction of the Russian and Ukrainian heavy equipment; as a result of fires, including forest and farmland fires, oil and gas, and leakage of gas pipelines; and, finally, as a result of forced migrations in addition of the climate costs and benefits of rebuilding the Ukrainian economy using renewable energy sources (Lipiński, 2022). Someone will say that such a report is premature, that the war is still ongoing, but don't we need such a diagnosis to formulate plans and recommendations for the future *now*?

Besides the above, social changes – the forced migrations of women and children, the costs of helping refugees and the social reality (still poorly recorded) of women's and men's everyday care for them in the face of the loss of their current positions and statuses in the face of an uncertain future – go along with the huge price of wars.

Those and other aspects of contemporary armed conflicts require, as highlighted in this volume, not only a reflection on the future but also a revision of our ideas about the past. Few people remember that during World War I and II, everyday life continued thanks to the involvement of women who developed priceless survival strategies that proved efficacious also in the war-ravaged areas of hunger, cold, homelessness, and disease. Until recently, little attention was paid in popular history to human efforts to restore ecosystems that might satisfy hunger in times of severe food shortages.

From the perspective of the present and the future, the issues identified above are invaluable indications not only of the destructive power of war, which affects, besides the environment, the people and their culture, but also the wish – despite the pain, the fear and the uncertainty – to imagine that the future would be different. There is a paradox in the fact that for centuries it was dictators and aggressors who shaped our human and nonhuman space of experience defined by wars and conflicts, while ordinary people and their efforts for harmony and peace were forgotten. And yet, thanks to these efforts, life after the war was possible to be rebuilt. This is a question of the tension between the space of experience and the horizon of expectations, and the burning question is who and what decides the nature of this tension? (Koselleck, 2001, pp. 359–388). Whether arising from the experience of war, fear, uncertainty, and helplessness in the face of the evil that contributed to this war, or the memory of the human capacity for sustainable development and peaceful coexistence. The last word should not belong to the aggressors, but to people of good will, truly concerned about the fate of the world for themselves and their successors. If this sounds like an utopia, let's at least avoid dystopia.

I.S.

As the North and South of the world have been – and are still being – invaded by weapons that brought death and devastation, in Rome – as I hear at this precise moment on TV (Benigni Roberto, 2024) – 70,000 children from all over the world are leaving the Olympic Stadium after their meeting with the Eminent old man who dresses in white, saying goodbye, and promising to come back in September for a renewed claim for peace. A guy (Oscar winning Roberto Benigni with his film "La vita è bella"), invited to syntonize the children with the Pope, told it right: "When children play 'war', as soon as one of them gets hurt, they stop. The game is over. So why, when adults wage war, don't they stop to help? Why? What cowardice is that? Wars must end."

In spite of the promised efforts toward a cease-fire, with the Russian President's peace terms being subjected to the recognition of four southeastern regions (Donetsk, Luhansk, Zaporizhzhia, and Kherson) as a permanent part of Russia, peace does not appear to be imminent. As Barbara Wejnert points out in her central chapter, then, autocracy diffusion has produced "a destructive effect on global peace and environmental protection" as derived by "the impact of democracy erosion." The consequences of such *diktat* are the downfall of temporary migrants', refugees', and asylum-seekers' hopes to return home. Compensations for that in terms of waiting patiently, socializing with the local community, practicing, or turning to, art and beauty – as I put it in my chapter focusing on a mother and child as refugees in Italy – will be to almost no avail for yourself and, if you are a mother, your progeny, until indefinite time. On this last point, the "ethics of care and justice," derived from an anthropological perspective, can come to rescue, but – as Skórzyńska and Chwieduk advise in their chapter – only as a disciplinary field to be reconsidered by students.

Education is an important sector for us to evaluate when we think of the need to realign the North and South of the world. Not surprisingly, it was Eleanor Roosevelt who, back in 1949, coined the slogan "Making human rights come alive" thus opening the UNESCO path toward the abolishment of gender discrimination and women's empowerment. "Women must not be left behind," she preached then; along the same lines today women must be granted access, as Leproni and Azara insist, to information technologies, a move vital in the efforts to prepare for the war and postwar diplomacy.

Memoirs and diaries are examined in four chapters dealing with different geographical areas. Witek-Dryjańska explores the work of women who, in the years between 1945 and 1956, organized the unfamiliar spaces of "Recovered territories" in Poland after the war. Halaburda, on another level, presents Ewa Zydorek's important role in the "victory of democratic opposition and socio-political transformation in Poland after 1989" as results of the activism of the "Independent Self-Governing Trade Union 'Solidarity'."

Away from the European interest, a study from 1950 to 2010 concerning Asia was undertaken by Chen who authored "a comprehensive examination of the dynamics" of conflicts dating to that period and, by means of a statistical analysis, presents "essential information on the duration and intensity of conflicts" during the era under consideration. The war in Burma and its impact on women's lives is the subject chosen by Win to focus her attention on the 2021 coup that "led to devastation and destruction in ethnic regions. ... gender-based violence and human trafficking." The chapter highlights "the women's involvement in political movement for peace, democracy, security, and sustainable development." Focusing on India, Vohra and Singh explain that, founded by the British rulers on the ruins of the Sikh Empire following the first Anglo-Sikh war, Jammu and Kashmir came into existence in 1846. The dominions, who desired to be independent, tried to resist belonging to India or Pakistan, so they were offered to the British as replacement for taxes. Jammu and Kashmir kept the existing system of political control, economic, and social arrangements. Immediately after independence, however, the Kabaili (tribal) invasion in October 1947, instigated and supported by the newly created Pakistan, changed the scenario. Kashmiri Pandits initially resisted exodus; later, Maharaja Hari Singh agreed to join India to save the lives of the people from brutality. Kashmiri Pandits form a unique religious and cultural minority in Kashmir; they were the largest, non-Muslim, religious minority in Kashmir before 1990. Vohra and Singh also analyze Rahul Pandita's childhood narrative, "Our Moon Has Blood Clots," a poignant narrative of pain, loss and survival.

Last but certainly not least, Niriella's investigation "of the effectiveness of existing legal instruments in safeguarding the rights and well-being of women and girl children" amidst noninternational armed conflicts is a judicial must. The author asks if "the mechanisms to address the protection of women and girl children" in noninternational conflicts can be enforced, which "strategies and reforms can enhance the efficacy of the international legal framework" in dealing with the vulnerabilities of the subjects, and which are the challenges involved. After examining Geneva Conventions, Optional Protocol II, Rome Statute, Convention on Certain Conventional Weapons (CCW), CEDAW, CRC, and the Beijing Platform, the author concludes that by implementing the proposed recommendations, the protection mechanisms for women and girls in noninternational armed conflicts can be strengthened, ensuring better adherence to international standards and improved outcomes for affected individuals – women and girl children.

M.A.S.

REFERENCES

Benigni Roberto. (2024). World's Children Day. RAI 1 Live, May 26, at about 6.30 p.m.
Comfort, E., & Atwood, R. (2024). *10 conflicts to watch in 2024*. International Crisis Group. https://foreignpolicy.com/2024/01/01/conflicts-2024-gaza-sudan-china-iran-myanmar-ukraine-ethiopia-sahel-haiti-armenia-azerbaijan-iran-hezbollah/
Koselleck, R. (2001). Przestrzeń doświadczenia i horyzont oczekiwań – dwie kategorie historyczne [The space of experience and the horizon of expectations – Two historical categories]. In H. Orłowski (Ed.), *Semantyka historyczna* [*Historical semantics*] (Trans. Kunicki, W., pp. 359–388). Poznań.
Lipiński, K. (2022). *Koszty klimatyczne rosyjskiej inwazji* [*Climate costs of the Russian invasion*]. Polski Instytut Ekonomiczny.
Szerszeń, T. (2024). Nie ma jednego obrazu wojny [There is no single image of war]. https://dzieje.pl/wywiad/tomasz-szerszen-nie-ma-jednego-obrazu-wojny-w-ukrainie

CRISSCROSSING WAR AND PEACE, DEMOCRACY AND AUTOCRACY VIEWED THROUGH AN ENVIRONMENTAL LENS

Barbara Wejnert

University at Buffalo, State University of New York, USA

ABSTRACT

The Ukrainian conflict, a real-world case study, vividly illustrates the threat autocratic regimes pose to democratic systems on a global scale, symbolizing a battle between freedom and authoritarianism. It is a stark reminder of the destabilizing effects of the spread of autocracy. This trend has replaced the previous wave of global democratic expansion and puts international peace and ecological sustainability at risk. Through a meticulous and comprehensive examination of contemporary autocratic rise, this study presents compelling evidence that clarifies the harmful outcomes of democratic erosion in emerging autocracies and their negative influence on global peacekeeping efforts and environmental preservation initiatives. In essence, this research study underscores the complex interplay between conflict and harmony and the dynamics of autocratic proliferation and democratic decline, all of which collectively shape the landscape of global security and environmental sustainability initiatives.

Keywords: Autocracy; democracy; war; peace; environmental sustainability; environmental politics; sustainability

INTRODUCTION

Commencing with the forceful Russian invasion of Ukraine in February 2022, a wave of alarming headlines flooded both American and global media platforms, including newspapers, news outlets, and magazines. These media outlets played a crucial role in unveiling the harsh realities of the invasion's brutality amidst a

Scars of War
Research in Political Sociology, Volume 30, 1–19
Copyright © 2025 Barbara Wejnert
Published under exclusive licence by Emerald Publishing Limited
ISSN: 0895-9935/doi:10.1108/S0895-993520250000030001

backdrop of Russian propaganda aimed at creating uncertainty about the state of hostilities. Despite claims from Russian sources of a halt in military actions, reputable journalistic entities like the BBC continued to report sustained bombardments on urban centers such as Kyiv, Kharkiv, and Chernihiv and rural communities. This narrative was further substantiated by firsthand accounts, including that of Chernihiv's mayor, who described the assault as "colossal" in its intensity.

Additionally, as the Director-General of the World Health Organization, Dr Tedros Adhanom Ghebreyesus underscored in his interview with the BBC international media on March 30, 2022, the indiscriminate nature of the violence and war's impact includes vital healthcare infrastructure, hospitals, and maternity wards. Notably, the timing of these attacks contradicted official Russian claims of de-escalation. The resumption of bombings shortly followed Russian assurances of military restraint.

Regardless of the massive force of 180,000 troops, convoys of tanks and artillery, surrounding and attacking Ukraine on three sides, Russia's plan to speedily roll over Ukraine did not materialize. Ukraine withstood, and two years later, it is withstanding Russian attacks. Ukrainians responded with courage and firm conviction that victory would prevail, defending their land and pushing back Russian troops toward the Ukrainian–Russian border. As the war continues, the Russian limitless bombing of schools, places of worship, hospitals, daycares, theaters, and residential buildings leaves remnants of homes, pain, and Ukrainian and global rage on its path of destruction. The broad use of landmines, attacks on nuclear power stations, and the use of cluster ammunition banned by the international community are striking reminders of the ruins of agricultural fields, forests, and clean water and air. The scares of this war are human casualties monumental for Ukraine and sobering reality manifested in the ongoing destruction endured by the country and its people.

Psychological warfare, through the spread of misleading claims of bombing reduction and propaganda about Ukraine's military and government corruption, aimed at weakening the Ukrainian determination, and Western allies military support augmented the velocity of civilian infrastructure destruction. Regardless of these efforts, brave Ukrainian civilians sign up for military duties, and women, from young girls to grandmothers, assist the men in combat. Millions of women and children initially immigrated to avoid bombing. However, after the first year of war, many returned and mobilized beyond the battlefield, providing logistics and noncombat support to defend their country. The civilians keep the economy growing despite the relentless Russian bombing; they rebuild services, including the energy sector and civilian infrastructure. In 2022, an article published in *Politico* journal specifies that residential buildings are uninhabitable because of Russia's military bombing (Banco et al., 2023). It attests that Putin's war is a war against the people, a war aimed at annihilation of Ukraine as it did not surrender to the Mighty Russia. This war is waged against civilians, with women and children paying a massive price for it. Already, it has destroyed nearly 70% of Ukrainian civil infrastructure. The invasion cost is global hunger, with food prices jumping to a six-year high (increasing by 92 points to 108 pts on the FAD

Food price index), as reported by the World Bank in 2022 (World Bank, 2022). Especially African countries, where 30% of wheat comes from Ukraine and Russia, suffer dire consequences.

For Ukrainians, it is a war for survival as a nation, a sovereign state, and a democracy against autocratic occupation. As the US National Public Radio reported on March 15, 2022, it is a clash of freedom vs tyranny (Gross, 2022). The attack on Ukraine galvanized countries in the defense of democracy worldwide. In the epic vote at the United Nations General Assembly on March 2nd, 2022, as many as 141 out of 193 assembly members denounced Russia for the attack on Ukraine. Only four countries, namely Belarus, Eritrea, North Korea, and Syria, voted against Russian condemnation. Authoritarian China was one of the 35 UN assembly members that abstained from voting on the resolution of Russian condemnation. The four UN members who voted against the resolution were countries with autocratic regimes, ruling with an iron fist against their people, aiding each other in aggressive tactics. All these autocracies suffer economic stagnation, high unemployment, and limited development and use the war as a job opportunity for their young men. Enlisted to fight in Ukraine received circa $7,000 for deployment, about the same as ISIS paid its soldiers (International Crisis Group, 2017). Among the enlisted are also Indian, Nepalese, and Sri Lankan nationals who are forced to serve in the Russian military invasion, being caught as illegal labor migrants (International Crisis Group, 2017).

The unleashed Russian military aggression represents not merely a brutal invasion but also a political struggle for democratic principles, national sovereignty, and independence. It serves as a sad reminder of the inherent peril autocratic regimes pose to democratic nations and the threat posed by autocracies to democratic states. The invasion of Ukraine is a symbolic reminder of the danger that autocrats pose to democracies worldwide. It is also a juxtaposition of democracy vs autocracy. The passed UN resolution attests to global solidarity in standing for peace, further verifying the conflict between democratic and autocratic values.

Eighty years of peace, cooperation, and prosperity in Europe have been ruined because of Russian aggression. In the past two years, Europe has focused its development on militarization, changing peace production to armaments, technological advancement, and innovation aimed at prosperity to countries' arms manufacture. It took only one autocrat's selfish desires to inflict intractable pain, destruction, and fear and to destabilize the world order. Since the end of Second World War, the European continent has symbolized a continent of unity, peace, cooperation, and thriving democracies. However, the pause on militarization is over, and the arms race between democratic and autocratic worlds restarted after prolonged demilitarization.

Autocratic Russia destroyed the peace. However, the Russian government falsely claims that its aggressive invasion is a war of Ukrainian liberation from the influence of Western tyranny, and the Russian government is supposedly a liberator of occupied Ukraine, its ethnic "brother" facilitating Ukrainian eagerness to join Mother Russia. Misleading propaganda failed. Russia is unable to be victorious as the West provides help. It is plausible that Russia, with the help of

Iran, attempted to divert global and Western ally attention from the war in Ukraine and helped to provoke a new war in Gaza. Inevitably, Russia would like to sidetrack global attention and reduce Western help in Ukraine.

Despite various attempts, Ukrainians' fight for national identity and the heroic defense of Ukrainian land continues; Western countries continue to provide military and humanitarian aid to prevent Russia from further escalation of the war. The prior Russian invasion of Ukraine in 2014 was met with a lack of Western support for Ukraine, leading to the annexation of Crimea and persistent war conflict in the Donbas and Luhansk regions, and is a reminder of the costs of Western democracies' inaction.

Prior events signaled a Russian attempt to incorporate Ukrainian land into Russia. It has been demonstrated since the start of the independent Ukrainian state in 1991 when 90% of Ukrainians from across the country voted for independence and a democratic political system. The call was repeated in 2014 (the year of the Euromaidan Revolution) and during the Orange Revolution of 2004 in response to Russian meddling in Ukrainian elections and spreading anti-Ukrainian propaganda (Wejnert, 2020, pp. 185–198). These events signaled Ukraine's upcoming defense of its national identity, sovereignty, and democracy, reminding the Western world that helping a fledgling democracy leads to autocracy inhibition and establishes peace.

This paper underscores the crisscross of war and peace, the diffusion of democracy countering autocracy diffusion, which shapes the world's security and environmental sustainability. It is a striking reminder of the danger diffusing autocracy poses to global peace and cooperation when replacing the prior trend of global democracy diffusion (Wejnert, 2014).

GLOBAL DEMOCRACY EROSION AND AUTOCRACY DIFFUSION

In contrast to the rapid increase of worldwide democratization at the end of the 20th century, where the number of democracies reached 79% of the existing 167 sovereign countries, in the 21st century, democracies are in steep decline. In the first 15 years of the new Millennium, democracies significantly decreased from 79 to 67% of all sovereign states (Wejnert, 2021). The strength of democracies also decreased, which is most commonly assessed on a scale of 0–10, with 0 meaning nondemocracy and 10 fully developed democratic systems (V-dem, 2021; Wejnert, 2014). Simultaneously, the number of autocratic regimes has surged, marking a striking reduction in the opportunities for global societies to live in a democratic system. Between 2010 and 2020, as V-dem Institute reports, within the first two decades of the 21st century, the number of people living in autocracies increased from 48% to 68% of the global population (V-dem, 2021), while the portion of the global population living in democracies declined from 52% to 32% within the same period. Freedom House Institute confirms these findings (Freedom House, 2020). The author's research on a global democratic regression, demonstrated in Fig. 1.1a and b, which extend prior discussions (Wejnert, 2020,

2021), also confirms the reduction of the number and strength of worldwide democracy.

Subsequently, as Fig. 1.1a and b reveal, democracy has a lengthy history. Nonetheless, the average level of worldwide democratization has weakened since 2008. In weakening democracies, elected leaders often embraced authoritarianism, the process called autocratization (Geddes et al., 2018), passing reforms, laws and policies limiting civil rights and civil society to control political power (Economy, 2022; Xia, 2021). With democratic regimes, autocratization, democratic norms, and political behaviors erode. Other changes include constrained individual freedoms, political appointment of judgeships that facilitated a decline in the impartiality of the judiciary system, limiting public trust in the rule of law, limiting freedom of the press, and constraints of the education system (Economy, 2022; Xia, 2021). In waking democracies, elected political leaders engage in sidelining, bribing, and silencing their political opposition from the mature US democracy to the relatively young postcommunist and postcolonial democracies (Applebaum, 2020; Levitsky & Ziblatt, 2018).

Several analyses devoted to the regression of democracy attempt to examine the causes of these changes, pointing to growing politics of supportive conditions for the global autocratic surge. Among the more crucial are the internal, domestic conditions within individual countries in the aftermath of democratic elections, when election losers refuse to concede power to incoming elected leaders and coordinate and lead democracies to fall (Huggard & Kaufman, 2021; Levitsky & Ziblatt, 2018; Przeworski, 2019). This process starts with growing intolerance, societal divisiveness, and disrespect for democratic values. It often stems from preexisting socioeconomic conditions, intense economic difficulties, and unmet needs of large portions of societies. Political instability and populism, at times verging on authoritarianism, become a more likely outcome (Huggard & Kaufman, 2021; Wejnert, 2020), and democratically elected government members use populist rhetoric to introduce antidemocratic behaviors and principles, initiating democratic decline and autocracy rise (Bauer & Becker, 2020; Markoff, 2013; Przeworski, 2019).

The world's population was exposed to such conditions at the start of the new millennium in the early 2000s, especially since the 2008 global economic crisis. The globalization of the market economy and related loss of industrial jobs due to automatization and industry relocation to less developed regions of an inexpensive labor force produced massively disfranchised populations in well-developed economies. For example, with the outsourced industrial jobs, the US industrial workers lost not only their jobs but also the dignity and pride associated with them, explained Williams (2016). Disfranchised populations succumb to extremism, conspiracy theories, and, most importantly, rapidly spreading anti-democratic populism, marked by global societal division and mistrust of governing regimes. These changes prepared a foundation for the rise of antidemocratic forces and led to the global erosion of support for democratic tolerance and collaboration. The profound decline of support for democratic values was associated with the progressive attrition of key democratic institutions

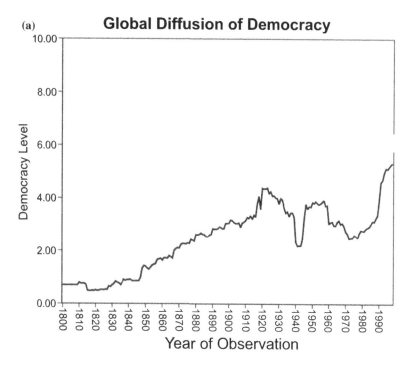

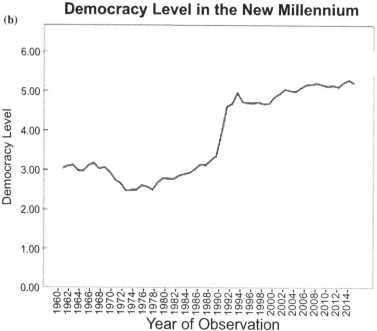

Fig. 1.1. Crisscrossing Diffusion of Democracy and Autocracy. (a) Democracy diffusion (1800–1998). (b) Democracy regression in the new millennium (1960–2015). *Source*: Modified figures from the author's prior work: (a) Wejnert (2014) and (b) Wejnert (2021). *Note*: The estimated democracy values on a scale of 0–10 were obtained using the database *Nations, Democracy and Development: 1800–2005* (Wejnert, 2007). Fig. 1.1b depicts the current work on extending this database to 2021 for use in the proposed project on democracy retrenchment and the rise of autocracy.

Table 1.1. Autocratic Behaviors Manifested by Democratically Elected Leaders in Eroding Democracies.

1	Losers Refuse to Accept Legitimate Elections (Pemstein et al. (2021)
	Pack courts with loyalists to the ruling regime – the practice of court-packing (Huggard & Kaufman, 2021)
2	Following populist's rhetoric, portray partisan rivals as criminals to disqualify them from political participation (Mollan & Geesin, 2020; Johnson, 2019)
3	Endorse or fail to condemn the violent behaviors of their supporters (Mollan & Geesin, 2020)
4	Support laws and policies that restrict civil liberties (Karolewski, 2020)
5	Appeal to violence to secure own power (Moffitt, 2016)
6	Restrict criticism of the ruling government (Cianetti et al., 2019).
7	Restrict freedom of independent press (Przeworski, 2019)
8	Undermine legitimate election if they lose the election (Przeworski, 2019)
9	Take legal or other punitive action against criticism of the government by media, civil society, or rival parties (Cianetti et al., 2019; Karolewski, 2020; Przeworski, 2019)
10	Praise repressions used by other authoritarian governments (Mollan & Geesin, 2020)

Note: Table constructed by the author based on literature review.

and a steady weakening of norms of democratic governing, facilitating an autocracy surge.

Elective leaders engage in autocratic behaviors to hold onto power after lost elections, as shown in Table 1.1.

Reduce justice, abstraction of law, and difficulty punishing regime members' corruption assisted the progressive autocratization of democratically elected leaders (Table 1.1). Elected state leaders slowly embraced more forms of autocratic governing. Illiberalism started to undermine democratic values, including support for human rights, tolerance, and diversity, preventing support for justice, checks and balances on the executive branches of government, and presidents. Although illiberalism and democracy erosion occur nationally, the "autocratization" of democratically elected leaders (Geddes et al., 2018) spills over to other countries in a process resembling autocracy's global diffusion. The diffusion process augments democratic weakening due to leaders' autocratization and adds another pathway of democratic regression.

The diffusion process encompasses adopting practices or behaviors by social institutions or other social or political entities (like individuals, social groups, or countries), where the adopters follow models and behavioral patterns of other social actors, organizations, national parties, or political regimes (Wejnert, 2005, pp. 55–56). Even though the diffusion studies began with a classic Book on *The Laws of Imitation* (Tarde, 1903), the development of this approach did not occur until Ryan and Gross (1943) published results on the spread of hybrid corn use among Iowa farmers 40 years later. Only recently, however, published important work on diffusion by Rogers (2003) initiated a surge of research focusing on the diffusion of social movements and political changes (Givan et al., 2010; Kneuer & Harnisch, 2016, pp. 548–556; Lee et al., 2011, pp. 444–544; Wejnert, 2014), farming and agribusiness (Mardiana & Kembauw, 2021, online), new technologies and market strategies (Wejnert, 2018), and political reforms and policies(Darian-Smith, 2022).

In the diffusion process, communication factors alter the plausibility of adopting a behavior or action by a political or social entity undertaking a similar action or practice following established patterns (Rogers, 2003; Starr, 1991; Wejnert, 2023). Amidst varied applications, a broad concept of diffusion evolved from the original diffusion views that required direct contact between prior and potential adopters to subsequent perspectives invoking additional diffusion modes. For instance, Rogers, in his classic definition, proposed a more general approach by defining diffusion as "[...] a process by which an innovation is *communicated through certain channels* over time among members of a social system" (Rogers, 2003, p. 5) or "...process by which institutions, practices, behaviors, or norms are transmitted between individuals and between social systems" (Starr, 1991, p. 359). Rogers himself clarified the process of diffusion by (a) distinguishing transmitters from adopters, (b) identifying classes of adopters based on the temporal rate of adoption (i.e., innovators, early adopters, early majority, late majority, and laggards), and (c) analyzing communication channels and specified conditions under which diffusion occurs. Consecutive studies have questioned the classic distinction between innovators and adopters and the roles of innovation and imitation in the diffusion process, arguing that adopters become innovators and vice versa.

This chapter, devoted to the worldwide rise of autocracy, approaches diffusion as a contributing factor to the erosion and weakening of democracy. It attempts to uncover possible examples of diffusion processes enhancing democracy backsliding and shows how and when democratic leaders imitate or adopt anti-democratic practices. To simplify the analysis of the diffusion of antidemocratic behaviors, this paper analyzes democratically elected leaders mimicking other leaders in backsliding democracies. Country leaders who imitate others are considered the followers being subjected to antidemocratic behaviors or rhetoric. The role modelers initiating antidemocratic practices are considered the initiators in the process of diffusion of autocracy. Both innovators and adopters constitute vital components of the rise of autocracy.

THE ILLUSTRATION OF THE DIFFUSION OF AUTOCRACY AND EROSION OF DEMOCRACY

According to Carter (2012), autocracies model each other and form alliances and networks of Like-Minded Groups and do not act alone. Formed networks provide legitimacy and justification for anti-democratic practices and endorsed values (Cianetti et al., 2019). For example, the initially democratically elected but autocratizing regime of Hungary and its Prime Minister, Viktor Orbán, was followed by Donald Trump, the prior president of the US Just like Orbán, Donald Trump accepted the far-right ideology endorsing the far-right groups and pushing the US into the proautocratic direction (Mollan & Geesin, 2020; New York Times, 2022). The prior US president also emulated Viktor Orbán's suppression of the free press and independent media broadcasting. The same practices of curbing press and media independence were copied by Poland and Serbia, which, like Hungary, are new democracies formed in the prior communist countries after the fall of the Soviet Union (Mollan & Geesin, 2020).

In Hungary, Victor Orbán, to hold into power, massively appointed judges in national and regional courts loyal to his agendas, the practice called court packing. Court-packing in a democratic country is a pre-step for democracy's regression since independent courts are essential for upholding a democratic constitution, ensuring the separation of executive and judicial powers, and implementing checks and balances on presidents and governing regimes. Substantial court-packing affects numerous democratic governing practices, signaling the rise of democracy regression and the increase in autocracy. Unsurprisingly, mandating sitting judges' earlier retirements, Orbán appointed new courts that supported his regime's proposal to change constitutional election rules. The new rule allowed Orbán to stay in office beyond the elected term. This anti-democratic model was replicated by the Polish president, who also issued a mandatory early retirement of judges by lowering the retirement age of Supreme Court Justices from 70 to 65 in 2018. This practice put 27 out of 72 sitting Supreme Court Justices at risk of being forced to retire, weakening the Polish rule of law and attacking judicial independence (Przeworski, 2019). The court-packing practice also took place in the US during the prior presidency, helping the former US President Trump to personalize his power. Moreover, the democratically elected head of the state of Turkey politically appointed judges to prevent the execution of justice and punishment for his obstruction of justice, tax evasion, and corruption.

Court-packing allows democratically elected state leaders to embrace authoritarian practices that curb human rights and citizens' freedoms. The classic example is the reversal of the half-century-old American reproductive rights law of Roe vs Wade by the conservative, loyal to former President Trump Supreme Court judges, with three out of seven Supreme Court judges appointed by Trump (the typical court-packing). The new law restricts or bans and criminalizes abortion in most American states. A similar law was enacted by Polish courts packed with loyalist judges during the prior presidency of Duda and his ruling party of Law and Justice (PiS). In Polish courts, newly appointed, conservative judges passed laws banning and criminalizing abortion in 2020 and limiting the reproductive rights Polish women enjoyed during communism and most of the post-communist period. The former Polish president Duda modeled his decision on Hungarian policies, further reinforced by growing limitations on the reproductive rights of women in the US.

Two democratic postcommunist countries of the Eastern European region – structurally similar and geographically proximate, modeled on Trump's anti-immigration stance and his promise to build a wall protecting the US southern border from crossing by undocumented immigrants. The restrictive anti-immigration policy established by the Hungarian government has been replicated by Polish policy (Applebaum, 2020, pp. 50–51). As European Union

(EU) countries, Poland and Hungary diverged from the general mandate of the EU (Reuters, 2021).

When democracy regresses, it also diffuses anti-democratic rhetoric. Trump's populist-like behaviors and rhetoric inspired other political leaders in democracies. For example, French presidential candidate Marine Le Pen accelerated attacks on ethnic and religious minority groups as well as the LGBTQ community, frequently using the political slogans and phrases used by then-U.S. president Trump (Applebaum, 2020; Ciobanu, 2021). The persistent lies and the aggressive, offensive language used by Trump helped Bolsonaro to use the same language during his political rallies, establishing a new form of acceptable communication in political debates. Institutionalized also a "mediatization" of politics, a form of direct communication of political leaders with followers broadly using media and social media and celebrity-like strategy to propagate agenda and increase the ranks of their followers (Economy, 2022, pp. 52–67; Xia, 2021, pp. 78–96). According to Moffitt (2016, p. 70 and 83), a new form of communication is broadly used by populist and authoritarian-like democratically elected leaders of states and governments.[1] For example, Georgia Meloni, the far-right politician and elected Prime Minister of Italy, copied such rhetoric. Mimicking antidemocratic leaders in faulting democracies, she presented her political agenda as standing against the establishment and for the disdained by the elite, forgotten underdog. She appealed to violence to defend these groups' rights, just like other leaders of failing democracies refused to condemn the violence of the extremists, e.g. Trump, Orbán, or Brazilian President Bolsonaro (Harlan, 2022).

Others soon replicate the prejudicial behavior and antiminority rights policies of one political leader. Subsequently, newly appointed judges in Poland and Hungary passed anti-LGBTQ laws, with Hungarian anti-LGBTQ laws copied by Polish laws. To further limit the rights of LGBTQ, both countries silenced LGBTQ activism (Human Rights Watch, 2022). Encouraged by acceptance of the anti-LGBTQ rights in Poland and Hungary, the prior president, Trump, issued an executive order of an anti-LGBTQ child welfare policy at the dusk of his term, copying a similar law passed by the Hungarian court (Cook, 2020).

The diffusion of autocratic behaviors also includes the refusal to accept election results by losers of the election. For example, when former US President Trump refused to accept the election results and incited the January 6, 2021, insurrection against the US Capitol, it set a precedent for other democratically elected leaders unwilling to concede power after losing elections. A notable instance is the January 2023 storming of Brazil's capital and Presidential Palace, incited by former President Jair Bolsonaro, who, after losing the presidential election, refused to cede power to his successor, President Luiz Inácio Lula da Silva. Bolsonaro's supporters, driven by his rhetoric, stormed the capital in an attempt to overturn the election results, mirroring the events at the US Capitol. Significantly, prior to this, Bolsonaro's son visited Trump and his advisors in Florida, suggesting that Trump's actions and strategies may have influenced Bolsonaro.

Following his electoral defeat, former Brazilian President Jair Bolsonaro refused to acknowledge the transition to President Luiz Inácio Lula da Silva. This refusal to recognize a legitimate change in leadership reflects broader authoritarian tendencies seen globally. In Turkey, President Recep Tayyip Erdoğan demonstrates similar autocratic behaviors, including the imprisonment of journalists, suppression of the free press, and labeling of opposition figures as "terrorists." During the 2023 election cycle, Erdoğan imprisoned Istanbul's mayor, Ekrem İmamoğlu, in December 2022, curtailing political rivalry through coercive means. Such actions parallel those of Belarusian autocratic leader Alexander Lukashenko, who falsified election results to secure his victory and used brutal force to quell protests demanding the integrity of the electoral process. These instances collectively illustrate a recurring strategy among authoritarian leaders who, when democratically elected, undermine democratic norms and maintain power through coercive and repressive means.

Significantly, democratic governments leaning towards autocracy have also amended school curricula to control the education of future generations. Restriction on science-driven and fact-driven knowledge and replacement of university administrations with appointed loyalists have been tiptoeing across the Eastern European higher education milieu since the early decade of the new millennium (Applebaum, 2020, pp. 49–54). Similar restrictions are imposed in selected conservative states of the US. The single-term presidency of Donald Trump did not result in significant changes to school curricula across the entire US. However, the appointment of a Trump ally as Secretary of Education laid the groundwork for potential educational reforms. Trump also advocated for expanding private educational options, referred to as "choice schools," while simultaneously proposing to diminish the role and funding of public schools. His administration proposed budget reductions for the US Department of Education by 13.5% in 2018, 5% in 2019, 10% in 2020, and 7.8% in 2021, enlarging the educational gap between privileged and less advantaged social strata in America and deepening social inequality (Lee, 2020).

An attempt to curb educational freedom was also observed in Poland, where in 2018, the democratic government of Poland, under President Andrzej Duda, sought to implement stringent regulations on the higher education system. The proposed reforms aimed to exert greater control over state-run universities, which are noted for their superior undergraduate and graduate programs compared to private institutions. The plan included appointing university councils composed of individuals lacking academic qualifications or affiliations tasked with overseeing curriculum reforms. According to Ciupka's (2018) report, the countrywide protests of students supported by university faculty members eventually forced the government to withdraw such a proposal.

Eroding democracies embolden autocrats by (1) offering examples of the seeming sameness of democracy and autocracy when rights and freedoms are restricted and political opponents are attacked and jailed during elections, (2) when elected democratic leaders praise authoritarian leaders' repressions of citizens' rights (Mollan & Geesin, 2020), and (3) when democratic countries support autocrats' policies, like Hungary supports Putin's agenda, voting against EU military support for Ukraine fighting the Russian invasion. In faulting democracies, it is common for presidents to display sympathy towards or express admiration for authoritarian leaders. Examples include the Hungarian leader's visit to Moscow following the Russian invasion of Ukraine. President Trump praised Philippine dictator Rodrigo Duterte and made favorable remarks about North Korean leader Kim Jong Un (Silva, 2018, p. 1). His admiration of autocrat Putin and China's leader Xi Jinping has been globally noted (Hamburger et al., 2016, p. 1) and so were his friendly meetings with turning authoritarian Brazilian President Bolsonaro.

The autocratization of democratic government emboldens autocratic politics and allows autocratic regimes to impose external pressure on democracies to accelerate democratic erosion (PCRCI, 2021). Regional democratic institutions often successfully challenge the impact; however, pressure applied through member states via bilateral connections is usually adequate to weaken democracies, especially in countries with strong Far-Right or Far-Left political parties that, together with Far-right members of parliament, help to channel authoritarian goals (PCRCI, 2021). Moreover, the influence of autocracies is exacerbated when duly elected democratic leaders endorse far-right ideology (Mollan & Geesin, 2020).

DIRE CONSEQUENCES OF AUTOCRACY DIFFUSION: ENDANGERED WORLD PEACE AND ENVIRONMENT

Consequences for Peace

Research shows undisputably that the rise of autocracy endangers world peace, showcased by the described in this paper's Russian invasion of Ukraine. In contrast to autocracies, democracies are rarely involved in wars and even less likely to be engaged in wars with other democracies. Democratic leaders are accountable to voters able to vote them out of office for unpopular decision-making and hence are selective about the wars they initiate or are engaged in (Tangerås, 2009). Hence, democracies rarely initiate wars and are called powerful pacifists. When democratic leaders engage in war, they tend to form overwhelming countercoalitions against expansionist autocracies and are more likely to win wars (Lake, 1992). The exceptions are democracies in the transitional phase of democratization, i.e. countries that transition from autocratic to democratic systems. Transitional democracies are more aggressive and war-prone, fighting wars with democratic states (Mansfield & Snyder, 2012). According to Mansfield and Snyder (2012), a classic example is Russia, a formally authoritarian state that rapidly transitioned from total autocracy to extensive mass democracy with rising democratic participation. Such countries are about twice as likely to fight wars in the decade after democratization as states that remained autocracies. The history of the Russian invasion of Georgia, followed by the annexation of Ukrainian Crimea and Donetsk, followed by the Russian full military invasion of Ukraine, proves that the authors were correct.

At the same time, the likelihood of autocracies initiating war is high, with the highest possibility of an autocracy attacking another autocracy (Tangerås, 2009). As Lake (1992) explains, autocratic regimes must control society to remain in power. Since social control costs are high, autocracies that govern without public consent are more expansionist and, in turn, war-prone. These states fight wars not only with autocracies but also with democracies.

Consequences for Environment

In addition to the threat to global peace, the rise of autocracies also endangers the environment. Research demonstrates that political institutions matter regarding official policies, laws, and regulations that protect environmental sustainability (Wilson, 2019). Autocratic "Chinese and Russian leaders did not even bother attending the U.N. climate summit in Glasgow, Scotland, in 2021," writes K. Roth in a recent issue of the *Foreign Affairs* journal (2022). It is broadly assumed that democratic governments are responsible for mitigating environmental degradation and disaster outcomes because they aim to protect citizens' health and well-being and guarantee environmental sustainability. However, scholarly discourse remains divided on the comparative efficacy of democracies versus autocracies in addressing environmental challenges and meeting the needs of citizens amidst environmental crises. This chapter contributes to this debate with three primary sets of arguments.

The first argument asserts that autocratic regimes are more effective in addressing environmental issues due to their centralized authority and the ability to impose control policies swiftly. Autocracies can curb overconsumption and pollution, while concerns about economic growth and private interests constrain democracies. This viewpoint, supported by environmentalists and economists such as William Ophuls (1977) and Paul Ehrlich (1968), gained prominence in the 1970s. Advocates claim that autocracies, compared to democracies, exhibit greater efficacy in managing societal overconsumption, pollution, and unrestrained population growth, collectively referred to as the "limits of growth." Centralized authority, authoritarian decision-making processes, and the imposition of control policies enable autocracies to swiftly and efficiently address issues such as the "tragedy of the commons," as delineated by Garrett Hardin (1968), thereby averting ecological calamities. According to Hardin, rational resource use at the individual level often leads to collective irrationality, where shared resources are exploited until depletion. Autocratic governments, through coercion, can implement regulations and taxes to curb consumption and pollution, thereby offsetting environmentally destructive practices of businesses and private consumers. In contrast, democratically elected leaders, beholden to their electorates, are less inclined to enforce stringent limitations. Consequently, environmental protection efforts in democracies are often impeded by the pursuit of economic growth, with profit-driven private enterprises hindering the implementation of effective environmental conservation measures in the absence of centralized political authority (Schweickart, 2010).

In contrast, the second argument suggests that authoritarian regimes typically do not prioritize environmental conservation efforts (Payne, 1995). Historical examples such as the Soviet Union, Putin's Russia, and Nazi Germany are often cited as instances of environmental negligence and abuse (Laakonen et al., 2019). Robert Wilson (2019) asserts that studying history can provide insights into the potential social ramifications of authoritarian environmental injustices. Studying Nazi Germany, the Chinese Mao period, the Stalin period in Russia, and other authoritarian regimes, he concludes that since citizens in autocratic countries had fewer political tools to influence government practices if doing so ran counter to the regimes' goals. Hence, severe environmental crimes like deforestation, pollution, or species depletion cannot be prevented in autocracies.

Hence, proponents argue democratic governance is better suited for environmental stewardship (Winslow, 2005). Margrethe Winslow (2005) provides empirical evidence supporting this claim, demonstrating a correlation between democracy and urban air quality. Using regression analysis on urban air pollutant concentrations – specifically sulfur dioxide (SO_2), suspended particulate matter (SPM), and smoke – and democracy metrics of the Freedom House Index and Polity III, Winslow finds a robust negative relationship: higher levels of democracy correspond to lower ambient pollution levels. Furthermore, democratic systems tend to adapt and learn from policy experiences in other democracies (Povitkina, 2018). Consequently, Freedman et al. (2005) argue that democratic governance enhances environmental protection by establishing regulatory frameworks and legislation, including measures to limit CO_2 emissions, enact clean water regulations, and safeguard residents' safety during environmental disasters and postdisaster recovery.

According to the *third set of arguments*, the support for the pros or cons of environmental protection is ambiguous, and neither democracy nor autocracy could be considered the sole supporter of the environment. When Freedman et al. (2005) and Hochstetler (2003) conducted comparative analyses of environmental protection legislation and practices in Eastern European and Latin American countries during transitions from autocracy to democracy, they found that both systems, to some degree, protected the environment. In Latin America, national environmental agencies were established before democratization, but robust and enduring policies were developed in the postdemocratic transition. For instance, in Brazil, the environmental agency's staff grew from three employees in 1973 to 6,000 by 1989 following democratization. Similarly, Chile witnessed substantial growth in its environmental agency post-transition in 1990, with personnel increasing from 6 to 4,758 and the budget rising from $76,000 to $21 million by 2000 (Freedman et al., 2005). The authors concluded that democratic regimes exhibit more effective environmental protection practices and legislation than authoritarian counterparts. In communist Eastern Europe, governments designated significant portions of land as pristine nature reserves, implemented forest protections, and initiated control over water and air pollutants. At the same time, the Eastern European region, governed by communist governments, was the most polluted region of Europe.

In autocracies, society actors can devise strategies to circumvent imposed regulations in specific autocratic regimes. Teets (2017), in his examination of contemporary Chinese policymaking, contends that civil society can influence and challenge strict regulations enacted by authoritarian governments. Teets illustrates how, in China, stringent rules aimed at controlling civil society, such as mandatory registration of civil organizations with a supervisory agency, inadvertently provided these organizations with a channel to access policy-makers. Consequently, in autocracies alike in democracies, civil society groups are the strong holders and the spokespersons for the environment, able to advocate for and effectuate policy changes, including governmental responses to environmental disasters, pushing the limits of governmental response to disasters (Wejnert, 2021).

Comparing the above investigations, both autocratic and democratic regimes are engaged in environmental protection. Nonetheless, democracy seems to be a superior environmental caretaker because it responds to citizens' demands (see Tables 1.2a and 1.2b).

Table 1.2a. Effect of Autocracy versus Democracy on the Environment.[a]

Political System	Positive Effects	Negative Effects
Autocracy	Robust response to limits of growth: Overconsumption, overpopulation (Ophuls, 1977)	Symbolically protect the environment (Freedman et al., 2005; Hochstetler, 2003)
	One-person/small group decision making	Do not develop environmental laws.
	Centralized power, easy to impose control (Ehrlich, 1968)	Environmental degradation is unchallenged & and unpunished (Payne, 1995)
	Regulate businesses to offset environmental degradation (Teets, 2017)	Autocracies are environmental criminals (Laaksonen et al., 2019)
	Central mitigation of climate change (Beeson, 2017)	
	Respond to environmental disasters by establishing law and order (Wejnert, 2021)	

Notes: Autocracy is the superior caretaker for the environment.
[a]Tables 1.2a and 1.2b were created by the author based on a literacy review.

Table 1.2b. Effect of Autocracy versus Democracy on the Environment.[a]

Political System	Positive Effects	Negative Effects
Democracy	Respond to voters and improve environmental regulations (Winslow, 2005)	Democratically elected leaders concerned with winning elections will not impose environmental control (Schweickart, 2010)
	Establish protective environmental laws (Freedman et al., 2005)	Protection is determined by the corruption of the democratic regime (Povitkina, 2018)
	Commitment to climate change mitigation, enlarge environmental protection agencies (Freedman et al., 2005)	Social justice unaddressed "sacrifice zones" (*The Ecologist*, 2010)
	Propose the inclusion of the roots of social inequality in environmental solutions (Ryder, 2017)	Political institutions matter for environmental protection (Wilson, 2019)
	Respond to environmental disasters by providing restoration assistance (Wejnert, 2021)	

Notes: Democracy is the superior caretaker for the environment.
[a]Tables 1.2a and 1.2b were created by the author based on a literacy review.

CONCLUSION

In the current climate of the Ukrainian war, crisscrossing war and peace, democracy and autocracy, is more than evident. At present, a critical juncture necessitates concerted efforts to counter the persistent menace posed by autocratic regimes to global security, sustainable development, and environmental well-being. In light of Russia's ongoing, unwarranted aggression, it is imperative to study the evolving autocratization of countries to mitigate the continuation of peace and environmental sustainability. Central to the agenda of global leadership is the imperative to translate peace and development initiatives into comprehensive strategies to foster sustainable coexistence among nations. International political leaders should also encourage leaders in democracies and autocracies alike to respect and honor the aspirations of citizens who seek to influence the course of their countries, particularly in pursuing and constructing a sustainable global future.

NOTE

1. This type of communication "uses spectacles and performances, derogatory language, and inflammatory comments . . . and celebrity-like strategy to propagate agenda" (Moffitt, 2016, p. 70). Such populist politicians "simultaneously embrace limits on freedom of the press" (Moffitt, 2016, p. 83).

REFERENCES

Applebaum, A. (2020). Twilight of democracy. In *The seductive lure of authoritarianism*. Doubleday.

Banco, E., Graff, G., Seligman, L., Toosi, N., & Ward, A. (2023, February 24). Something was badly wrong: When Washington realized Russia was actually invading Ukraine. *Politico*. (article 1, online). https://www.politico.com/news/magazine/2023/02/24/russia-ukraine-war-oral-history-00083757

Bauer, M. W., & Becker, S. (2020). Democratic backsliding, populism, and public administration. *Perspectives on Public Management and Governance*, 3(1), 19–31. https://doi.org/10.1093/ppmgov/gvz026

Beeson, M. (2017). Coming to terms with authoritarian alternative: The implications and motivations of China's environmental policies. *Asian and the Pacific Policy Studies*, 5(1), 34–46.

Carter, B. L. (2012). Unite and rule. A theory of compulsory elite social networks in autocracies. In *APSA 2012 Annual Meeting Paper*. https://ssrn.com/abstract=2105386

Cianetti, L., Dawson, J., & Hanley, S. (2019). *Rethinking "democratic backsliding" in central and Eastern Europe*. Routledge.

Ciobanu, C. (2021, June 10). *Polish ruling party's education reform: God and Country*. Balkan Investigating Reporting Network. Reporting Democracy. https://balkaninsight.com/2021/06/10/polish-ruling-partys-education-reforms-god-country/

Ciupka, M. (2018). This is our space. *Students at Polish universities unite in protest against new higher education reform*. Political Critique. Krytyka Polityczna & European Alternatives. http://politicalcritique.org/cee/poland/2018/polish-reform-higher-education-gowin-protest/

Cook, C. (2020). Trump signs anti-LGBTQ child welfare executive order. *Lambda Legal (online)*. https://www.lambdalegal.org/blog/20200630_trump-admin-child-welfare-executive-order?gclid=CjwKCAiAvK2bBhB8EiwAZUbP1N5-edDezn3JD5lyHthSYtxqssYNTbToOSpH7unY7-UXeH-Y8z35BoC5uYQAvD_BwE

Darian-Smith, E. (2022). *Global burning. Rising antidemocracy and climate change*. Stanford University Press.

Economy, E. (2022). Xi Jinping's new world order. *Foreign Affairs, 101*(1), 52–67.

Ehrlich, P. (1968). *The population bomb*. Ballantine Books.

Freedman, E. J., Hochstetler, K., & Clark, A. M. (2005). *Sovereignty, democracy, and global civil society: State–society relations at UN world conference*. State University of New York Press.

Freedom House. (2020). *Freedom in the world 1994-2020*. Electronic manuscript. Freedom House. www.freedomhouse.org/template.cfm?page=363&year=2020

Geddes, B., Wright, J., & Frantz, E. (2018). *How dictatorships work. Power, personalization, and collapse*. Cambridge University Press.

Givan, R. K., Roberts, K., & Soule, S. (2010). *The diffusion of social movements. Actors, mechanisms, political effects*. Cambridge University Press.

Gross, T. (2022, March 15). Former Ambassador Marie Yovanovitch warns Putin will move west if he wins in Ukraine. *NPR Fresh Air News*. https://www.npr.org/2022/03/15/1086427993/marie-yovanovitch-ukraine-ambassador-lessons-from-the-edge

Hamburger, T., Helderman, R. S., & Birnbaum, M. (2016). Inside Trumps financial ties to Russia and his unusual flattery of Vladimir Putin. *Washington Post*. https://www.washingtonpost.com/politics/inside-trumps-financial-ties-to-russia-and-his-unusual-flattery-of-vladimir-putin/2016/06/17/dbdcaac8-31a6-11e6-8ff7-7b6c1998b7a0_story.html?utm_term=.1e96c2c47830. Accessed on June 17, 2016.

Hardin, G. (1968). The tragedy of the commons. *Science, 162*(3859), 1243–1248.

Harlan, C. (2022, November 4). In the midterm, Trump Republicans look to Georgia Meloni as a model for success. *The Washinton Post*. https://www.washingtonpost.com/world/2022/11/04/giorgia-meloni-trump-right-maga/

Hochstetler, K. (2003). Fading green: Environmental politics in the Mercosur free trade agreement. *Latin American Politics and Society, 45*(4), 349–371. https://doi.org/10.2307/3177129

Huggard, S., & Kaufman, R. (2021). *Political economy of democratic transitions*. Princeton University Press.

Human Rights Watch. (2022). *Poland: Rule of law harms women and LGBT people*. https://www.hrw.org/news/2022/12/15/poland-rule-law-erosion-harms-women-lgbt-people?gclid=CjwKCAiA2fmdBhBpEiwA4CcHzYJiZQPoZebHJ8PIzTYkbXunsdvoyFv0tWlgCBmBsxr0HDZLQUoQIhoCE5AQAvD_BwE

International Crisis Group. (2017, July 24). *How the Islamic state rose, fell, and could rise again in Maghreb*. Report 178/Middle East & North Africa. Crisis Group.

Johnson, R. (2019). *Children of the dream: Why school integration works*. Basic Books.

Karolewski, I. P. (2020). Towards a political theory of democratic backsliding? Generalizing the East-Central European experience. In *Palgrave studies in European Union politics* (book series) https://link.springer.com/content/pdf/10.1007%2F978-3-030-54674-8.pdf

Kneuer, M., & Harnisch, S. (2016). Diffusion of e-government and e-participation in democracies and autocracies. *Global Policy, 7*(4), 548–556. https://doi.org/10.1111/1758-5899.12372

Laakonen, S., Tucker, R., & Vuorisalo, T. (2019). *The long shadows: A global environmental history of the Second World War*. Oregon State University Press.

Lake, D. A. (1992). Powerful pacifists: Democratic states and war. *American Political Science Review, 86*(1), 24–37. https//doi.org/10.2307/1964013

Lee, T. (2020, September 17). Comparing Trump and Biden's K-12 education plans. *American Action Forum*. https://www.americanactionforum.org/insight/comparing-trump-and-bidens-k-12-education-plans/

Lee, Ch, Chang, K., & Stokes Berry, F. (2011). Testing the development and diffusion of E-government and E-democracy: A global perspective. *Public Administration Review, 71*(3), 444–544.

Levitsky, S., & Ziblatt, D. (2018). *How democracies die*. Crown.

Mansfield, E. D., & Snyder, J. (2012). Democratization and war. In R. K. Betts (Ed.), *Conflict after the cold war* (Vol. VII, pp. 380–393). https://doi.org/10.4324/9781315664484

Mardiana, H., & Kembauw, E. (2021). Earth environmental science. IOP Conference Series (Vol. 755, p. 012074). *Annual Conference on Health and Food Science Technology*, November 25, 2020, Yogyakarta, Indonesia. https://doi.org/10.1088/1755-1315/755/1/012074

Markoff, J. (2013). Democracy's past transformations, present challenges, and future prospects. *International Journal of Sociology, 43*(2), 13–40.

Moffitt, B. (2016). *The global rise of populism. Performance, political style, and representation.* Stanford University Press.

Mollan, S., & Geesin, B. (2020). Donald Trump and Trumpism: Leadership, ideology, and narrative of business executive turned politician. *Organization, 27*(3), 405–418. https://doi.org/10.1177/1350508419870901

New York Times. (2022, January 3). Trump endorses Viktor Orban, Hungary's far-right prime minister. Online. https://www.nytimes.com/2022/01/03/us/politics/trump-endorses-viktor-orban-hungary.html

Ophuls, W. (1977). *Ecology and the politics of scarcity: Prologue to a political theory of the steady state.* W. H. Freeman.

Payne, R. A. (1995). Freedom and the environment. *Journal of Democracy, 6*(3), 41–55. https://doi.org/10.1353/jod.1995.0053

PCRCI. Political Capital. (2021). *The specter of authoritarian regimes is haunting Europe.* Political Capital Research and Consulting Institute- PCRCI Report. https://www.ned.org/democracy-research-news-September-2021/

Pemstein, D., Marquardt, K. L., Tzelgov, E., Yi-ting, Wang, Medzihorsky, J., Krusell, J., Miri, F., & von Römer, J. (2021). V-dem Institute. V-dem working paper series 2021, 21. https://www.v-dem.net/media/publications/Working_Paper_21.pdf

Povitkina, M. (2018). The limits of democracy in tackling climate change. *Environmental Politics, 27*, 411–432. https://doi.org/10.1080/09644016.2018.1444723

Przeworski, A. (2019). *Crises of democracy.* Cambridge University Press.

Reuters. (2021). Hungary to defy the EU Court ruling over the immigration policy, Orban says. https://www.reuters.com/world/europe/hungary-defy-eu-court-ruling-over-migration-policy-orban-says-2021-12-21/

Rogers, E. M. (2003). *Diffusion of innovations.* Free Press.

Roth, K. (2022). How democracy can defeat autocracy. *Foreign Affairs.* https://foreignpolicy.com/2022/01/13/how-democracy-can-defeat-autocracy

Ryan, B., & Gross, N. (1943). The diffusion of hybrid seed corn in two Iowa communities. *Rural Sociology, 8*, 15–24.

Ryder, S. (2017). A bridge to challenging environmental inequality: Intersectionality, environmental justice, and disaster vulnerability. *Social Thought and Research, 34*, 85–115. https://doi.org/10.17161/1808.25571

Schweickart, D. (2010). Is sustainable capitalism possible? *Procedia Social and Behavioral Sciences, 2*(5), 6739–6752. https://doi.org/10.1016/j.sbspro.2010.05.020

Silva, D. (2018, April 30). Trump on North Korea's Kim Jong Un: 'He's a pretty smart cookie'. *NBC News.* https://www.nbcnews.com/politics/donald-trump/trump-north-korea-s-kim-jong-un-he-s-pretty-n753006

Starr, H. (1991). Democratic Dominos. Diffusion approaches to the spread of democracy in the international system. *Journal of Conflict Resolution, 35*, 356–381.

Tangerås, T. P. (2009). Democracy, autocracy, and the likelihood of international conflict. *Econ Gov, 10*, 99–117. https://doi.org/10.1007/s10101-008-0055-6

Tarde, G. (1903). *The laws of imitation.* Hold.

Teets, J. (2017). The power of policy networks in authoritarian regimes: Changing environmental policy in China. *Governance. An International Journal of Policy, Administration, and Institutions, 31*(1), 125–141.

The Ecologist. (2010, September 10). Privileged opposition holding back wind farm development. https://theecologist.org/2010/sep/10/privileged-opposition-holding-back-wind-farm-development. Accessed on September 10, 2021.

V-dem. (2021). *V-Dem dataset v 11.1.* Compiled by Coppedge M., Gerring J., Knutsen C. H., Lindberg S. I., Teorell J., Alizada, N., ... & Ziblat, D. Variety of Democracies.

Wejnert, B. (2005). Diffusion, development, and democracy, 1800–1999. *American Sociological Review, 70*(1), 53–81.

Wejnert, B. (2007). Database Nations, democracy and development: 1800–2005. Inter-university Consortium for Political and Social Research.

Wejnert, B. (2014). *Diffusion of democracy. Past and future of global democracy.* Cambridge University Press.

Wejnert, B. (2018). Democratization, globalization, and women's empowerment: A critical review and conceptual framework. *European Journal of Social Sciences (EJSS), 1*(1), 20–32. https://doi. org/10.29198/ejss1805

Wejnert, B. (2020). Populism, democracy, and the Ukrainian uprisings of the Orange revolution and Euromaidan. In A. Ron & M. Nadesan (Eds.), *Mapping populism: Approaches and methods* (pp. 185–198). Taylor & Francis Group.

Wejnert, B. (2021). Educating on democracy in a time of environmental disasters. *London Review of Education, 19*(1), 1–16. https://doi.org/10.14324/LRE.19.1.30

Wejnert, B. (2023). The tenets of Trumpism and the assault on American and global democracy. In A. Akande (Ed.), *US democracy in danger: The American political system under pressure (Ch. 3,* pp. 53–75). Springer Studies on Populism, Identity Politics and Social Justice. Springer Nature Switzerland.

Williams, J. (2016, November 16). What so many people don't get about the U.S. working class. *Harvard Business Review.*

Wilson, R. (2019). Authoritarian environmental governance: Insights from the past century. *Annals of the American Association of Geographers, 109*(2), 314–323.

Winslow, M. (2005). Is democracy good for the environment? *Journal of Environmental Planning and Management, 48*(5), 771–783. https://doi.org/10.1080/09640560500183074

World Bank. (2022, December 6). *Local and global economic impact of the war in Ukraine.* https://www. worldbank.org/en/events/2022/12/06/local-and-global-economic-impacts-of-the-war-in-ukraine

Xia, C. (2021). The party that failed: An insider breaks with Beijing. *Foreign Affairs, 100*(1), 78–96.

"WOMEN MUST NOT BE LEFT BEHIND": THE UNESCO PATH TOWARDS WOMEN'S EMPOWERMENT

Raffaella Leproni and Liliosa Azara[1]

Roma Tre University, Italy

ABSTRACT

This proposal aims to retrace the efforts of the international community in defining and implementing the "functional education," allowing women to access the necessary knowledge and competences to stimulate the socioeconomic development, combat the effects of conflicts on their empowerment, and become protagonists of the transition to the digital era. Education and training become the privileged field for international confrontation on gender equality, resulting in a commitment to grant equal opportunities in education and training as an intrinsic right of women. In a diachronic perspective, however, despite the positive afflatus of the first attempts, a substantive approach centred on the individual's capacity to access rights, resources, services and technologies is only later envisaged, which then finds a new definition in the concept of capability approach. *UNESCO's dedication to abolish gender discrimination in accessing education in its different grades and fields (adopted as a case-study) makes it apparent that in the colonial and postcolonial era, the commitment of the international community has been directed to sustain equal access for women to all grades and modes of education, within the wider and more complex frame of*

---

[1]R. Leproni wrote the Introduction, sections "Education and Training as Battlegrounds for Gender Equality," "The Commitment of the International Community in the Colonial/Post-Colonial Era: Eleanor Roosevelt's Audacious Vision," and the Conclusions; L. Azara wrote sections "Competing on Equal Footing in Future Professions: UNESCO and National Governments' Role in Reducing the Digital Divide Through the Decades" and "A Further Step Ahead: The Learning Cities Concept".

Scars of War
Research in Political Sociology, Volume 30, 21–46
Copyright © 2025 Raffaella Leproni and Liliosa Azara
Published under exclusive licence by Emerald Publishing Limited
ISSN: 0895-9935/doi:10.1108/S0895-993520250000030004

promoting gender equality and women's empowerment. Today, Eleonor Roose-velt's slogan Making Human Rights Come Alive *(Columbia University, 1949) has become one of the guiding principles of the 2030 Agenda and of its development goals.* Women must not be left behind*: women must be granted equal access to technology education, where they must be able to compete with men for future professions, through policies, strategies, and programmes aiming to reduce/delete digital divide adopted by national governments.*

Keywords: UNESCO; women education for empowerment; gender equality; technology; digital divide; women in conflict

INTRODUCTION

In the contemporary global landscape, the role of women in socioeconomic development is undeniably crucial. However, at the joints of the web of progress and development, certain pivotal questions emerge, demanding attention and introspection. Among these questions, one stands out prominently: what factors have shaped and continue to shape women's access to information and communication technology (ICT), a linchpin for fostering the socioeconomic development imperative for bridging the gap between the North and South of the world?

This inquiry examines the complex interplay between gender, technology, and development, necessitating an analysis of the existing obstacles that hinder women's access to the digital domain. Additionally, it examines some of the repercussions of historical prejudices embedded in educational policies and programs, contributing to the stark under-representation of women in specific fields crucial to the ongoing industrial revolution. Embarking on this exploration, the many and diverse layers on which women's empowerment is (supposedly) built become apparent, underlining the urgency of facing and dismantling obstacles that have persistently held women back from harnessing the full potential of ICT and participating equitably in the transformative processes shaping our world.

It becomes more and more evident that women encounter a myriad of barriers in accessing ICT, ranging from sociocultural norms that dictate gender roles to economic disparities that limit educational opportunities. Discrimination within workplaces and insufficient representation in decision-making positions further exacerbate these challenges. Unpacking these barriers is essential for formulating effective strategies to dismantle them. Even education, often heralded as a beacon of empowerment, can paradoxically be a source of perpetuating gender biases, as educational policies and programs have, at times, reinforced stereotypes, channeling women away from certain fields deemed "male-dominated." Examining the biases embedded in educational systems greatly helps to understand and possibly rectify the under-representation of women in strategic fields vital to the ongoing industrial revolution.

HISTORICAL PERSPECTIVES ON WOMEN AND TECHNOLOGY

To comprehend the contemporary challenges faced by women in accessing ICT, a retrospective analysis of historical factors is needed. The intersection of gender norms and technological advancements throughout history has influenced women's participation in the digital sphere and contributed to prevent a consistent realigning the North and South of the world. From the Industrial Revolution to the Information Age, women's involvement in technological fields has undergone an intermittent evolution, where societal expectations and stereotypes have played a significant part in framing women's roles and opportunities.

During the Industrial Revolution, as societies transitioned from agrarian economies to industrialized structures, women found themselves at the nexus of shifting norms. Educational opportunities for women during the early stages of the Industrial Revolution were often limited: formal education was not widely accessible for them, especially in higher education; societal norms and expectations dictated that women's primary role was in the domestic sphere, and education was sometimes considered unnecessary beyond basic literacy and numeracy (see Taylor & Knott, 2005). Despite these constraints, the 19th century saw the emergence of movements advocating for women's education: pioneering individuals and organizations began to push for expanded educational opportunities for women; some religious institutions and philanthropic organizations established schools for girls, providing them with basic education.[2] While the prevailing narrative reinforced gender roles, some women broke through societal expectations, engaging in professions traditionally dominated by men, as was the case of women employed in textile mills and artisanal workshops, who challenged stereotypes and demonstrated the adaptability of women in the face of economic transformations. Factories, particularly textile mills, employed a considerable number of women during this period. In the United Kingdom (UK), policymakers also started to consider women's working conditions: the Factory Acts of the early 19th century in the UK aimed to regulate working conditions, including those for women and children; while these acts were primarily concerned with working hours and conditions, they indirectly contributed to the recognition of women as a part of the industrial workforce. In France, women were involved in various artisanal and craft workshops in urban areas, contributing to the economy and challenging traditional gender roles. While the Napoleonic Code, established in the early 19th century, reinforced patriarchal norms, it also granted women certain property rights, providing some legal recognition. In Russia, where peasant women traditionally played essential roles in agricultural labour, the transition to industrialization saw some women moving to urban areas to work in factories. In the Soviet era, policies aimed at achieving gender equality were implemented; women were encouraged to participate in the workforce, receive education, and pursue professional careers. In Germany, Italy, and other countries, as industrialization progressed, women increasingly found employment in factories, challenging conventional gender roles.

The industrialization era coincided with the first wave of feminism in the US Women such as Susan B. Anthony and Elizabeth Cady Stanton (1815–1902) advocated for women's rights, including the right to work and access to education. Catherine Beecher (1800–1878), an American educator and author, advocated for women's education in the United States during the 19th century. She emphasized the importance of education for women in various fields, including teaching and domestic science. Beecher's work influenced the establishment of women's seminaries and teacher training schools (Woody, 1929; Seller, 1989).

As the world entered the World Wars Era, women's roles in the workforce expanded due to the absence of men in various industries. This period marked a temporary shift in perceptions, as women took on nontraditional roles, including those in technological and manufacturing sectors. However, these opportunities were often circumscribed by wartime exigencies, and the postwar period witnessed a resurgence of traditional gender norms in many countries. Recent conflicts have marked a dangerous reawakening of such perceptions, which not only hinder the full participation of women in the active citizenship of the 21st century but also impede the realigning the north and south of the world, as well (or as bad) as peaceful coexistence and safety. The effects of the ongoing conflicts will be long-lasting in terms of school drop-outs and the deskilling of women's labour.

The advent of the Information Age in the mid-20th century brought about unprecedented technological advancements, accompanied by both opportunities and challenges for women. Initially, women played determining roles as computer programmers and operators, contributing significantly to early developments in computing.[3] However, as the field gained prestige, a marked gender divide emerged, perpetuated by societal expectations and reinforced stereotypes, mostly relegating women to the peripheries of the burgeoning tech industry.[4] To contrast this tendency, amid the Second Wave Feminism of the 1960s and 1970s, concerted efforts were made to dismantle barriers hindering women's participation in STEM fields. Advocacy for equal opportunities in education and the workplace gained momentum, yet systemic challenges persisted. The Dot-com Boom and subsequent bust in the late 20th century marked another inflection point, showcasing the industry's rapid growth but also laying bare persisting gender disparities.

In the 21st century, the digital divide and challenges related to access and representation persist, influencing women's participation in the digital sphere. Contemporary initiatives focus on dismantling barriers through education, mentorship, and altering workplace cultures.[5] Despite strides towards inclusivity, women continue to face obstacles, and the path toward equitable participation in technology fields remains an ongoing endeavor, underscoring the need for comprehensive and sustained efforts to redefine gender dynamics in the evolving landscape of the Information Age.

FUNCTIONAL EDUCATION: AN ESSENTIAL ELEMENT IN OVERALL DEVELOPMENT

The concept of functional education is one of the responses envisaged by policymakers at worldwide level to foster equal empowerment opportunities; the international community has been long working in defining and implementing it, specifically focusing on how it enables women to access the necessary knowledge

and competences to stimulate socioeconomic development and become protagonists of the transition to the digital era:

> [Functional literacy was accepted] as an essential element in overall development, closely linked
> to economic and social priorities and to present and future [man]power needs. [The delegates]
> accepted the new concept of functional literacy, which implies more than the rudimentary
> knowledge of reading and writing that is often inadequate and sometimes chimerical. Literacy
> instruction must enable illiterates left behind by the course of events and producing too little, to
> become socially and economically integrated in a new world order where scientific and
> technological progress calls for ever knowledge and specialization. (UNESCO, 1965, p. 29)

The quote from the World Congress of Ministers of Education in 1965 in Teheran
underscores the evolving nature of education, emphasizing the shift from a basic
understanding of reading and writing to a more dynamic concept – functional
education. This novel approach to education surpasses the mere acquisition of
rudimentary skills, recognizing the inadequacy of traditional literacy in a world that
demands continuous adaptation to scientific and technological progress. In the
context of functional education, illiteracy is not just a lack of basic skills; it represents
an exclusion from the broader socioeconomic landscape (on the definition of functional literacy and its relevance in education, see Bhola, 1965).

Over the decades, the international community has recognized the critical role
of functional education in shaping a sustainable future. Efforts have been dedicated to defining and implementing functional education, focusing on providing
individuals, particularly women, with the knowledge and competences necessary
for active participation in the rapidly evolving global landscape in different
perspectives.

One key objective of functional education is to empower individuals with the
skills needed for meaningful participation in the workforce. For women, historically marginalized in various societies, functional education becomes a gateway
to economic independence; by offering comprehensive knowledge and practical
competences, functional education equips women with the tools to contribute
significantly to the socioeconomic development of their communities and nations,
breaking down barriers and challenging traditional gender roles, fostering an
environment where women are not just passive participants but active contrib-
utors to economic progress.

In addition, in the current epoch dominated by digital advancements, functional education becomes even more important when the ability to navigate and
contribute to the digital era is a skill set that holds immense significance. For
women, who may face additional barriers in accessing technology, functional
education acts as a leveling force: it ensures that women are not left behind in the
technological transition but instead become protagonists in shaping the digital
landscape. From digital literacy to specialized skills in emerging technologies,
functional education paves the way for women to harness the power of information and communication technologies, thereby narrowing the gender gap in
the tech industry.

As envisioned by the international community, functional education stands as
a transformative force; it goes beyond traditional literacy, recognizing the need

for practical knowledge and competences in a world driven by constant change and progress. For women, it emerges as a catalyst for socioeconomic empowerment and active participation in the digital era. As the global community continues its pursuit of sustainable development, ensuring that women have access to functional education becomes not just a priority but a fundamental step towards a more inclusive and equitable future.

EDUCATION AND TRAINING AS BATTLEGROUNDS FOR GENDER EQUALITY

Education and training have emerged as focal points in the international struggle for gender equality; consequently, the recognition that equal access to education and training is not just a privilege but a fundamental right for women has gained prominence on the global stage.

Translating functional education into practice through professional training is meant to provide the necessary knowledge and competences to trigger and foster socioeconomic development, which must be paralleled by an intense activity of support to highly unalphabetized countries; research, technical assistance, and experimental projects can be promoted in cooperation with the United Nations Development Program (UNDP), UNESCO (United Nations Educational, Scientific and Cultural Organization) and other ONGs though primary action responsibilities depend on local governments.

At the heart of the international agenda for gender equality lies a commitment to viewing education and training as intrinsic rights for women. This commitment transcends regional and cultural boundaries, signifying a collective understanding that empowering women through education is not just a matter of societal progress but a human right imperative. The goal is not only to enroll women in educational programs but to ensure that they have equal opportunities to excel and contribute meaningfully to various domains.

The growing recognition of the need for a substantial approach to address the many challenges hindering women's access to education and training claims for actions that go beyond mere rhetoric and policy declarations, focusing on the individual's capacity to access essential elements such as rights, resources, services, and technology, acknowledging that gender equality is not achieved through a one-size-fits-all solution but demands tailored interventions that consider the unique circumstances and barriers faced by individual women. The commitment to breaking down gender-based barriers in these fields is not merely a symbolic gesture; considering the need for a substantial approach centered on individual capacity and introducing a new definition within the concept of the capability approach represents a strategic move to reshape societies and economies by leveraging the untapped potential of women.

The involvement of women in conflicts poses many issues to the international community, which need to be considered and addressed through concrete actions; by focusing on education, advocacy, and the protection of cultural heritage, UNESCO aims to enhance the role of women in conflicts and ensure their contributions are recognized and valued, keeping them as safe and protected as possible.

Women play different roles in conflicts. They frequently bear the brunt of conflicts, facing sexual violence, displacement, and the loss of family members, their experiences as victims highlighting the need for gender-sensitive approaches in conflict zones. Over the world, they participate in conflicts both as combatants and peacemakers; while they may take up arms, they also play crucial roles in peace negotiations and postconflict reconstruction, often leading their communities through crises, providing essential services and support. Their involvement in grassroots movements can drive peacebuilding efforts.

Promoting education as a fundamental right and a tool for empowerment, UNESCO works on providing education to women and girls in conflict zones to ensure they have the skills and knowledge to participate in peace processes and decision-making bodies, emphasizing the importance of gender equality in achieving sustainable peace and protecting cultural heritage. UNESCO particularly supports initiatives that involve women in safeguarding intangible cultural heritage, among which are educational programs for girls in conflict-affected areas, such as in Syria and South Sudan, ensuring continuity of learning even in crisis. UNESCO also works in line with the UN Security Council Resolution 1325, which calls for increased participation of women in all stages of peace processes, promoting research and policy recommendations to support this agenda. As to cultural preservation projects, in Mali, for instance, UNESCO has sustained projects where women are involved in the preservation of cultural heritage sites threatened by conflict.

UNESCO has envisaged some main areas of intervention, encompassing ensuring safety and security, overcoming stereotypes, and resources allocation: women in conflict zones face significant risks, and UNESCO works to create safe spaces for them to learn, work, and lead, so to combat gender stereotypes that limit women's roles in peace processes and conflict resolution is an ongoing challenge. To do so, securing adequate funding and resources for initiatives that support women's involvement in conflict resolution and peacebuilding remains critical.

Some key initiatives and proposals by UNESCO to empower women through education include the Global Citizenship Education (GCED) initiative, aiming to empower learners of all ages to assume active roles in resolving global challenges, focusing on gender equality and the promotion of peace, with special attention to the involvement of women. Also, Women Make the News (WMN), launched annually on International Women's Day (8 March), is an international initiative meant to encourage media organizations to give fair coverage to women in all sectors, including in conflict zones, highlighting the contributions of women and ensure their voices are heard. UNESCO has also promoted Chairs in Gender Equality and Women's Empowerment in various countries around the world; these chairs aim to advance gender equality through research, training, and policy development, focusing on areas such as women's leadership in peacebuilding.

The Capability Approach Reimagined

Traditionally associated with economist Amartya Sen, Nobel Laureate in 1998, who reimagined it connecting its value with the quality of the individual's life, the capability approach emphasizes the importance of expanding individuals' capabilities to lead lives they value.[6] In the context of gender equality in education and training, this redefined approach recognizes that women's capabilities extend beyond mere academic achievements: it encompasses their ability to access and utilize rights, resources, services, and technology that are essential for their educational and professional advancement.

In this reimagined framework, the capability approach becomes a dynamic tool for evaluating the effectiveness of interventions, which potentially prompt policymakers and stakeholders to consider not just enrollment numbers but the holistic development of women's capabilities, ensuring they have the skills, knowledge, and access to resources necessary to navigate and excel in diverse fields. The international commitment to gender equality in education and training seems therefore to surpass symbolic gestures; it is a strategic imperative rooted in the acknowledgment of women's intrinsic right to equal opportunities. The substantial approach redesigning capabilities, centered on individual capacity, reframes the discussion, emphasizing the need to address unique challenges faced by women. Within this paradigm, the redefined capability approach becomes a guiding framework, ensuring that women not only enter educational and training programs but also have the capabilities to shape their destinies and contribute meaningfully to a more equitable and inclusive global society.

UNESCO's Pledge to Abolish Gender Discrimination in Education

At the heart of UNESCO's overarching mission to eradicate gender discrimination in accessing education lies a commitment to fostering inclusive educational environments. UNESCO recognizes that genuine empowerment commences with dismantling barriers hindering equal access to education for both genders; this commitment manifests through concrete actions, such as initiatives aimed at eliminating illiteracy. By addressing the root cause of illiteracy, UNESCO strives to equip individuals with foundational skills necessary for personal development and active citizenship, adopting a holistic vision which underscores UNESCO's dedication to creating a merit-based educational landscape, where individuals are judged on their capabilities rather than gender, establishing a robust foundation for broader socioeconomic progress.

UNESCO's allegiance to abolishing gender discrimination in education and its emphasis on functional education, especially through the leading concept of "Literacy for Empowerment," testifies the Organization's role in professional training and its intensive efforts to combat illiteracy in collaboration with the UNDP and nongovernmental organizations (NGOs).

UNESCO champions the concept of "Literacy for Empowerment," which serves as a guiding principle in its efforts to combat illiteracy as it outreaches conventional notions of literacy, incorporating functional education into practice.[7] The emphasis, in fact, is not solely on acquiring basic reading and writing skills but on empowering individuals with practical knowledge and competences that are essential for active participation in socioeconomic development. In this perspective, professional training becomes a catalyst for economic empowerment, enabling individuals, especially women, to participate meaningfully in various professional spheres.

THE COMMITMENT OF THE INTERNATIONAL COMMUNITY IN THE COLONIAL/POST-COLONIAL ERA: ELEANOR ROOSEVELT'S AUDACIOUS VISION

In the wake of the colonial and postcolonial era, the international community recognized the imperative to address gender disparities, especially in the realm of education. A seminal moment in this pursuit came with the establishment of the United Nations Commission on the Status of Women (UNCSW) in 1946. This groundbreaking initiative marked a decisive step towards dismantling systemic barriers that impeded women's progress, particularly in the crucial domain of education.

The overarching goal of the Commission was clear: to ensure equal access for women to all grades and modes of education, encompassing not only basic education but also advanced academic pursuits, vocational training, and professional development. The vision was comprehensive, acknowledging that true gender equality could only be achieved when women had unrestricted access to education at all levels.

While the focus was on education, the Commission's mission extended to the broader and more complex frame of promoting gender equality and women's empowerment. Education was viewed as a catalyst for societal change, a means through which women could not only uplift themselves but also contribute significantly to the advancement of their communities and nations. The Commission recognized that achieving gender equality required addressing heterogeneous challenges, ranging from legal frameworks to sociocultural norms that perpetuated discrimination.

At the forefront of this historic endeavor was Eleanor Roosevelt, First Lady of the United States from 1933 to 1945, a passionate advocate for human rights, who attempted seminal pioneering steps toward the educational empowerment of women across the globe. Her audacious vision went beyond conventional norms, daring to challenge ingrained prejudices and biases that perpetuated gender inequality: recognizing the transformative power of education, Roosevelt ardently championed equal access for women to all grades and modes of education, a tireless effort that laid the foundation for a paradigm shift in international discourse, pushing for educational equity as a fundamental right for women.

The Commission on the Status of Women held its first meeting in February 1947, with Roosevelt serving as chairperson. The Commission's mandate was to address issues such as political participation, economic empowerment, education, and legal rights for women; in its first session (10–24 February 1947), the

Commission declared that one of the guiding principles informing its action was "to raise the status of women, irrespective of nationality, race, language or religion, to equality with men in all fields of human enterprise, and to eliminate all discrimination against women in the provisions of statutory law, in legal maxims or rules, or in interpretation of customary law." (UN Commission on the Status of Women, Report to Ecosoc (E/281/Rev.1, 25th Feb. 1947), Lake Success, New York)

The audacious vision set forth by the Commission on the Status of Women and championed by Eleanor Roosevelt left an enduring legacy, as it catalyzed subsequent international efforts to advance gender equality and women's empowerment. The commitment to equal access to education for women became a cornerstone of global initiatives, shaping policies and frameworks that aimed to break down barriers and promote inclusivity.

The Universal Declaration of Human Rights (1948) – Overcoming Gender-Biased Language

One of the Commission's most significant achievements was the drafting of the *Universal Declaration of Human Rights*, adopted by the United Nations General Assembly in 1948, and still standing as a landmark document in the history of human rights.

The UNCSW's contribution to the Declaration was transformative as to the formulation of the Declaration, actively challenging resistances within the Commission on Human Rights to ensure gender-respectful normative grammar, a point on which Eleanor Roosevelt played a crucial role. Roosevelt particularly fought on challenging gender-biased language and advocating for the recognition of women's rights within the broader framework of human rights, ensuring that the document enshrined the principle of gender equality as a fundamental human right, so that the UNCSW shaped not only the document itself but also the underlying philosophy. The term «right of men» was prevalent, reflecting an ambiguity that simultaneously referred to the broader category of human beings and the specific gender of males. The UNCSW protested against this expression, recognizing that language shapes perceptions and influences the realization of rights. To address this issue, they advocated for the replacement of «right of men» with the more inclusive term "human rights"; this shift signalled the Commission's commitment – thanks in particular Roosevelt – to recognizing and addressing the specific identities, including gender, within the realm of universal rights.

The insistence on using the term "human rights" instead of "right of men" was not merely a linguistic adjustment but a profound philosophical shift. It aimed to convey that human rights concern individuals not only as abstractly equal beings in front of the law but as subjects with specific personal identities. This shift was particularly crucial in recognizing the fundamental identity of gender. By emphasizing that human rights encompass the rights of women, the UNCSW laid the foundation for acknowledging the specific and diverse challenges and rights associated with gender, which necessitates the adoption of a canon of social justice: canon that surpasses the abstract notion of equality, encompassing the specific challenges and needs of women, acknowledging the historical and systemic injustices they face. Despite progress, though, this vision of social justice is often not fully achieved, and the UNCSW's advocacy serves as a reminder of the ongoing work required to attain true gender equality.

Eleanor Roosevelt's Discourse at Columbia University (1949): Making Human Rights Tangible

Eleanor Roosevelt's discourse at Columbia University in 1949 ("Making Human Rights Tangible") laid the groundwork for making human rights tangible; still today, the guiding principle of the 2030 Agenda, particularly its development goals, echoes the commitment to ensuring women are not left behind, especially in the realm of technology education.

In her discourse at Columbia University in 1949, Eleanor Roosevelt set a milestone in making human rights more than just theoretical concepts: she emphasized the need to breathe life into these rights, ensuring they resonate with the everyday lives of individuals. Her vision transcended legal documents, aiming to instil in people the understanding that human rights are not abstract ideals but practical principles that should guide social and political progress.

The language she used was much informed with what today we can refer to as "feminine" characteristics: the use of the pronoun "we" to introduce all topics in the discourse not only scaffolds the commonality of the process but strongly underlines the shared responsibility of the decisions made and the global involvement they mark. She also stressed the importance of becoming aware and cope with the issues brought forward by the Declaration of Human Rights, as well as of the process its rafting implied:

> Perhaps the first Covenant will not cover all the things that we will want to have covered in the future. We will keep our minds open and we will be prepared to meet new needs and new circumstances as they arise, but we have to make a beginning, and the beginning can only be made if we really make the Declaration a living document, something that is not just words on paper but something which we really strive to bring into the lives of all people, all people everywhere in the world. Now to do that we, all of us, will have to study this document. We will have to understand how it came to be written, why certain things are in it. (Roosevelt, 1949, p. 23)

Also, Roosevelt's discourse is highly marked with irony, which she purposely uses to have people react to some ideas, and to trigger them to some critical thinking on what may have seemed a natural consequence of words, being instead the outcome of much discussion – sometimes arising from something "which we had not given much thought to" (Roosevelt, 1949, p. 23). This is the case of the aforementioned use of "all men" in the document, where the orator uses specific ironic narration techniques to involve the audience and drive it towards her thinking, making them feel involved in the discourse leveraging on their emotional intelligence.[8] It is also the case of translation acceptance for words that sounded "neutral" in the sort of "Anglo–Saxon" English Roosevelt says was used to draft the Declaration but had to be culturally negotiated and accepted by all, the purpose of the document being "come to mean something in the lives of people all over the world" (Roosevelt, 1949, p. 23).[9] This of course also applies to the culturally-oriented meaning of some keywords in the document, as the word "freedom," which Roosevelt reports as being perceived differently in different countries:

> [...] in Japan, for instance, freedom only means license. There was no character in the Japanese language which meant freedoms as we understand it, so that when we tried to explain what freedom meant, they had to evolve a new character, because when they speak of a child who acted with complete irresponsibility and complete license, they said he was acting with freedom. That is something we must remember [...]. (Roosevelt, 1949, p. 27)

Roosevelt rounds up her discourse with a personal appeal intended to involve the whole audience in a "sustainable" common effort towards cooperation in democracy to build a better global society:

> [...] I hope, therefore, that we will concentrate on making our own selves, our own communities, our own country, the real democracy that we have given lip service to for so many years. {Applause) And in doing that, that we will be the spearhead and the spiritual and moral leader of all the other democracies that really want to see human rights and human freedoms made the foundation of a just and peaceful world. (Roosevelt, 1949, p. 27)

Roosevelt's Legacy: Guiding Principle of the 2030 Agenda and Development Goals

Fast forward to the 2030 Agenda for Sustainable Development, which guiding principle remains firmly rooted in the tangible realization of human rights: the development goals outlined in the Agenda are a testament to the global commitment to address multifaceted challenges, including gender inequality; central to this commitment is the acknowledgment that women must not be left behind: within the context of the 2030 Agenda, the recognition that women must have equal access to technology education is a crucial component. Eleanor Roosevelt's legacy of making human rights tangible extends to ensuring that women, too, have the knowledge and skills to engage with evolving technologies and the power to contribute actively to various sectors and compete on an equal footing with men for future professions.

COMPETING ON EQUAL FOOTING IN FUTURE PROFESSIONS: UNESCO AND NATIONAL GOVERNMENTS' ROLE IN REDUCING THE DIGITAL DIVIDE THROUGH THE DECADES

The commitment to gender equality in technology education is not just about access: it concerns empowering women to compete on equal footing with men in professions shaped by technological advancements, a perspective which goes beyond addressing immediate disparities, in a strategic move to create a work-force that leverages the diverse talents and perspectives of both genders in driving innovation and progress.

Realizing the vision of equal access to technology education requires concerted efforts from national governments at a global level; policies, strategies, and programs become essential tools in reducing and eliminating the digital divide. Governments must invest in educational infrastructure, formulate inclusive policies, and design strategies that bridge gaps in access to technology; this includes addressing socioeconomic disparities, ensuring that women from all backgrounds have the opportunity to engage with and benefit from technological advancements.

The XV International Conference on Public Education (Geneva, 1952)

The XV International Conference on Public Education held in Geneva in July 1952, jointly organized by the International Bureau of Education and UNESCO, marked a significant moment in the global discourse on education, one of its key outcomes being the adoption of Recommendation (*The Right to Education*, MC.52/II.8/A, 1952) addressed to the Ministries of Education of all countries exhorting them to promote a comprehensive vision towards equality in education and laying the groundwork for addressing barriers faced by women in accessing education.[10]

The key points from the recommendation were meant to address some main areas of intervention. On first instance, the conference emphasized the importance of promoting the access of all, women included, to education and science teaching in secondary schools, in a conscious, collective effort to eradicate illiteracy so to improve social conditions and well-being:

> Paradoxical though it may seem in an age of aviation, radio and nuclear physics, it is nevertheless a fact that more than half the world's population cannot read or write. [...] It is easy to see what disastrous results may ensue from this situation and to understand why it is the duty of men and women who have enjoyed the benefits of education to see that those benefits are extended to people who have had no education at all. [...] Today, ignorance breeds want. It stands in the way of scientific and technical progress and the use of modern means to improve the general state of health, preserve natural resources, increase agricultural production and develop industrial undertakings. The eradication of illiteracy cannot, of course, suffice in itself to raise the peoples' standards of living. The problem as a whole is not strictly educational, but social. (UNESCO, 1952, pp. 1–4)

This called for a departure from traditional gender norms that might have restricted women's participation in certain educational levels. The goal was to create an inclusive educational landscape where women could pursue education at all stages of their learning journey.

Second, the recommendation strived towards the extension of compulsory education to both sexes, recognizing the transformative power of education, urging Ministries of Education to ensure that education became a fundamental right for all but also addressing gender disparities in access to basic education, laying the foundation for a more equitable society.

Third, the text called for equal opportunities for women across various educational paths; equal opportunities which encompassed not only secondary education but also technical-professional education and training, as well as tertiary education leading to university degrees. The goal was to break down gender-based barriers that might have limited women's choices and opportunities in pursuing diverse educational paths.

Fourth, a forward-thinking aspect of the recommendation was its lifelong learning perspective: recognizing that education is not a one-time endeavour but a continuous process, the recommendation aimed at highlighting the importance of providing opportunities for women to engage in continuous learning and skill development throughout their lives.

The recommendation made at the 1952 conference was historically significant as it aligned with the global shift towards recognizing the importance of gender equality in education, setting the stage for subsequent international efforts and initiatives that aimed at dismantling barriers to education for women and promoting their equal participation in all spheres of learning. In essence, the *XV International Conference on Public Education*, and the subsequent recommendation by UNESCO and the International Bureau of Education provided a framework that encouraged nations to actively work towards ensuring that women had equal opportunities to access education at all levels, reflecting a broader vision of social and gender equity in education.

Along with the testimony of the contemporary international effort to overcome gender barriers in education, additional details from the 1952 recommendation provide insights into the prevailing gender norms, expectations, and attitudes toward women's education during that era. The language used in the recommendation illustrates a delicate balance between advocating for equal access to education and conforming to traditional gender roles and stereotypes: while the recommendation advocated for equal access to education for women, it also reflected certain societal expectations and stereotypes regarding women's roles. For example, the recommendation suggested the provision of courses preparing girls for their family responsibilities, reflecting the prevailing societal norms of the time, where women were often expected to fulfil traditional roles within the family. The language of the text suggests a gendered perspective on education, emphasizing preparation for domestic responsibilities as a key component of women's education. Furthermore, in the context of higher education, the recommendation indicated that university studies should permit women to specialize in fields particularly suited to feminine aptitudes; a notion which aligns with gender stereotypes that associate certain professions or fields with so-called "feminine" qualities and highlights a societal belief in inherent gender differences that influence career choices. The recommendation also pays particular attention to professional training in care works and assistance, remarking an expectation that women might naturally gravitate towards professions related to caregiving; while the intention may have been to acknowledge and value these roles, it also reinforces traditional gender roles that limit women's career choices to certain predefined sectors.

According to the recommendation, women should be offered a practical, effective, and moral education, emphasizing the "natural role" of women in the family and society – a traditional perspective that views women primarily in caregiving and nurturing roles, which aligns with the societal expectations prevalent during that time, as well as with a belief in inherent gender differences that were often used to justify gender-specific educational approaches taking into account differences in the psychophysiological development between the sexes.

Equality and Equity: Transitioning From the 1960s to the 1970s

The United Nations Assembly resolutions in the late 1960s and early 1970s marked a further significant step in advancing the global conversation on gender equality, a turning point in international efforts to define and pursue gender equality beyond mere formal acknowledgment of women's rights; in particular, the 1967 Declaration on the Elimination of Discrimination against Women and the early 1970s Programme of Concerted Action for the Advancement of Women set the stage for UNESCO to engage in a deeper reflection on the role of women in the development process.

The 1967 Declaration on the Elimination of Discrimination against Women laid the foundation for articulating the rights of women on an international scale, acknowledging that discrimination based on gender was a violation of fundamental human rights. Later on, the early 1970s Programme of Concerted Action for the Advancement of Women built upon the momentum generated by the 1967 Declaration. The Programme represented a commitment to taking concrete actions to advance the status of women globally, as it recognized the need for coordinated efforts to overcome systemic barriers and promote gender equality in various spheres, including education and economic development.

In response to these resolutions, UNESCO was prompted to engage in a deeper reflection on the role of women, recognizing its intrinsic relevance to the development process. The acknowledgment of women's rights underscored the imperative of integrating women into the broader narrative of development and triggered further resolutions, which in turn prompted a need to substantially define "equality" (gender equality in particular), transcending formal acknowledgment of women's rights. The concept demanded a comprehensive understanding that went beyond legal frameworks and emphasized the need for substantive equality, addressing underlying social, economic, and cultural factors that perpetuated gender disparities.

Notably, the works of Ester Boserup, *Woman's Role in Economic Development*, and Jacqueline Chabaud, *The Education and Advancement of Women*, both published in 1970 during UNESCO's International Year of Education, contributed significantly to the discourse, highlighting women's roles in economic development and underscoring the importance of education in advancing women.

The International Commission on the Development of Education (1971)

The International Commission on the Development of Education, chaired by Edgar Faure in 1971, and its report *Learning to Be: The World of Education Today and Tomorrow*, holds an instrumental importance in shaping UNESCO's strategic direction towards lifelong learning and lifelong education.

The Faure Report generated significant debate and was unanimously considered a foundational document for UNESCO's new educational paradigm:

it advocated for a profound shift, emphasizing the importance of lifelong learning; it recognized that education should not be confined to specific stages of life but should be a continuous process that adapts to the evolving needs of individuals throughout their lives. This strategic choice marked a departure from traditional, more compartmentalized educational models towards a more holistic and adaptable approach that accommodates the learning needs of individuals at every stage of life.

A central concern of the report was the need to prevent new forms of marginalization within industrialized countries in the emerging "learning society," where combating the risk of leaving segments of the population behind needed to become a priority, through inclusive educational strategies to address the diverse needs of learners. In response to the recommendations of the report, UNESCO adopted and relaunched the indications emphasizing the need to deeply modify teaching methods, shifting the focus from traditional, teacher-centred approaches to learner-centred methods aimed to align education more closely with the diverse needs, interests, and capabilities of learners.

The Faure Report left a lasting legacy, influencing educational policies and practices globally, its emphasis on centring education on the diverse learners' needs being a crucial aspect of its impact: education should no longer be provided with a one-size-fits-all model but should be responsive to individual characteristics, pace, and aspirations.

The Report's insights into preventing marginalization and adapting education to the needs of learners continue to resonate in contemporary discussions on inclusive and equitable education, and Lifelong learning has since become a fundamental principle in education, shaping discussions and initiatives to this day.

UN Women's Decade (1976–1985)

The UN Women's Decade from 1976 to 1985 was a crucial period marked by significant international efforts to address gender inequality and improve the condition of women globally, an initiative which gained momentum following the Declaration of Mexico City in 1975 on the equality of men and women and their contribution to development and peace. During this decade, UNESCO played a key role by adopting the "Thinking Ahead" medium-term project (1977–1982), which prioritized overcoming the condition of inferiority faced by women, particularly in the context of education.

The World Action Plan, stemming from the Declaration of Mexico City, served as a significant document that outlined guidelines for improving the condition of women. It called upon member states and the international community to address issues related to development and socioeconomic structures that relegated women to inferior positions.

In response to this imperative, UNESCO adopted the "Thinking Ahead" medium-term project in 1977, by which it made a priority of the improvement of women's conditions with a special focus on ensuring the effective exercise of their rights, starting from access to education. The Thinking Ahead project reflected a deeper understanding of the societal barriers that perpetuated gender inequality, and underscored the need for an emancipated change in social constructs, particularly challenging traditions, preconceived ideas, and stereotyped distinctions between the roles of men and women. The project highlighted the challenges faced by women in accessing education, acknowledging sociocultural and economic conditions that were often unfavourable; such challenges that hindered women's educational opportunities included indifference, traditional customs, early marriages, domestic responsibilities, and the preeminent role of boys' education over girls'. The project also drew attention to the role of media and school textbooks in perpetuating gender stereotypes; it emphasized the need to challenge portrayals that reinforced traditional roles and distinctions between men and women and drew attention on the importance of media literacy and inclusive educational materials in fostering gender equality.

The efforts undertaken during the UN Women's Decade prepared the ground for continued global initiatives to advance gender equality. The recognition of barriers to women's education, as highlighted by UNESCO's Thinking Ahead project, contributed to ongoing discussions and policies aimed at dismantling systemic obstacles and promoting equal access to education for all, irrespective of gender.

The Status of Women (1985)

The outcomes of the UN World Survey on the Role of Women in Development in 1985 had a significant impact on UNESCO's approach to gender and education. Following these findings, UNESCO launched a new program on the Status of Women. Unlike previous efforts that primarily focused on ensuring educational equality, this program aimed to surpass the concept, assisting member states in offering equality through education. The program sought to address not only the issue of access but also the content, values, and impact of education in perpetuating or challenging gender hierarchies. This involved a shift in focus from merely ensuring equal access to education to a more comprehensive approach that addressed the broader socio-cultural context, including the contents and values transmitted within educational processes.

The program recognized the importance of not only equal access to education but also the need to address the contents and values embedded in educational systems; while it acknowledged that educational materials and curricula could play a role in perpetuating or challenging traditional gender roles and stereotypes, it emphasised the promotion of gender-sensitive education to foster equality.

"Status of Women" subscribed to the diversified impact of scholarization, recognizing that the benefits and challenges of education are experienced differently by men and women. The program consequently paid higher attention to the inequality experienced by women in accessing work, careers, and roles in the public domain, a recognition that reflected a broader understanding of the link between education and employment, highlighting that gender disparities persist beyond the educational phase and extend into the professional realm.

The acknowledgment that this period is considered one of the darkest in UNESCO's history suggests that addressing gender inequality was met with significant challenges or controversies. It might reflect internal or external pressures, resistance to progressive initiatives, or difficulties in effectively implementing the program's objectives. Internally, UNESCO faced bureaucratic inertia and a lack of consensus among its diverse member states, some of which were resistant to rapid social changes and the progressive gender policies promoted by the program. Externally, UNESCO encountered opposition from governments and influential groups that viewed the emphasis on gender equality as a threat to traditional social structures and cultural norms. This resistance was not just ideological but also practical, as many member states struggled with limited resources and competing priorities.

Moreover, the period was marked by broader geopolitical tensions and financial crises that affected UNESCO's operations. The organization had to cope with the complexities of the Cold War, which influenced international cooperation and the prioritization of development goals. Financial constraints, partly due to reduced contributions from key member states, hindered the effective rollout and sustainability of the new initiatives aimed at gender equality. These financial and political pressures led to a slowdown in progress and, in some cases, the scaling back of ambitious programs.

Despite these challenges, UNESCO's efforts during this period laid crucial groundwork for future advancements. The program's emphasis on the sociocultural dimensions of education and gender equity highlighted the need for systemic change and set the stage for subsequent international efforts to promote gender equality in education. While progress was slow and often met with resistance, the period underscored the complexity of achieving gender equality and the importance of sustained commitment and adaptation in the face of adversity.

1990, the International Year of Literacy

The year 1990 marked the International Year of Literacy, and during this significant period, the World Conference on Education for All was convened in Jomtien. This conference, promoted by UNESCO, the World Bank, UNICEF, and UNDP, resulted in the approval of the World Declaration of Education for All and the Framework for Action to Meet Learning Needs. The outcomes of this conference represented a crucial step in advancing global efforts to address education challenges and promote literacy.

The Jomtien Conference reflected a continuity with the ideas theorized at the Teheran World Congress of Ministers of Education in 1965, emphasizing the concept of functional literacy, recognizing that literacy should go beyond basic reading and writing skills, so to equip individuals with the practical knowledge and skills needed to actively participate in society. Basic Cognitive Tools in education were recognized as fundamental to ensure development, acknowledging that their relevance might vary from country to country based on their developmental stage, economic complexity, technological infrastructure, and administrative apparatus.

Despite these variations, there was a call for alignment with the more homogeneous reality of the global economy and the concept of a "global village": a crucial section of the declaration following the Conference emphasized the importance of "globalizing access to and promoting equity," reflecting the participants' commitment to ensuring that education is accessible to all, with a particular focus on granting access to female children and women. The declaration underscored the need to improve the quality of education offered to women and remove all obstacles hindering their active participation in the educational process, and it gave rise to the "Education for All" campaign. The main aim of the campaign was to mobilize global efforts to achieve universal access to quality education, fostering a comprehensive and inclusive approach, which recognized the interconnectedness of education, development, and social equity.

The commitment to functional literacy, the recognition of the globalized nature of education, and the emphasis on promoting equity, especially for women and girls promoted through the Conference and the following Campaign, marked a paradigm shift in international educational goals. The legacy of these initiatives can be seen in the continued emphasis on inclusive and quality education as a fundamental human right and a key driver of sustainable development.

The Commission on Education for the 21st Century (1995)

Five years later, the Commission on Education for the 21 Century, chaired by Jacques Delors in 1995, stands as a further landmark initiative that sought to redefine global strategies for education as the world entered the new century. The report produced by the commission presented a vision that went beyond traditional educational goals, emphasizing the transformative role of education in achieving broader ideals of peace, freedom, and social justice. The commission recognized the evolving nature of educational challenges and aimed to move the fulfilment of literacy goals for all into the new century, adopting a forward-looking approach to respond to the changing demands and opportunities of a rapidly evolving global landscape. Education was agreed to be an indispensable resource that enables all of humanity to progress toward the ideals of peace, freedom, and social justice, a transformative force enabling a broader understanding of the sociohistorical panorama, therefore acquiring a new role in shaping not only individuals but entire societies: the report advocated a shift "from the basic community to the world society," a transition towards recognizing the interconnectedness of global issues as well as the need for an educational approach to prepare individuals to engage in a complex, interdependent world. A notable aspect of the report was the acknowledgment that, in the process of defining a new global ethic, women represented a crucial subject of change: UNESCO identified women as privileged interlocutors in the elaboration and diffusion of peace, and this recognition reflected the evolving understanding of the role of women in society and their potential as agents of positive change.

The Delors Report had a profound impact on global education policies and discussions. The emphasis on a holistic approach to education, the transition

from local to global perspectives, and the recognition of women as key con-
tributors to peace and change influenced subsequent initiatives. The report's
vision has left a lasting legacy, contributing to ongoing efforts to redefine and
enhance the quality and inclusivity of education worldwide. The work of the
commission laid the foundation for a comprehensive approach to education,
emphasizing four pillars: learning to know, learning to do, learning to live, and
learning to be; through these pillars, the commission aimed to provide a holistic
framework which surpasses traditional academic knowledge, encompassing
practical skills, social engagement, and personal development. Almost 30 years
later, the goals of the 2030 Agenda still build upon the same pillars the whole
scaffolding of education declined in the different key-life skills it promotes.

The World Conference on Women, Beijing (1995)

Organized by the Commission on the Status of Women and the UN Division for
the Advancement of Women, the World Conference on Women held in Beijing in
1995 focused on various aspects of women's empowerment, including the crucial
role of equality in education as a key driver for achieving broader societal goals.

The conference underscored that equality in education is a foundational
prerequisite for achieving other essential aspects of women's empowerment. This
included the full respect of women's rights, the expression and utilization of their
creative potential, and equal participation in decision-making processes.
Recognizing education as a cornerstone, the conference aimed to address systemic barriers that hindered women's access to quality education, while calling
for a new orientation of social and economic policies that granted equal
opportunities and transformed gender relationships. The outcome of the Commission's works reflected a broader understanding that achieving gender equality
requires structural changes in societal norms, policies, and economic frameworks.

The action plan adopted by the conference outlined strategic goals for
women's empowerment. Beyond addressing women's illiteracy, it aimed for a
wider definition of literacy, an expanded view which included the acquisition of
scientific and technical competences to enhance women's access to professional
education. The programs were designed to cover a broad spectrum, ranging from
science and mathematics to environmental sciences, technology, information
technology, high tech, and company management.

An essential aspect of the action plan was the strategic goal of elevating
women's access to professional education, breaking traditional barriers that
limited women's participation in fields that were often dominated by men. By
encouraging women to pursue education in science, technology, and management, the conference aimed to bridge gender gaps in professional and technical
fields. At the same time, the efforts to enrich the definition of literacy by incorporating scientific and technical competences reflected a commitment to preparing women for roles in an increasingly complex and technologically advanced
world; this approach sought to ensure that women were not only literate but also
equipped with the skills and knowledge necessary for active participation in
diverse professional domains. The emphasis on expanding definitions of literacy

and promoting women's participation in science, technology, and management set by the Beijing Conference's action plan continues to influence policies and initiatives aimed at breaking down gender barriers in education and the workforce.

The UNESCO Gender Action Plans and Beyond

The UNESCO Gender Action Plan, and subsequent initiatives like the EU Gender Action Plans (GAPs), launched in the first decade of the 21st century, promote a further advancement in fostering and implementing gender equality and women's empowerment on a global scale.

The UNESCO GAPs, spanning from 2008 to 2021, are strategic frameworks that guide UNESCO's efforts to integrate and advance gender equality considerations into all activities within UNESCO's mandate, and to support Member States in achieving gender equality by addressing gender disparities in various sectors, including education, culture, natural sciences, social and human sciences, and communication and information, through targeted actions and strategies.[11] The key objectives they set include mainstreaming gender equality by integrating gender perspectives into all policies, programs, and initiatives to ensure that both women and men benefit equally; advancing women's empowerment and promoting women's leadership and participation in decision-making processes across sectors; strengthening the capacities of Member States, partners, and UNESCO staff to address gender equality effectively, while developing mechanisms to monitor progress and assess the impact of gender equality initiatives.

The implementation phases of the Plans have integrated one another: GAP I (2008–2013) focused on establishing gender equality as a global priority for UNESCO, key initiatives including promoting girls' education, women's literacy, and gender-sensitive media; GAP II (2014–2021) built on the achievements of GAP I, with an emphasis on deepening gender mainstreaming efforts and enhancing partnerships with other organizations and stakeholders.

Almost in parallel, the EU also launched GAPs, strategic frameworks designed to promote gender equality and women's empowerment in the EU's external relations and international cooperation efforts. These plans reflect the EU's commitment to advancing gender equality globally through its development and humanitarian aid policies, covering specific time frames (GAP I: 2010–2015, GAP II: 2016–2020, GAP III: 2021–2025), with the aim to mainstream gender considerations across EU external policies, projects, and programs. As for the UNESCO Plans, key objectives and strategies focus on promoting economic and social rights to ensure women's access to education, healthcare, economic resources, and decent work; empowering women and girls, supporting women's leadership and participation in political, economic, and social spheres; ending gender-based violence through fostering institutional change, to enhance the gender responsiveness of EU institutions and their partners.

However, as afore mentioned, despite concerted efforts the goals outlined in these action plans were only partially fulfilled, and challenges such as persistent gender disparities, cultural barriers, and gaps in implementation hindered the comprehensive achievement of gender equality objectives. Furthermore, limited resources and funding are available for gender equality initiatives, and there is still need for stronger monitoring and accountability mechanisms to ensure effective implementation.

The *Re-Linking Women's Empowerment and Gender Equality (2015 and Beyond)* conference, held in Paris, highlighted some of these challenges and underscored the need for a critical examination of progress. The report it originated emphasized a critical perspective on the progress made and identified issues that needed further attention.

Agenda 2030: Universal Sustainability

The Agenda 2030 for Sustainable Development represents a comprehensive global plan for progress, extending beyond the economic dimension to encompass environmental and societal aspects. Its most distinctive feature is universality, emphasizing the shared responsibility of all countries in achieving Sustainable Development Goals (SDGs) that transcends geographical and economic boundaries. The universality of Agenda 2030 is a ground-breaking feature, emphasizing that sustainable development is a shared responsibility: all countries, regardless of their development status, are called upon to contribute to the achievement of its 17 SDGs, recognizing the interconnectedness of the dimensions highlighted in the document, which underscores the need for integrated solutions, and fostering a collaborative and global approach.

The SDGs cover a wide range of issues, including poverty, hunger, health, education, gender equality, clean water, climate action, and more. Goal 5 specifically focuses on achieving gender equality and empowering all women and girls.

While the Agenda 2030 represents an ambitious and holistic framework, challenges persist in its implementation, including financing, political will, and the need for effective global cooperation. Ongoing efforts involve continuous monitoring, assessment, and adjustments to strategies to overcome obstacles and ensure progress towards sustainable development and gender equality.

A FURTHER STEP AHEAD: THE LEARNING CITIES CONCEPT

The UNESCO Global Network of Learning Cities, launched in Beijing in 2013, represents a commitment to promoting lifelong learning for all within urban contexts, with the goal to create cities that embrace education as a central component of their future development. The concept of Learning City not only focuses on theoretical principles, but also emphasizes pragmatic approaches to ensure quality, equal, and inclusive education, where gender equality and empowerment, along with socioeconomic interdependence and sustainability are key features embedded in the framework of learning cities. The initiative is structured around some key-pillars that guide the vision and mission of learning cities, which serve as fundamental principles for creating an environment conducive to lifelong learning. One of these is the guarantee of gender equality, emphasizing the importance of ensuring equal opportunities and rights for individuals of all genders.

"Lifelong Learning for All is Our City's Future," leaving no one behind, is a slogan that encapsulates the core ethos of the UNESCO Global Network of Learning Cities.[12] It underscores the belief that education is not limited to specific life stages but should be a continuous and accessible process for all individuals within a city, irrespective of age, gender, or background. The concept emphasizes the importance of providing education that is not only of high quality but is also equal and inclusive, addressing disparities in access, resources, and opportunities; Learning Cities aim to ensure that education is a universal right for all resident citizens. In this perspective, the commitment to guaranteeing gender equality is a prominent feature; it involves creating environments where women and men have equal opportunities to access and benefit from education.

Education is a crucial aspect in empowering individuals, especially women, to actively participate in societal development in particular when it comes to socioeconomic interdependence and sustainability. Learning cities recognize the interdependence of education with socioeconomic factors, to educate individuals as well as to integrate education into the broader fabric of societal sustainability, aligning educational practices with economic and social development goals. In doing so, involving the community in educational initiatives fosters a sense of ownership and ensures that educational programs are relevant to the local context.

The Guidelines for Learning Cities suggest an inclusive and accessible strategic approach to planning complying with the overall goals of the initiative, involving setting clear objectives, identifying key challenges, and developing action plans to address those challenges; a process which should ensure that education is available to all residents, regardless of socio-economic status, age, gender, or other factors, with the aim of removing barriers and creating environments that cater to diverse learning needs. Continuous monitoring and evaluation are essential components of the learning city strategic approach, prioritizing the assessment of the impact of educational programs, identifying areas for improvement, and adapting strategies to meet evolving needs. Partnerships and collaboration with various stakeholders, including government bodies, educational institutions, businesses, and community organizations, are critical for the success of learning cities: collaborative efforts leverage resources and expertise to create a more comprehensive and effective learning environment.

CONCLUSIONS (SO FAR)

Addressing the disparities in women's access to ICT and dismantling the prejudices ingrained in educational systems are significant steps toward achieving gender equality in the global development narrative. The UNESCO path towards women's empowerment emerges as a beacon of hope, providing a roadmap for overcoming these challenges and fostering an environment where women are not left behind, especially in those contexts where wars, and unsecure conditions undermine basic respect and force weaker voices to silence, migration, or death. As we seek to tackle the complexities of our interconnected world, it is paramount to advocate for inclusivity, eliminate barriers, and ensure that women occupy a central and equitable role in shaping the socioeconomic future of our global community.

UNESCO's many-sided and evolving approach to combating gender discrimination and illiteracy is rooted in its commitment to inclusive and functional education. The emphasis on "Literacy for Empowerment" underscores the transformative power of education in shaping individuals and societies. Treasuring the structural ideas triggered and championed by Eleanor Roosevelt, and by extending its reach to professional training and collaborating with international partners, UNESCO epitomizes a holistic commitment to socioeconomic development through education. As the organization continues to focus on the challenges of illiteracy, it remains dedicated to fostering a world where education is not just a privilege but a fundamental right, accessible to all, irrespective of gender or geographical location. The UNESCO Global Network of Learning Cities functions as a transformative initiative that places education at the centre of urban development; through its key pillars and strategic guidelines, the Learning Cities network aims to create inclusive, accessible, and sustainable learning environments, with a specific focus on guaranteeing gender equality and empowerment.

Only becoming aware of the deep interconnection between inequality, marginality/exclusion and poverty, human rights, gender equality, and women empowerment can be fulfilled responding to the imperative of an inclusive development.

Leaving no one behind.

NOTES

2. In the United Kingdom, Maria Edgeworth (1767–1849), working with her father, Richard Lovell, first spoke about the "science of education," aiming at a practical education based on Truth, Justice and Humanity, and confined to no particular rank or circumstance (Edgeworth, 1796, *Preface*); her educational writings were addressed to both boys and girls, and her works often feature exemplary female characters. She also wrote Letters for Literary Ladies (1795), an epistolary work satirising the bias in women's education at her time, "a text that uses writing and narrative not only as a means to configure feminine identity but as a means to fashion a female authorial self" (Narain, 1998, p. 267).
Emily Davies (1830–1821) was a prominent English feminist and suffragist who, along with Barbara Bodichon (1827–1891), founded Girton College in Cambridge in 1869, the first residential college in England for the education of women. Davies advocated for women's access to university education and fought for the admission of women to Cambridge University.
3. A notable case is the invention of the frequency-hopping spread spectrum, patented as *Secret Communication Service* in 1942 by Hedy Kiesler Markey (1914–2000, worldwide known as Hedy Lamarr, the Hollywood diva) and George Antheil. Kiesler Markey had been married to Fritz Mandl, who provided weapons to the Nazi Germany; once the

marriage was annulled, she fled to the USA, where she sat at work to help the Allies against Hitler. Considered to be the forerunner of wireless, although the credit will only be recognised by the international scientific community years later, the frequency-hopping spread spectrum, modified into CDMA - Code Division Multiple Access was adopted by the US Navy in 1962.

4. See for instance Grace Murray Hopper (1906–1992), Rita Levi-Montalcini (1909–2012), Sister Maria Kenneth Keller (1913–1985), Katherine Johnson (1918–2020), Margherita Hack (1922–2013), Karen Spärck Jones (1935–2006).

5. A few examples:

- Focussing on education and skill development, Girls Who Code (https://girlswhocode.com/) is a non-profit organization dedicated to closing the gender gap in technology and engineering fields. The initiative offers coding programs, clubs, and summer immersion programs specifically designed for girls. By providing hands-on coding experience and fostering a supportive community, Girls Who Code aims to empower young women to pursue careers in technology.

- Named after its founder, Anita Borg, AnitaB.org (https://anitab.org/) is a global organization operating since 1987; it advocates for the advancement of women and non-binary individuals in technology. The organization works towards creating inclusive and diverse workplaces by providing resources, hosting conferences (such as the Grace Hopper Celebration), and promoting initiatives that support women in technology careers. AnitaB.org also collaborates with companies to implement policies that foster gender diversity.

- #MeTooSTEM (https://metoostem.com/) is a movement within the scientific and technology communities that addresses issues of sexual harassment and gender-based discrimination. This initiative sheds light on the challenges faced by women in STEM fields and advocates for changes in workplace cultures to ensure safe and equitable environments for all professionals.

- TechWom@n (https://www.techwomen.org/) is an Initiative of the U.S. Department of State's Bureau of Educational and Cultural Affairs; a program that connects women in STEM fields from the Middle East, Africa, and Central Asia with their counterparts in the United States through mentorship and cultural exchange, TechWomen aims to empower women to pursue leadership roles in technology and create a global network of professionals committed to supporting each other.

6. Amartya Sen's approach to capability theory constitutes a theoretical framework underpinned by two fundamental normative propositions. Primarily, it posits that the ethical significance of attaining well-being rests on the foundational value of freedom. Additionally, it asserts that the comprehension of freedom in the pursuit of well-being necessitates an understanding grounded in the capabilities of individuals. Robeyns and Fibieger Byskov (2020) summarised the concept: "Capabilities are the doings and beings that people can achieve if they so choose [. . .]; functionings are capabilities that have been realized." See also the *Stanford Encyclopedia of Philosophy* (2011). https://plato.stanford.edu/entries/capability-approach/

7. In regions facing high levels of illiteracy, UNESCO engages in intense activities and provides support through research, technical assistance, and experimental projects. Recognizing the complexity of illiteracy-related challenges, UNESCO collaborates closely with the UNDP and NGOs. While UNESCO plays a supportive role, it acknowledges that primary action responsibilities lie with local governments, emphasizing the importance of tailored solutions that consider the unique contexts and needs of each country.

8. See the narration of the episode in Roosevelt (1949, pp. 23–24).

9. See the report of the discussion on article II, Roosevelt (1949, pp. 24–25).

10. See https://unesdoc.unesco.org/ark:/48223/pf0000128322. It is worth noting that, though some language biases persist, as in the quote from Jean Piaget, *Le droit de*

l'éducation dans le monde actuel, p. 14 (p. 5), or in the use of the word "mankind," and again in the referring Adult education to "Men" (p. 17), the general attitude of the Resolution is to explicitly address to men and women, using the two terms simultaneously in all possible occasion, and to adopt the word "human" to imply both sexes/genders.

11. The UNESCO initiatives on gender comprise the Gender Action Plan (2008–2013) and the UNESCO Priority Gender Equality Action Plan 2014–2021 (37 C/4-C/5).

12. See Valdés-Cotera, R., & Wang, M. (2018). Lifelong learning for all: Our city's future. In J. James, J. Preece, & R. Valdés-Cotera (Eds.), *Entrepreneurial learning city regions*. Springer.

REFERENCES

Bhola, H. S. (1965). *Functional literacy, workplace literacy and technical and vocational education. Interfaces and policy perspectives*. UNEVOC – International Project n Technical and Vocational Education. UNESCO. https://unevoc.unesco.org/fileadmin/user_upload/pubs/Studies-05e.pdf

Edgeworth, M. (1796). *The parent's assistant, or stories for children*. Joseph Johnson.

Narain, M. (1998). A prescription of letters: Maria Edgeworth's "Letters for Literary Ladies" and the ideologies of the public sphere. *Journal of Narrative Technique, 28*(3), 266–286. http://www.jstor.org/stable/30225498

Robeyns, I., & Fibieger Byskov, M. (2020). The capability approach. In E. N. Zalta & U. Nodelman (Eds.), *Stanford encyclopedia of philosophy* (Summer 2023 ed.). https://plato.stanford.edu/entries/capability-approach/

Roosevelt, E. (1949, September). Making human rights come alive. Discourse at the …. *Phi Delta Kappan, 31*(1), 23–33.

Seller, M. S. (1989). A history of "Women's Education in the United States": Thomas Woody's classic—60 years later. *History of Education Quarterly, 29*(1), 95–107.

Taylor B., & Knott, S. (Eds.). (2005). *Women, gender and enlightenment*. Palgrave Macmillan.

UN Commission on the Status of Women. (1947). *Report to ECOSOC of the first session of the Commission on the Status of Women*. Lake Success, New York, from 10 to 24 February 1947: E/281/Rev.1. https://digitallibrary.un.org/record/198580?ln=en. Accessed on February 25, 1947.

UNESCO. (1952). *The right to education, MC.52/II.8/A, UNESCO and its programme* (Vol. 8, Issue 31). https://unesdoc.unesco.org/ark:/48223/pf0000128322

UNESCO. (1965). *World conference of ministers of education on the eradication of illiteracy*, Teheran, 8–19 September 1965. Final report. Paris, UNESCO.

Woody, T. (1929). *A history of women's education in the United States*. The Science Press.

REVIEW ON THE INTERNATIONAL LEGAL FRAMEWORK FOR THE PROTECTION OF WOMEN AND GIRL CHILDREN IN NON-INTERNATIONAL ARMED CONFLICTS

Muthukuda Arachchige Dona Shiroma

Jeeva Shirajanie Niriella

University of Colombo, Sri Lanka

ABSTRACT

The international legal framework for protecting women and girl children in noninternational armed conflicts (NIACs) faces critical scrutiny regarding its adequacy. This research investigates the effectiveness of existing legal instruments in safeguarding the rights and well-being of women and girl children amidst such conflicts. To unpack the main problem, this study focuses on three primary research questions to guide the inquiry. First, how comprehensive and enforceable are the existing international legal mechanisms specifically addressing the protection of women and girl children in NIACs? Second, what are the major challenges in the implementation and the gaps in the legal frameworks at the international level? Third, what strategies and reforms can enhance the efficacy of the international legal framework in addressing the vulnerabilities of women and girl children in such conflicts? This review research aims to achieve three main objectives: first, to critically analyze the existing international legal instruments pertinent to the protection of women and girl children in NIACs, second, to identify the key obstacles hindering the effective implementation of these legal provisions, and thirdly, to propose practical measures and policy recommendations aimed at

Scars of War

Research in Political Sociology, Volume 30, 47–60

Copyright © 2025 Muthukuda Arachchige Dona Shiroma Jeeva Shirajanie Niriella

Published under exclusive licence by Emerald Publishing Limited

ISSN: 0895-9935/doi:10.1108/S0895-993520250000030005

strengthening the international legal framework and improving the protection mechanisms for women and girl children in such conflicts. This legal research engages in content analysis of the available relevant secondary sources in the completion of the study.

Keywords: Women; girl children; noninternational armed conflicts; international legal framework; protection

INTRODUCTION

In noninternational armed conflicts (NIACs), several groups are particularly vulnerable to suffering and exploitation (Freedman, 2015). These include women and girl children, elderly and disabled individuals, minority groups, displaced people, and children (https://www.iiss.org) (Armed Conflict Survey, 2023). This study is focused only on the women and girl children who are often subjected to sexual violence, sexual exploitation, slavery, forced marriages, and other forms of gender-based violence. For example, in conflicts such as those in Sudan and Afghanistan, women and girls have faced systematic abuses, including restrictions on education and employment, and targeted violence. In recent years, women and girls have faced severe suffering in NIACs due to various forms of violence, exploitation, and deprivation (Bendavis et al., 2021).

In the common parlance, these conflicts (NIACs), characterized by fighting between government forces and non-state armed groups (NSAGs), or between such groups themselves, exacerbate the vulnerabilities of women and girl children.

A significant issue is sexual violence, which is often used as a weapon of war. A report presented in 2022 to the UN Security Council documented 3,293 UN-verified cases of sexual violence in conflict, marking an increase from previous years. Women and girls comprised 97% of these cases, highlighting the gendered nature of such violence. This report emphasized the need for prosecution to combat the culture of impunity surrounding these crimes. In Syria, for instance, nearly 10,000 women are detained in conditions where sexual violence is routinely employed to punish, humiliate, and extract confessions. Similar atrocities have been reported in other conflict zones like northern Iraq, where thousands of Yazidi women were subjected to sexual slavery by ISIL.

The reports from organizations such as Amnesty International (2023) and Human Rights Watch (2023) have documented widespread sexual violence against women and girls in Syria's conflict, including in detention centers and by various armed groups. These reports have also highlighted the vulnerability of Syrian women and girls to trafficking and exploitation in displacement camps both within Syria and in neighboring countries such as Turkey and Lebanon. Studies conducted by organizations like UN Women (2023) and the International Organization for Migration (IOM, 2022) have documented cases of sexual violence and trafficking of women and girls by ISIS militants in areas under their control in Iraq. Reports from the United Nations Children's Fund (UNICEF) and the UN Population Fund (UNFPA) have highlighted the increased risk of displacement and child marriage for Iraqi girls as a result of the conflict. Recent UN information such as a newsletter in 2023 published by World Health Organization – Sudan- Top UN Officials Sound Alarm at Spike in Violence Against Women and Girl Children, and some NGO studies have documented sexual violence against women and girls, including in the context of the conflict in Darfur, Sudan. These reports highlighted that the displacement has also led to increased vulnerability to exploitation and abuse. Human Rights Watch (2019) has highlighted the recruitment and use of child soldiers, including girls, by armed groups in Sudan's conflicts. The facts and statistics mentioned in this paragraph and the above paragraph respectively reveal the vulnerabilities faced by women and girls in conflict settings.

Henceforth, investigating the sufficiency of the international legal framework concerning the safeguarding of women and girl children in NIACs is presently of paramount significance. To find the solutions to the three research questions focused in this study, engaged in an introduction to NIAC, discussion on the international instruments concerning NIAC, dialog on the legal mechanisms specifically addressing the protection of women and girl children in NIACs with a critical analysis on its adequacy, the feasible enforceability of the relevant international standards on safety of women and girl children in nonarmed conflict, merits and demerits of the existing international standards on security of women and girls in NIACs. Finally, it proposes recommendations to strengthen the international legal framework and improve the protection mechanisms for women and girls in such conflict areas.

WHAT IS NONINTERNATIONAL ARMED CONFLICT?

A NIAC refers to a situation of armed hostilities within the borders of a single country, involving either sustained combat between government (state) forces and organized armed groups or between such groups themselves. In NIACs, hostilities must reach a certain threshold of intensity beyond irregular/illegal acts of violence or internal disturbances. The nonstate actors involved must be organized, possessing a command structure and the capability to sustain military operations to demand what they want. Unlike international armed conflicts (IACs), involved two or multiple states, NIACs occur within a single state's territory but can have significant implications for international law and humanitarian efforts. The legal framework governing NIACs is primarily derived from international humanitarian law (IHL – which is also known as the law of war and the law of armed conflict); specifically, Article 3 common to the four Geneva Conventions of 1949 and the Additional Protocol II of 1977 having the primary objectives to limit the impact of armed conflict on civilians ensure humane treatment of all persons who are not or no longer participating in hostilities and maintain some measure of order and legal standards amidst conflict.[1,2] These instruments set out the fundamental protections for those not take part in hostilities, including civilians and surrendered combatants. Furthermore, Human Rights law also continues to apply during NIACs, (Dilawar Khan & Sudipta, 1995), ensuring the protection of the fundamental rights of people including women and girls (Rome Statute of the International Criminal Court (ICC) (last amended 2010) – UNGA, 1998). Generally, there are two distinctive/characteristics of NIACs. They are, first, the fighting/dispute/conflict must reach a certain level of intensity, amounting to hostilities and second, NSAG involved in the conflict must possess a sufficient degree of organization to be considered a "party" to the conflict. In a conflict that does not fulfill the above-stated two requirements does not fall into NIAC.

International Instruments Concerning Noninternational Armed Conflict

International instruments on NIACs are crucial for setting legal standards and protections in conflicts within a single state, involving either government forces andNSAGs or between such groups. The most important instruments are as follows:

• Common Article 3 of the Geneva Conventions, August 12, 1949 – Common Article 3 applies to NIACs and sets minimum standards for humane treatment. It prohibits violence to life and person, taking hostages, degrading treatment, and unfair trials (Saandesh, 2011).
• Protocol Additional to the Geneva Conventions of August 12, 1949, and relating to the Protection of Victims of NIACs (Protocol II), June 8, 1977 – Protocol II elaborates on and supplements Common Article 3. Both instruments provide specific protections for those who do not get involved in hostilities, including the wounded and sick, and it regulates the conduct of hostilities (Jean-Baptiste, 2017).
• Rome Statute of the ICC, July 17, 1998 – The Rome Statute criminalizes serious violations of Common Article 3 Geneva Convention and other acts such as intentionally directing attacks against civilians and humanitarian assistance personnel in NIACs. It also includes provisions on war crimes committed in NIACs (Shane, 2010).
• International Covenant on Civil and Political Rights, December 16, 1966 – While not specifically tailored to armed conflicts, the ICCPR provides fundamental protections for individuals' rights that apply at all times, including during NIACs. It protects rights such as the right to life, prohibition of torture and guarantees fair trial standards.
• Convention on Prohibitions or Restrictions on the Use of Certain Conventional Weapons (CCW) which may be deemed to be excessively injurious or to have indiscriminate effects (CCW), October 10, 1980, and its Protocols – The CCW and its various protocols regulate or ban the use of specific types of weapons that cause unnecessary suffering or have indiscriminate effects. Protocol II, for instance, specifically addresses landmines and booby traps in NIACs.
• Convention on the Rights of the Child, November 20, 1989 and Optional Protocol to the Convention on the Rights of the Child on the Involvement of children in armed conflict, May 25, 2000 – The CRC and its Optional Protocol protect children in armed conflicts, prohibiting their recruitment and use in

hostilities and ensuring their rights are protected during and after conflicts (Coomaraswamy, 2021).

- Convention on Elimination of All Forms of Discrimination Against Women adopted in 1979 (CEDAW) by the United Nations General Assembly is another key international treaty focusing on the rights of women. This convention is considered the *Magna Carta* document in respect of the protection of women's rights although it is not directly focused on NIACs. CEDAW could apply at any time – at wartime or ordinary time and at any time of war (IAC or NIAC).
- Beijing Platform for Action, adopted at the Fourth World Conference on Women in 1995, is a comprehensive policy document aimed at promoting gender equality and empowering women. It addresses various critical areas, including the protection of women and children during conflicts. The Platform includes strategic objectives and specific actions to ensure the protection of women and children in NIACs, emphasizing their rights and needs in these challenging circumstances.
- Sustainable Development Goals adopted in 2015 that aim better future for all.
- Furthermore, other than the above-stated treaties the customary IHL also deals with the rules concerning NIACs. Customary IHL, as identified by the International Committee of the Red Cross (ICRC), applies to all armed conflicts, including noninternational ones. It includes rules derived from consistent state practice and a sense of legal obligation (Henckaerts & Doswald-Beck, 2005). However, in this article, the customary laws are not considered as the research focuses on the same separately in another paper.

By adopting international instruments concerning NIACs, the international community expects to achieve the following key objectives.

- Protection of noncombatants – these instruments aim at ensuring the humane treatment of all persons who are not taking an active part in hostilities, including civilians, the wounded and sick, and those who have laid down their arms.
- Prohibition of certain acts of people – these international instruments establish clear prohibitions against acts such as murder, torture, mutilation, taking hostages, unfair trials and degrading treatment.
- Regulation in conduct of hostilities – these soft law documents set standards for the conduct of hostilities, including the protection of civilian objects, the prohibition of indiscriminate attacks, and the principle of proportionality in the use of force.
- Accountability for violations – these instruments provide mechanisms for holding individuals accountable for war crimes and serious violations of IHL, including through international criminal courts and tribunals.
- Specific protection for vulnerable groups – these international legal documents offer additional protections for vulnerable groups such as children and ensure that their recruitment and use in hostilities are prohibited.

- Minimization of suffering – this limits the use of certain types of weapons that cause unnecessary suffering or have indiscriminate effects, thus reducing the human cost of conflicts.
- Humanitarian assistance –these international instruments facilitate and protect humanitarian assistance and ensure that aid reaches those in need without undue interference.

Therefore, it is clear that the adoption of these instruments aims to mitigate the horrors of war, uphold human dignity, and ensure that basic humanitarian principles are respected even in conflict.

Legal Mechanisms Specifically Addressing the Protection of Women and Girl Children in Noninternational Armed Conflicts and Critique

As said earlier in NIACs, women and girl children are mostly susceptible to violence, including sexual violence, varied types of exploitation, and displacement. IHL and international human rights law (IHRL) offer various protections to mitigate these risks. First, briefly discuss the relevant legal mechanism available for addressing the protection of women and girl children in NIACs and then engage in the criticism of the available standards.

The Geneva Conventions and their Additional Protocols form the bedrock of IHL. Common Article 3 of the Geneva Conventions applies to NIACs and mandates humane treatment without adverse distinction. Specifically, it prohibits violence to life and person, taking hostages, and outrages upon personal dignity, including humiliating and degrading treatment. Additional Protocol II relating to NIACs, provides further protections. It explicitly prohibits violence against women and children, including rape, enforced prostitution, and any form of indecent assault (Article 4). This protocol also emphasizes the special protection of children and the need for their care and education (Article 4(3)).

Article 7 of the Rome Statute prohibits crime against humanity includes some provisions to protect women and girls both in IACs and NIACs. Article 7 (1) (g) criminalizes rape, sexual slavery, enforced prostitution, forced pregnancy, forced sterilization, and any other form of sexual violence of comparable gravity whilst Article 7 (2) (f) includes the crime of enforced sterilization which can specifically impact women. Article 8(2) (c) and Article 8(2) (e) specifically address war crimes committed in NIACs. Article 8(2) (c) addresses serious violations of Common Article 3 of the Geneva Conventions, including: Violence to life and person, in particular murder of all kinds, mutilation, cruel treatment, and torture; Committing outrages upon personal dignity, in particular humiliating and degrading treatment; The passing of sentences and the carrying out of executions without previous judgment pronounced by a regularly constituted court. This article enumerates other serious violations of the laws and customs applicable in armed conflicts not of an international character, within the established framework of international law, including: Rape, sexual slavery, enforced prostitution, forced pregnancy, as defined in Article 7(2) (f), enforced sterilization, and any other form of sexual violence also constituting a serious violation of article 3 common to the four Geneva Conventions; Conscripting or enlisting children under the age of 15 years into armed forces or groups or using them to participate actively in hostilities. Article 8(2) (e) (vii) prohibits the conscription, enlistment, or use of children under 15 in hostilities, ensuring their protection from being forced into combat roles. This provision is common to all children with no gender difference. Article 21 (3) provides a general principle on the application and interpretation of law. According to this Article, it must be consistent with internationally recognized human rights, and be without any adverse distinction founded on grounds such as gender.

Articles 2–10 and 24–26 which focus on the protection of some basic human rights of the people are applicable at all times regarding any person.

The ICCPR's Human Rights Committee, which monitors the implementation of the Covenant, has also issued General Comments providing interpretive guidance on how these rights should be upheld, including during times of conflict. The Committee emphasizes the importance of ensuring that measures taken during NIACs comply with the Covenant's provisions, particularly in protecting vulnerable groups such as women and children.

The Convention on Prohibitions or Restrictions on the Use of CCW. Protocol I (nondetectable fragments) prohibit the use of weapons whose primary effect is to injure by fragments that cannot be detected by X-rays. This reduces the risk of severe injury to all civilians, including women and children, ensuring better medical treatment outcomes if they are injured. Protocol II (mines, booby-traps and other devices), prohibits the indiscriminate use of mines, booby traps, and other devices. This is crucial for protecting women and children who are often noncombatants and more vulnerable to the effects of such weapons. Also, it requires that parties to a conflict take feasible precautions to protect civilians from the effects of these weapons, including marking, monitoring, and removing mines, which can dispro- portionately affect women and children during and after conflicts. Protocol III (incendiary weapons) restricts the use of incendiary weapons, particularly in areas with concentrated civilian populations. This is significant for protecting women and children from the severe burns and injuries such weapons cause. Protocol IV (blinding laser weapons) prohibits the use of laser weapons designed to cause per- manent blindness. Women and children, who are often noncombatants, benefit from this protection against a particularly cruel and incapacitating form of injury. Pro- tocol V obligates parties to a conflict to clear explosive remnants of war (ERW) such as unexploded ordnance (UXO) and abandoned explosive ordnance and requires states to take measures to ensure the safety of civilian populations from ERW, including risk education and victim assistance. This is particularly important for women and children who are at higher risk of encountering ERW while carrying out daily activities such as gathering food or water. It is important to note that all these protocols, while not explicitly targeting women and girl children, include general provisions that indirectly benefit them by aiming to reduce civilian casualties and injuries caused by CCW.

IHRL remains applicable during armed conflicts. Other than the ICCPR, key instruments include the Convention on the Elimination of All Forms of Discrimination Against Women (CEDAW) and the Convention on the Rights of the Child (CRC). CEDAW requires states to take appropriate measures to eliminate discrimination against women and ensure their protection and rights during armed conflict. Similarly, the CRC mandates the protection of children from all forms of physical or mental violence, injury, abuse, and exploitation (Article 19). The Optional Protocol to the CRC on the Involvement of Children in Armed Conflict further safeguards children by raising the minimum age for direct participation in hostilities to 18 years and obligating states to ensure that children are not recruited into armed forces or groups.

The United Nations Security Council (UNSC) has passed several resolutions under the Women, Peace, and Security (WPS) agenda, emphasizing the protection of women and children in armed conflicts. Resolution 1325 (2000) calls for the protection of women and girls from gender-based violence and their involvement in peace processes. Subsequent resolutions, such as 1820 (2008) and 1888 (2009), specifically address sexual violence in conflict, mandating measures to prevent and respond to such acts.

Some provisions of the Beijing Platform for Action, adopted at the Fourth World Conference on Women in 1995 could be considered the protection of women and girl children specifically. Strategic objective E1 says that the necessity to increase the participation of women in conflict resolution at decision-making levels and protect women living in situations of armed and other conflicts or under foreign occupation. Strategic objective 4 emphasizes promoting women's contribution to fostering a culture of peace. Strategic objective E 5 highlights the protection, assistance, and training of refugee women, other displaced women in need of international security, and internally displaced women. Strategic objective I 1 aims to promote and protect the human rights of women through the full implementation of all human rights instruments especially the Convention on the Elimination of All Forms of Discrimination Against Women (CEDAW). Strategic objective L 5 suggests necessity of the eliminating discrimination against girls in education, skills development, and training during all time.

Despite the (comprehensive) legal framework above-stated, substantial and noteworthy challenges remain in the protection of women and girl children in NIACs. One of the primary criticisms is the gap between legal norms and their enforcement. NSAGs, often key perpetrators of violence in non-international conflicts, are not formal signatories to international treaties, complicating enforcement. While there are mechanisms to hold state actors accountable, such as the ICC, there is limited recourse against NSAGs.

As another criticism, I may argue that in many conflict zones, engrained cultural/social norms and social structures obstruct the protection of women and girls. Patriarchal/male-dominated societies may not prioritize the rights and protections of women and children, leading to a lack of local support for international norms. Women and girls in such war zones are not protected due to this reason.

Ensuring access to justice and accountability for violations remains problematic. Conflict zones often lack functioning legal systems, and victims may be unable or unwilling to report abuses due to fear of retaliation or stigma. This reason also contributes to the nonprotection of women and girls in war zones.

Effective protection requires substantial international support and resources. Humanitarian aid, legal assistance, and psychosocial support are critical, yet often insufficiently provided. International Organizations must prioritize these areas to ensure the effective implementation of protective measures.

While international legal frameworks provide robust protections for women and girl children in NIACs, the effectiveness of these mechanisms is hindered by implementation challenges, societal barriers, and resource constraints. Addressing these gaps requires a concerted effort by the international community, including robust enforcement mechanisms, cultural sensitization programs, and enhanced support for victims. Only through such comprehensive measures can the legal protections translate into tangible safety and security for women and girl children in conflict zones (Baines, 2017; Bellal, 2018).

Adopted in 2015, the SDGs include specific targets for gender equality (Goal 5) and the protection of children from violence (Goal 16.2). These goals provide a framework for integrating gender-sensitive and child-protective policies into national development agendas.

Feasible Enforceability and Merits and Demerits of the Relevant International Standards on the Safety of Women and Girl Children in Nonarmed Conflict

The above discussion demonstrates that the safety of women and girl children in nonarmed conflict settings is governed by a range of international standards including treaties, conventions, and resolutions aimed at preventing violence, ensuring justice, and promoting gender equality. This part of the paper explores the enforceability of these standards, highlighting their merits and demerits in practice.

As far as the practicable enforceability of the Geneva Conventions is concerned, the Conventions primarily address armed conflicts, making their direct application to nonarmed conflicts challenging. National laws inspired by these conventions could be adapted, but inconsistent enforcement and cultural barriers pose significant obstacles. International institutions like the ICRC would require expanded mandates and resources to monitor nonarmed conflicts effectively. Some merits could be seen in the conventions such as establishing international standards (norms) to facilitate global cooperation and protection, prioritizing the rights and safety of women and children considering them vulnerable groups, and applying humanitarian principles by emphasizing humane treatment applicable across various contexts. The provisions of the Geneva Conventions may not fully address issues like domestic violence or human trafficking, feebler mechanisms and varied national legal systems hinder effective enforcement, absence of strong provisions to face the societal norms in some regions may resist the application of these standards outside armed conflict contexts are some of the demerits in the Conventions.

The Optional Protocol II to the Geneva Conventions, focusing on the safety of women and girl children, aims to address their protection in nonarmed conflicts. Its enforceability, however, is hindered by its optional and nonbinding nature, leading to varied implementation across different legal jurisdictions (ICRC,

2024). The protocol's merits lie in its potential to raise global awareness, provide a framework for advocacy and offer guidelines for enhancing the safety and rights of vulnerable populations (Amnesty International, 2023). However, on the downside, the lack of mandatory enforcement mechanisms means that compliance is largely voluntary, often resulting in inconsistent application and limited effectiveness. Additionally, the varying capacities of national legal systems to adopt and enforce these guidelines can lead to significant disparities in protection levels. Thus, while the protocol is a positive step towards recognizing and addressing these issues, its impact is contingent upon broader international commitment and national legislative support.

The Rome Statute's provisions on the safety of women and girl children in non-armed conflict are marked by both significant merits and notable challenges in enforceability. The Statute explicitly criminalizes acts such as sexual violence, offering a robust legal framework to address these crimes globally (Bensouda, 2018). This establishes a precedent for holding perpetrators accountable, thus serving as a deterrent. However, the enforceability of these provisions is often hindered by the ICC's reliance on state cooperation, which can be inconsistent due to political and jurisdictional issues (Kreß & Sluiter, 2019). Furthermore, while the Statute sets high standards, the practical implementation at the domestic level frequently falls short due to inadequate legal infrastructure and cultural resistance. It may be said that while the Rome Statute provides critical international standards for protecting women and girls, its effective enforcement requires enhanced international collaboration and strengthened domestic legal systems.

As far as CEDAW is concerned it, adopted in 1979 by the United Nations General Assembly, is a key international treaty focusing on the rights of women. It obligates state parties to take measures to eliminate discrimination against women in all forms, ensuring their full development and advancement (Article 2). The CEDAW Committee monitors implementation and reviews state parties' reports, issuing recommendations and general comments to guide states in fulfilling their obligations. While CEDAW establishes a comprehensive legal framework, its enforceability is limited by the reliance on State reporting and the absence of binding enforcement mechanisms. Compliance is primarily driven by political and moral pressure rather than legal compulsion.

Adopted in 1989, the CRC emphasizes the protection of children from violence, exploitation, and abuse (Articles 19 and 34). It mandates state parties to undertake all appropriate legislative, administrative, and other measures for implementation. The CRC benefits from widespread ratification and robust monitoring by the Committee on the Rights of the Child. However, similar to CEDAW, enforcement is limited to periodic reviews and recommendations, lacking direct legal mechanisms to compel state compliance.

The Convention on Prohibitions or Restrictions on the Use of CCW primarily addresses the use of specific weapons in armed conflicts, but its principles can indirectly enhance the safety of women and girl children in nonarmed conflicts by promoting general humanitarian norms. As the Human Rights Watch 2023 states the convention's merits include raising awareness about the indiscriminate effects of certain weapons and establishing guidelines that can influence broader international standards, thereby indirectly benefiting civilians in nonarmed situations. However, its limitations are evident as it does not specifically target nonarmed conflicts, limiting its direct applicability and effectiveness in such contexts. Additionally, enforcement is contingent on the commitment of state parties, which can vary significantly. Despite these challenges, the CCW contributes to the overarching goal of protecting vulnerable populations by fostering a culture of compliance with humanitarian principles.

It is not wrong to say that the International Covenant on Civil and Political Rights also provides essential protections for the safety of women and girl children in nonarmed conflict (as it includes all time and all people) through its provisions on non-discrimination and the right to security (Nowak & Engel, 2019). These provisions establish a framework for safeguarding against gender-based violence and ensuring equal treatment under the law. The enforceability of the ICCPR, however, faces significant challenges. While the Human Rights Committee monitors compliance, it relies on state reports and lacks direct enforcement mechanisms (Joseph & Castan, 2013). This limits the effectiveness of the ICCPR in compelling states to act against violations. Additionally, cultural and sociopolitical barriers often impede the domestic application of these international standards.

The Beijing Platform, which was mentioned earlier, is a nonbinding yet influential policy document advocating for gender equality and the empowerment of women. It outlines strategic objectives and actions to prevent and address violence against women and girls. As a non-binding agreement, the Beijing Platform relies on political will and international cooperation for implementation. Its strength lies in setting normative standards and mobilizing global advocacy rather than enforcing compliance.

The SDGs are aspirational and nonbinding, with progress monitored through voluntary national reviews. Their enforceability depends on national commitment and the availability of resources for implementation.

Recommendations to Strengthen the International Legal Framework to Improve the Protection Mechanisms for Women and Girls in Noninternational Armed Conflict

To strengthen the protection mechanisms for women and girls in NIACs, the following recommendations can be made for the Geneva Conventions, Optional Protocol II, Rome Statute, Convention on CCW, CEDAW, CRC, and the Beijing Platform.

(1) Geneva Conventions and Optional Protocol II:
   • Enhanced training: Implement comprehensive training programs for military and nonstate actors on gender-sensitive approaches and the specific protections afforded to women and girls under these instruments.
   • Stronger enforcement mechanism: Establish more robust monitoring and enforcement mechanisms to ensure compliance by all parties in conflicts.

(2) Rome Statute:
  - Increased legal cooperation of the countries: promote greater international cooperation to ensure that states assist in the enforcement of ICC mandates, particularly regarding gender-based violence.
  - Victim support programs: Develop and fund comprehensive victim support and rehabilitation programs for women and girls affected by conflict-related crimes.
(3) Convention on CCW:
  - Ban on gender-specific weapons: Advocate for the prohibition of weapons that disproportionately affect women and girls, such as certain types of landmines and explosive devices.
  - Data collection: Enhance data collection and reporting on the gendered impact of conventional weapons to inform policy and operational changes.
(4) Convention on Elimination of All Forms of Discrimination Against Women
  - National Action Plans: encourage states to develop and implement National Action Plans specifically addressing the protection of women and girls in conflict zone.
  - Periodic Reviews: Conduct regular reviews and updates of state reports with a focus on compliance with obligations related to conflict situations.
(5) Convention on the Rights of the Child
  - Child-specific protection: Strengthen provisions and enforcement related to the protection of girl children in conflict, including preventing recruitment and sexual exploitation.
  - Education programs: Implement educational programs in conflict zones that focus on the rights and protection of girl children.
(6) Beijing Platform for Action
  - Gender mainstreaming: Ensure that the gender perspectives are integrated into all peacekeeping and humanitarian missions.
  - Grassroots involvement: Support grassroots organizations working on the ground to protect and empower women and girls in conflict zones.

CONCLUSION

In conclusion, while significant strides have been made in developing an international legal framework to protect women and girl children in NIACs, challenges persist regarding the adequacy of its implementation and enforcement. The Geneva Conventions and Optional Protocol II, Rome Statute, CEDAW, CRC, and other instruments discussed above provide crucial standards and mechanisms for safeguarding their rights. However, gaps remain in translating these standards into effective action on the ground. Strengthening state compliance, enhancing monitoring and enforcement mechanisms, promoting gender-sensitive approaches, and prioritizing the needs of women and girl children in conflict zones are essential steps toward improving the adequacy of the international legal framework. Continued efforts are necessary to ensure that legal protections translate into tangible improvements in the lives of those most vulnerable to the horrors of armed conflict. Finally, the research suggests that by implementing the proposed recommendations, the protection mechanisms for women and girls in NIACs can be strengthened, ensuring better adherence to international standards and improved outcomes for affected individuals – women and girl children.

NOTES

1. Article 3 of the Geneva Conventions of 1949, often referred to as Common Article 3, is a key provision that applies to noninternational armed conflicts (such as civil wars) and sets minimum standards for the humane treatment of individuals who are not actively participating in hostilities. It is called "Common Article 3" because it is included in all four of the Geneva Conventions. Common Article 3 sets out fundamental rules to protect those who are not directly involved in the conflict, including civilians, members of armed forces who have laid down their arms, and wounded, sick, or detained combatants. The key provisions of Article 3 are as follows:

- Humane treatment: It mandates that all persons who are not actively participating in hostilities be treated humanely, without adverse distinction based on race, color, religion, or other criteria.
- Prohibited actions: The article specifically prohibits certain acts against these persons, including violence to life and person, including *murder, mutilation, torture,* and *cruel treatment.* Taking of hostages. Outrages upon personal dignity, including *humiliating and degrading treatment.* Sentences or executions without a prior *judgment* by a properly constituted court that provides all necessary judicial guarantees.
- Care for the wounded and sick: It emphasizes that the wounded and sick should be cared for and treated with the same considerations as others, without any form of discrimination.

2. Protocol additional to the Geneva conventions of August 12, 1949, and relating to the protection of victims of NIACs (Protocol II), of June 8, 1977

Article 1: Material field of application.

(1) This Protocol, which develops and supplements Article 3 common to the Geneva Conventions of August 12, 1949, without modifying its existing conditions of applications, shall apply to all armed conflicts which are not covered by Article 1 of the Protocol Additional to the Geneva Conventions of August 12, 1949, and relating to the Protection of Victims of International Armed Conflicts (Protocol I) and which take place in the territory of a High Contracting Party between its armed forces and dissident armed forces or other organized armed groups which, under responsible command, exercise such control over a part of its territory as to enable them to carry out sustained and concerted military operations and to implement this Protocol. (2) This Protocol shall not apply to situations of internal disturbances and tensions, such as riots, isolated and sporadic acts of violence, and other acts of a similar nature, as not being armed conflicts.

Article 2: Personal field of application.

(1) This Protocol shall be applied without any adverse distinction founded on race, colour, sex, language, religion or belief, political or other opinion, national or social origin, wealth, birth or other status, or on any other similar criteria (hereinafter referred to as "adverse distinction") to all persons affected by an armed conflict as defined in Article 1. (2) At the end of the armed conflict, all the persons who have been deprived of their liberty or whose liberty has been restricted for reasons related to such conflict, as well as those deprived of their liberty or whose liberty is restricted after the conflict for the same reasons, shall enjoy the protection of Articles 5 and 6 until the end of such deprivation or restriction of liberty.

REFERENCES

Armed Conflict Survey. (2023). From global jihad to local insurgencies: The changing nature of Sub-Saharan Jihadism. https://www.iiss.org/publications/armed-conflict-survey/2023/from-global-jihad-to-local-insurgencies. Accessed on January, 2024.

Amnesty International. (2023). *Syria: Conflict-related sexual violence and the exploitation of women and girls.* Amnesty International Report.

Baines, E. (2017). *Buried in the heart: Women, complex victimhood and the war in northern Uganda.* Cambridge University Press.

Bellal, A. (2018). *Non-state armed groups in international humanitarian law: Nature, scope, and consequences.* Geneva Academy of International Humanitarian Law and Human Rights.

Bendavid, E., Boerma, T., Akseer, N., Langer, A., Malembaka, E. B., Okiro, E. A., Wise, P. H., Heft-Neal, S., Black, R. E., Bhutta, Z. A., & BRANCH Consortium Steering Committee members. (2021). *The effects of armed conflict on the health of women and children.* National Library of Medicine, National Centre for Biotechnology Information. European PubMed Central.

Bensouda, F. (2018). Gender and the Rome statute of the international criminal court. *International Review of the Red Cross*, 100(907–909), 537–558.

Coomaraswamy, R. (2021). The optional protocol to the convention on the rights of the child on the involvement of children in armed conflict – Towards universal ratification. *The International Journal of Children's Rights*, 18(4), 535–549.

Dilawar Khan, M. D., & Sudipta, B. (1995). Protection of the rights of women, children and elderly: A dynamic perspective. *International Journal of Law and Legal Jurisprudence Studies.* ISSN 2348-8212. https://ijlljs.in/protection-of-the-rights-of-women-children-and-elderly-a-dynamic-perspective

Freedman, J. (2015). *Gender, violence and politics in the Democratic Republic of Congo.* Routledge.

Henckaerts, J.-M., & Doswald-Beck, L. (Eds.), (2005). *Customary international humanitarian law* (Vols. I and II). Cambridge University Press.

Jean-Baptiste, M.-C. (2017). Cracking the toughest nut: Colombia's endeavour with amnesty for political crimes under additional protocol II to the geneva conventions. *Notre Dame Journal of International & Comparative Law*, 7(1), 4.

Joseph, S., & Castan, M. (2013). *The international covenant on civil and political rights: Cases, materials, and commentary.* Oxford University Press.

Human Rights Watch. (2019). *Trafficking and exploitation of women and girls in Syria and neighboring countries.* Human Rights Watch Report.

Human Rights Watch. (2023). *Syria: Women and girls subjected to sexual violence in conflict zones.* Human Rights Watch Report.

International Committee of the Red Cross (ICRC). (2024). *Syria: Humanitarian impact of armed conflict and sexual violence against women.* International Committee of the Red Cross Report.

International Organization for Migration (IOM). (2022). *Trafficking and sexual violence in conflict: Case studies from Iraq and Syria.* International Organization for Migration Report.

Kreß, C., & Sluiter, G. (2019). Enforcement of the Rome statute: A challenge for international criminal justice. *Journal of International Criminal Justice*, 17(1), 1–20.

Nowak, M. (2019). *U.N. Covenant on civil and political rights: CCPR commentary.* N.P. Engel.

Saandesh, S. (2011). Revisiting the international law of armed conflict. *European Journal of International Law*, 22(11), 219–264.

Shane, D. (2010). Prosecuting the war of collective punishment: Is it the time to amend the Rome statute? *Journal of International Criminal Justice*, 8(1), 29–51.

UN Women. (2023). *Sexual violence against women in conflict zones: Syria and Iraq.* UN Women Report.

United Nations General Assembly (UNGA). (1998). *Rome Statute of the International Criminal Court.* UNGA Res. 2187.

World Health Organization (WHO). (2023). *Sudan: Top UN officials sound alarm at spike in violence against women and girl children.* UN Newsletter, WHO Sudan. https://www.who.int/news/item/05-07-2023-sudan-top-un-officials-sound-alarm-at-spike-in-violence-against-women-and-girls

HOW DID ARMED CONFLICTS IMPACT WOMEN IN ASIA: A STUDY FROM 1950 TO 2010

Xingyu Chen

University at Buffalo, State University of New York, USA

ABSTRACT

The period from 1950 to 2010 in Asia witnessed numerous conflicts that profoundly shaped the sociopolitical landscape of the region. This study provides a comprehensive examination of the dynamics of these conflicts, with a particular focus on conflict-induced displacement and gender-based violence (GBV). By synthesizing existing research and employing descriptive statistical analysis, this study presents essential information on the duration and intensity of conflicts during this era. Conflict-induced displacement and GBV emerge as significant challenges, profoundly affecting millions of lives and altering the demographic and social fabric of numerous countries. In this study, descriptive statistical data analysis serves as a preliminary tool, providing a foundational exploration of these issues. While this approach reveals important trends and patterns, it does not quantify the extent of impact. Instead, it sets the stage for future research to delve deeper into causality and the underlying mechanisms driving these phenomena. This study underscores the importance of addressing conflict-induced displacement and GBV as critical aspects of conflict dynamics. By highlighting these challenges and the specific impacts on women, it contributes to the ongoing discourse on conflict resolution and postconflict reconstruction in Asia, paving the way for more nuanced and in-depth investigations in the future.

Keywords: Conflict dynamics; gender-based violence; conflict-induced displacement; women and conflict; conflict duration; Asia

Scars of War
Research in Political Sociology, Volume 30, 61–87
Copyright © 2025 Xingyu Chen
Published under exclusive licence by Emerald Publishing Limited
ISSN: 0895-9935/doi:10.1108/S0895-993520250000030006

INTRODUCTION

In the year 2000, about one-fifth of the 1.6 million violence-related deaths globally were attributed to war, totaling approximately 310,000 (WHO, 2002). Notably, violence-related deaths in low-to-middle-income countries in 2000 reached 32.1 per 100,000 population, nearly double the rate in high-income countries (WHO, 2002). Furthermore, war-related violence often displays disproportionate distributions across genders and regions, resulting in increased GBV against women and girls as a tactic of war (OHCHR, 2022). These disparities underscore the unequal impacts on specific populations, such as women and girls, during times of conflict and instability.

During periods of conflict and instability, essential services, such as sexual and reproductive health services, are often suspended or shut down, leaving women and girls particularly vulnerable. This interruption increases the risk of unplanned pregnancy, maternal mortality, severe sexual and reproductive injuries, and sexually transmitted infections due to conflict-related sexual violence. The United Nations Population Fund (UNFPA)'s flagship State of World Population report underscores how crises and conflicts can profoundly impact women, stripping them of agency, perpetuating gender inequality, and constraining their full participation in society (United Nations Population Fund [UNFPA], 2022). These challenges are compounded by disruptions to healthcare systems and restricted access to maternal health services, heightening the risks to women's health and well-being (United Nations Population Fund [UNFPA], 2022). The ramifications of crises and conflicts on women's agency and health can significantly impede global progress toward achieving the Sustainable Development Goals (SDGs) set by the UN, with the target date set for 2030.

Women's health during armed conflicts is one of the least understood issues afflicting developing countries (Brueck & d'Errico, 2019; DeRose & Kravdal, 2007; Ghimire & Pun, 2006; Iqbal, 2010; Urdal & Che, 2013). Almost 295,000 women died from pregnancy-related causes in 2017, with 94% of these maternal deaths occurring in low-income and lower-middle-income countries (WHO, 2019). The problem is particularly acute in Asia; nearly 20% (58,000) of the total global maternal deaths occurred in South Asia while over 5% (16,000) occurred in Southeast Asia (WHO, 2019). Despite the very high maternal mortality rate between 2000 and 2017, South Asia achieved a significant reduction in maternal mortality, decreasing from 384 per 100,000 live births to 157 in 2017, marking a decline of nearly 60% (WHO, 2019). Additionally, Central Asia and East Asia nearly halved the maternal mortality rate from 2000 to 2017 (WHO, 2019).

While systematic studies on women's health in Asian conflict zones remain limited, insights from related regions, such as Sub-Saharan Africa (SSA), offer valuable perspectives. For instance, examining fertility rates in conflict-affected regions, such as SSA, provides a lens through which to understand the broader implications of armed conflict on women's health. Among the 11 countries in SSA, the total fertility rate (TFR) is higher above 6.0, meaning that women in those countries are, on average, having more than six children during their reproductive years (15–49 years old). Eight of these countries had experienced recent protracted high-intensity, armed conflicts with at least 1,000 battlefield deaths annually (UN Population Fund, 2007). These countries were also considered to be "very high alert" or "high alert" according to The Fragile State Index, ranking in high vulnerability in state security, economic, political, and social indicators by The Fund for Peace in 2017.

Despite high fertility levels being common in conflict settings, relatively little systematic research has been conducted on how armed conflicts affect women. We lack a comprehensive understanding of how conflicts in these regions – considering their duration, intensity, and impact – lead to large-scale displacement and GBV. Consequently, we do not fully understand why and how women in developing countries suffer and die at higher rates in conflict-affected areas.

This study provides a comprehensive examination of conflict dynamics in Asia from 1950 to 2010, focusing on conflict-induced displacement and GBV. By synthesizing existing research and applying descriptive statistics, this study presents basic information on the duration and intensity of conflicts during this period, highlighting the significant challenges posed by conflict-induced displacement and GBV in the region.

It is important to note that this study employs descriptive statistical data analysis as a preliminary step to understand the general picture of conflict, displacement, and GBV in Asia from 1950 to 2010. While descriptive statistical data reveal trends and patterns, they do not quantify the extent of impact. Instead, they serve as a foundational exploration, paving the way for future research to investigate causality and the underlying mechanisms.

Through the analysis of empirical evidence and statistical data, this study contributes to a deeper understanding of the specific challenges confronting women in conflict-affected areas. Furthermore, the study advocates for targeted interventions to address these pressing concerns, emphasizing the critical importance of prioritizing women's health initiatives within the broader discourse on sustainable development in Asia.

THEORETICAL BACKGROUND

After World War II (WWII), 90% of all military conflicts took place in developing countries. Women and girls have disproportionately suffered from the indirect and long-term consequences of these conflicts, from damage to infrastructure and health services, GBV, and economic deterioration, as well as from displacement and dislocation during and after conflicts. However, the impact of armed conflict on women' health in developing countries is rarely studied. Unlike developed countries in North America or Europe, where changes in demography are well-documented (e.g. Bongaarts, 1977; Davis & Blake, 1956; Henry, 1972; Hobscraft, 1996; Sheps, Menken, & Radick, 1973; Wynn & Wynn, 1993), the issue is less clear in war-affected areas of developing countries due to challenge in obtaining sufficient data as well as difficulty in obtaining self-reported information.

Asia offers an appropriate case for examining of the effects of war on women's health. After WWII , Asian countries underwent abrupt changes of regimes, gained independence from colonial powers, re-organized political communities, and sparked new disturbances during and after the Cold War. The region has seen persistent political instability and significant conflict-induced displacement. Unfortunately, reliable information during periods of military conflict in this region is limited.

There is ample evidence to suggest that women's health is influenced by the social environment, including political instability, regional violence, battlefield and civilian casualties, and GBV (Chukwuma et al., 2021; Ekzayez et al., 2021; Namasivayam et al., 2017; Price & Bohara, 2013; Ramos Jaraba et al., 2020; Ziegler et al., 2020; Ziegler et al., 2021). This study focuses on variables related to conflict-induced political instability and regional violence, including conflict-related deaths, duration of war, the number of internally displaced persons (IDPs) by conflict and violence, and conflict-related GBV.

Military conflicts are major triggers of global refugee crises. The lingering social impact of such conflicts often poses severe challenges to the resulting displaced populations. Women's health, in particular, is heavily influenced by conflict-induced displacement. This is especially evident among conflict-induced displaced populations in three areas: women's reproductive health, rape or other forms of GBV, and mental health.

According to the World Population Report (2002), 75% of displaced and refugee populations are women and children, and 25% of these are women of reproductive age (15–49 years old). Among these women, 20% will be pregnant. Though women may not be an intrinsically vulnerable group, an increased potential vulnerability can be seen among women concerning reproductive health outcomes during times of conflict-induced displacement (Black et al., 2014). While traditional views often associate women's vulnerability with gender roles and power dynamics, the term "intrinsic vulnerability" here refers specifically to the increased potential vulnerability observed during times of conflict-induced displacement.

Though some military conflicts may not cause high numbers of casualties or create a large number of conflict-related disabilities amongst displaced populations, conflict-induced populations often suffer from shortages in human resources and a lack of provision for basic needs, in addition to a general absence of public health infrastructure (Holtzman & Nezam, 2004; Kottegoda et al., 2008; Lozano-Gracia et al., 2010; McGinn, 2000).

Previous studies suggest that conflict-induced displacement is frequently associated with a mixed response to women's reproductive health. After reviewing the data on pregnancy outcomes of refugees living in stable camp settings since 1990s, McGinn (2000) stated that poor pregnancy outcomes are very common in many war-affected populations and can worsen during active stages of conflicts. Once a situation stabilizes allowing for health services to become available to refugees at camp sites, maternal mortality and neonatal mortality rates lower, which has an adverse effect on pregnancy outcomes both for host and home countries as they respond to pressure to replace deceased numbers of children and warriors. However, fertility rates fall again, as McGinn

(2000) has pointed out, due to the stress and uncertainties of refugee life being less conducive to childbearing.

This is particularly evident in developing countries, which have seen 90% of the conflicts since WWII. Conflicts in such countries have a greater tendency to exacerbate existing problems connected with a lack of obstetric services. One of the examples is the Democratic Republic of Congo. The war-torn eastern area has higher maternal mortality rate, 1,174 deaths per 100,000 live births, compared with the relatively peaceful western area which had 881 deaths (Black et al., 2014). The WHO's report (2019) on emergency obstetric care also suggests that about 15% of displaced pregnant women will encounter life-threatening obstetric complications and that more than 170,000 maternal deaths happen among forced migrants during humanitarian crises every year. The challenges escalate for the internally-displaced population, particularly during periods of active conflict. In war-affected areas such as Afghanistan, internally-displaced refugees face a higher maternal mortality rate of 820 per 100,000 live births. In comparison, refugees displaced to established camps experience a notably lower rate of 291 per 100,000 live births (O'Heir, 2004). It is essential to highlight that the difference in maternal mortality rates is significant and emphasizes the distinct vulnerabilities faced by internally-displaced refugees and those in refugee camps.

Conflict-induced social instability and GBV also add risk factors to the overall well-being of a displaced population, especially women and adolescent girls (Black et al., 2014; Lischer, 2007; Patel et al., 2012; Stark et al., 2010; Wirtz et al., 2014). The current review of available data is limited in scope to rape and domestic violence among conflict-affected populations that are forced to migrate. Rape is often used by armies as a weapon of war, while violence by intimate partners or acquaintances is more prevalent in the stable phase of war. The prevalence of GBV is widespread in conflict situations. An estimated 250,000–400,000 women were raped during the Bangladesh War in 1971, and 39% of Vietnamese women aged from 11 to 40 years old were abducted or raped when they fled the country by sea in 1985 (Swiss & Giller, 1993). McGinn (2000) has pointed out that it is difficult to quantify the degree to which refugee women are affected by rape and domestic violence, compared with their counterparts in settled populations.

Studies suggest that refugee women are at higher risk of rape or other forms of GBV than those in settled populations. Studies show that the vulnerability of women often increases in areas of conflict and displacement, and this vulnerability is further exacerbated by prevailing cultural norms and practices. This risk and vulnerability are enhanced in times of conflict-induced displacement for various reasons: the collapse of livelihoods, being left unsupervised in camps or idle during the day, commuting within camp at night away from the family hut, and having inadequate access to appropriate sexual health information and services (Patel et al., 2012). Additional factors contribute to an increase in domestic conflict and violence: the lack of employment opportunities for young, men and the lack of living space in displaced settings (Kottegoda et al., 2008). This is consistent with the study of GBV in internally-displaced people's camps of conflict-affected northern Uganda. As a major issue among women and girls,

57.8% of respondents spontaneously mentioned intimate partner violence and 22.5% spontaneously mentioned rape (Stark et al., 2010). Research into the relationship between intimate partner violence and outsider violence – for example, violence perpetrated by military or para-military personnel, police officers, jail or prison guards, community members, or fellow refugees – found that women in Rwanda who had previously experienced violence from outsiders had a higher risk of intimate partner violence in conflict-affected settings (Wako et al., 2015).

DATA AND METHOD

This study creates a database detailing the intensity and duration of conflicts, the number of IDPs, and incidents of GBV in selected Asian countries from 1950 to 2010. It provides a clear understanding of the duration and intensity of armed conflicts, with a particular focus on displacement and increased GBV, thereby highlighting the humanitarian and social challenges that arise from such conflicts. The data are analyzed using the IBM SPSS Statistics 28 software package and organized as country-year observations to facilitate detailed analysis and interpretation.

Data on the number of battle-related deaths and conflict duration are retrieved from the Peace Research Institute Oslo (PRIO) and the Correlates of War Project (1816–2010) by Meredith Reid Sarkees. Most of the data on conflict-related GBV are retrieved from the Sexual Violence in Armed Conflict (SVAC) dataset, which covers conflict-related sexual violence committed by government/state military, pro-government militias, and rebel/insurgent forces between 1989 and 2019. Data prior to 1989 are obtained from official reports by the United States Institute of Peace, UN Human Rights Office of the High Commissioner, Women's International League for Peace and Freedom, the International Institute for Strategic Studies, the Geneva Center for Security Sector Governance, UN Women, and the World Bank.

Data on conflict-related IDPs are retrieved from the World Development Indicators (1960–2020) by the World Bank. For countries involved in conflicts before 1960, information is supplemented by other sources, including the Report of the Representative of the Secretary-General on the Human Rights of IDPs by the United Nations Commission on Human Rights (1995), the Internal Displacement Monitoring Center (2022), and studies such as *Indonesia's Internally Displaced* (2000) and the *UN' Guiding Principles on Internal Displacement* (2000). Additional sources include research on the relational displacements of Vietnamese refugees and the Indigenous Aetas by the Philippine Refugee Processing Center (Le Espiritu & Ruanto-Ramirez, 2020; Ratih, 2000).

The time frame from 1950 to 2010 is chosen strategically for practical reasons. First, the year 1950 marks a period when many countries began systematically recording data about displacement, facilitating relatively easier access to information. Second, concluding the study in 2010 ensures a substantial time span for analysis without introducing excessive complexity to the research process.

In this study, only Asian countries involved in war conflicts with one or more countries after 1950 are selected. There are two phases in selecting countries that meet the criteria, involving data derived from two datasets. In phase 1, the primary data source is *The Correlates of War Project 1816–2007 (COW Datasets v4.0)* by Sarkees and Wayman (2010). The COW Datasets are compiled by dedicated research teams that systematically determine the presence of conflict using consistent and comparable definitions across countries and years. The COW Datasets use "war event" as the unit of analysis and define war as "sustained combat involving organized armed forces, resulting in a minimum of 1,000 battle-related fatalities."

Based on the links between conflicts and regime types in the context of Asia after 1950, there are five thematic patterns: intercommunal violence, cross-border insurgency and terrorism, GBV, and land/natural resource conflicts. However, after cross-referencing with reports from *The State of the World's Refugees: The Challenge of Protection* (UNHCR, 1993), three types of war specifically feature significant battlefield deaths and forced migrations: inter-state wars, ethnic conflicts, and nonethnic civil conflicts. In the COW Datasets, these conflicts are categorized as interstate war (War Type 1), intra-state war (War Types 4, 5, 6, and 7), and extra-state war (War Types 2 and 3).

In this study, Asian countries are selected based on regions where combat involving the state occurred (Value 7 = Asia) and the time frame (1950–2010). Fifteen countries meet the criteria in Phase 1: Afghanistan, Burma, Cambodia, China, India, Indonesia, Laos, Nepal, North Korea, Pakistan, Philippines, South Korea, Sri Lanka, Thailand, and Vietnam.

The COW Datasets set the threshold of conflict as those with a minimum of 1,000 battle-related deaths, excluding conflicts with less than 1,000 battle-related deaths (Correlates of War Project, 2010). To achieve a comprehensive portrayal of war conflict situations, conflicts with fewer than 1,000 battle-related deaths are added, using data from the Uppsala Conflict Data Program (UCDP) to avoid missed cases (Uppsala Conflict Data Program, 2024). The UCDP defines conflict as "a contested incompatibility that concerns government and/or territory where the use of armed force between two parties results in a minimum of 25 battle-related deaths in a calendar year." The UCDP dataset uses a unit called the conflict year. Each conflict is listed according to fighting in one or more countries/territories with a minimum threshold of 25 battle-related deaths.

By combining the COW datasets with the UCDP dataset, both large conflicts with over 1,000 battle-related deaths and smaller conflicts with 25 battle-related deaths per year are included, depicted as country-year observations. This approach ensures a comprehensive analysis of conflict dynamics in Asia from 1950 to 2010.

AN OVERVIEW OF ARMED CONFLICTS IN ASIA (1950–2010)

Over the past 60 years, approximately one-third of the total countries in Asia have found themselves entangled in military conflicts. These conflicts have been further exacerbated by interventions from global powers like the United States and the Soviet Union, continuing to ignite violence in the region to this day. These consequences underscore the emergence of risks that transcend national borders. However, existing studies have predominantly associated military conflicts with shifts in population dynamics, sex ratios, age structures, conflict duration, and human casualties. Despite this body of work, the precise role and directional impact of military conflicts remain enigmatic. While international war and homicide datasets offer insights into violence in Asia, their focus often gravitates toward specific types of violence, such as categorizations of civil disturbance, political violence, or terrorism. Alternatively, these datasets amalgamate all forms of conflict into a single metric, masking the underlying causes of these disputes (Asia Foundation, 2017). Our comprehension of how these distinct forms of violence interconnect remains limited. For instance, we lack understanding regarding whether a country undergoing a particular type of conflict, like cross-border insurgency or ethnic riots, is also susceptible to other forms of strife, such as local political violence or GBV.

Given this information gap, the primary aim of this research is to scrutinize the basic information on armed conflicts, such as their duration and battle-related deaths, and their impact on IDPs and GBV among populations affected by conflicts in Asia from 1950 to 2010. This approach provides a comprehensive understanding of the dynamics of conflict, displacement, and violence in the Asian context.

The State of Conflict and Violence Report examines nine types of conflict at the transnational, national, subnational, and local levels: (1) national civil war; (2) national political conflict; (3) transnational terrorism; (4) separatism and autonomy; (5) communal and ideological conflict; (6) local political and electoral violence; (7) local resource conflict; (8) urban crime and violence; and (9) domestic and GBV (Asia Foundation, 2017). Based on the links between these nine conflict types and regime types, there are five separate thematic patterns: intercommunal violence, cross-border insurgency, terrorism, GBV, and land/natural resource conflicts. After cross-referencing with reports from *The State of the World's Refugees: The Challenge of Protection* (UNHCR, 1993), three types of war are particularly noteworthy, featuring a significant number of battlefield deaths and many forced migrations. These are discussed below.

Inter-State Wars

In the time span from 1950 to 2010, wars between nation states usually generated a high intensity of war, with many battlefield deaths and a significant number of forced migrations. Two examples of this are the Soviet Invasion of Afghanistan in 1978 and the US invasion of Afghanistan in 2001. Together, these two conflicts created one of the largest conflict-induced migrations since WWII. Another example is the war between North and South Vietnam from 1955 to 1975. It caused 1.2 million conflict-induced migrations in Vietnam, as the result of the fighting between US and South Vietnamese forces against communist guerrillas and North Vietnamese forces. The Vietnam War also caused over 250,000 conflict-induced displacements in Laos, as the result of the recruitment by the US of Hmong tribal members to attack the North Vietnamese forces.

Ethnic Conflicts

Ethnic conflicts often create many IDPs. A typical example is Burma, which has a population of 55 million but over 100 ethnic groups, including ethnic Burman (50%–70%), Shan (9%), Karen (7%), and other smaller ethnic groups such as the Mon, Rakhine, Kareni, Kachin, Chin, Akha, Lahu, Wa, Kayan, Danu, Naga, Kokang, Palaoung, Pa-O, Rohingya, Tavoyan, Chinese, and Indian (Allden & Murakami, 2015). Ethnic-based military conflicts began shortly after Burma gained independence from the British colonization. As a result, civilians in these ethnic regions suffered the harshest treatment and were eventually forced to relocate. Other examples include wars featuring India, Pakistan, Bhutan, Bangladesh, and Sri Lanka from 1962 to the present. These conflicts include the Second Kashmir (1965), the Bangladesh Liberation War (1971), the Pakistan-Bengal War (1972), the Baluchi Separatists (1974), conflicts between Tamil separatists and Sinhalese government in Sri Lanka, the Kashmir Insurgency (1989), the Kargil War (1998), and the Waziristan insurgency (2005). In fact, ethnic conflicts remain among the most common causes of GBV and refugee flows in the newly independent states after WWII (UNHCR, 1993).

Nonethnic Civil Conflicts

Nonethnic civil conflicts, feature with large numbers of internally displaced populations and significant war intensity. The number of these wars increased after WWII. Typical examples include the conflicts between the Kampuchean People's Revolutionary Party and the Khmer Rouge in Cambodia, and the conflicts between the defeated royalists and the communist Pathet Lao regime in Laos.

First, military conflicts did not uniformly affect Asian countries. Different characteristics and intensity of war varied by the geopolitical environment. However, Asian countries have been routinely categorized into six sub-regions based on geographic characteristics: South Asia, East Asia, South-East Asia, West Asia, Central Asia, and North Asia. As countries geographically close to each other are treated as an undifferentiated category of "South-East Asia" or "South Asia," this categorization has frequently overlooked and masked accurate information about conflicts, as well as aggregate causal conditions within the countries in refugee-generating conflicts. Based on this oversimplification of regions, researchers may encounter difficulties in understanding why one country could have different variations in fertility patterns from another in the same "Asian sub-region" group.

Second, not all Asian countries have the same form of domestic disturbance or foreign intervention nor do they respond to conflicts in the same manner. Take the Vietnam War (1955–1975) as an example. Vietnam, Cambodia, Thailand, the Philippines, and South Korea all participated in the same war, but not all of them were exposed to the same war intensity, owing to their different level of participation in the war (whether they were direct adversaries/allied forces), their colonial/post-colonial history, their ethnic characteristics (whether they were multi-ethnic or mono-ethnic), or their levels of foreign military intervention or humanitarian aid.

Third, compared with other regions in the developed countries, Asian countries have a greater risk of generating the kind of conflict that leads to sizeable populations (Weiner, 1996). Intensely politicized ethnic and religious identities often lead to violence. The trend should be seen a risk factor for the future. In India, for example, it has been a strategy for politicians to manipulate religious riots to in order to win elections, a practice that has led to massive civilian deaths and further deepened cleavages between different ethnic or religious groups.

Fourth, the extent and impact of GBV might be substantially underestimated in Asia. This is an area that has been under-researched by previous studies. The GBV against Rohingya women is an example. The UN documented sexual violence against women and girls by Myanmar border police and military against the Rohingya minority after conflicts broke out in Rakhine in 2012, 2016, and 2017 (UN Security Council, 2017). The UN report on the Rakhine case suggests that conflict-related sexual violence is widespread and systematic. However, the actual levels of GBV could not be reflected, due to restricted humanitarian access, fears of retaliation, and a mistrust of health services.

In short, these military conflicts present typical case examples of post-WWII and Cold War political violence. Many of these wars were fought in civilian-populated areas affected by chronic poverty and significant disparities in basic health infrastructure. Examples include the Maoist insurgency in Nepal and the post-Cold War conflicts in Burma, such as the Kachin rebellion, the Karen conflicts, and the Rohingya insurgency. This political violence is rooted in deep-seated structural causes. By examining these conflicts, we can better understand the intricate dynamics and far-reaching impacts on affected populations, particularly in terms of displacement and GBV.

CONFLICT DURATION AND INTENSITY

During the past 60 years, one-third of Asian countries have been involved in military conflicts at some point. Compounded by the intervention of the US and Russia during the Cold War, these conflicts have continued to impact the region into the present day. Though most combatants in armed conflict are men, women on average suffer more from the damage to the health, economic, and other infrastructure, as well as from displacement during and after conflict (Plumper & Neumayer, 2006). The World Health Organization Report on during conflict and displacement has noted that GBV against women and girls have become increasingly common during armed conflicts (WHO et al., 2002).

This study has four key variables: (a) battle-related deaths, (b) conflict duration, (c) IDPs, and (d) conflict-related GBV. These variables provide a comprehensive understanding of the impacts of armed conflicts in Asia from 1950 to 2010. Detailed descriptions of these variables can be found in Appendix. In this study, the data are aggregated into country-year observations, and armed conflict is present in 279 out of 920 (30.3%) country-years between 1950 and 2010. There is a considerable variance within conflict-related variable of battlefield intensity, which is stratified for analysis. The largest number of battle-related deaths was observed in China during the Korean War in 1950, with approximately 422,612 fatalities. The second-largest number of battlefield deaths occurred in Vietnam during Vietnam War Phase Two in 1972, with 282,703 fatalities. The smallest number of battlefield deaths was observed in Indonesia, 12, was observed in Indonesia in the last year of the East Timorese War in 1979. To analyze battle-related deaths, the data are stratified into four groups based on the number of fatalities.[1]

According to Table 4.1 and Fig. 4.1, one conflict-year recorded 1–25 battle-related deaths, categorized as low-intensity conflict, comprising 0.4% of the total. Medium-intensity conflicts, with 26–999 battle-related deaths, accounted for 20.4%. High-intensity conflicts, defined by over 1,000 battle-related deaths, constituted the majority, making up 79.2% of the total 279 conflict-years. From 1950 to 2010, more than half of the country-year observations across the 15 Asian countries were classified as high-intensity conflicts, marked by battle-related deaths exceeding 1,000.

Such intense conflicts have significant impacts on the affected areas, leading to widespread disruption of social and healthcare services. This finding aligns with Iqbal's (2006) study on war and health, which highlights the profound short- and long-term effects of frequent and intense conflicts on populations' health and well-being.

Iqbal's (2006) analysis of summary measures of public health across all states from 1900 to 2001 revealed that a significant number of high-intensity conflicts leads to the breakdown of social structures. This breakdown is driven by the displacement of populations, the destruction of infrastructure, and the disruption of community cohesion. The loss of infrastructure, resources, and access to essential services during conflicts disproportionately affects vulnerable populations, further widening the gap between different social groups. The pervasive and ongoing impact of numerous

Table 4.1. Conflict Intensity in Selected Asian Countries Between 1950 and 2010 by Country-Year.

Observations	Frequency	Percentage
Total	920	100
No	641	69.7
Yes	279	30.3
Intensity of armed conflicts		
Low intensity (1–25 battle deaths)	1	0.4
Medium intensity (25–999 battle deaths)	57	20.4
High intensity (>1,000 battle deaths)	221	79.2

Notes: Number = 920
Data Source: United Nations Population Division, World Development Indicators by World Bank, UNICEF/WHO Database, Correlates of War Dataset, and UCDP.

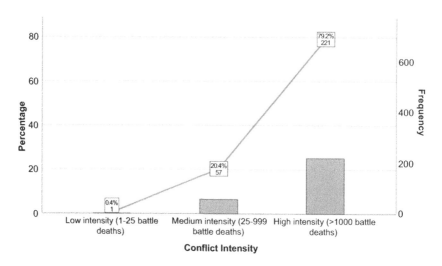

Fig. 4.1. Proportional and Frequency of Conflicts by Intensity Categories in Selected Asian Countries From 1950 to 2010. *Note*: Total values are presented for the indicators. The dataset includes $N = 279$ observations across $n = 15$ countries.
Battle-related deaths data is sourced from the PRIO and the Correlates of War Project, covering the period from 1816 to 2010, compiled by Meredith Reid Sarkees. A low-intensity conflict is defined as up to 25 battle-related deaths in one calendar year, a medium-intensity conflict as 25–999 battle deaths in a year, and a high-intensity conflict as 1,000 or more battle-related deaths in a year.

high-intensity conflicts underscores the critical need for effective interventions to mitigate these adverse effects.

In this study, the duration of conflicts ranges widely, from 1 to 7,396 days, with duration measured in days and analyzed by country/year observations.[2] Table 4.2 and Fig. 4.2 present findings regarding the distribution of conflict duration among the 279 conflict-years examined.[3]

Short-duration conflicts, lasting from 1 to 91 days, represented 13.6% of the total, with 38 conflict-years falling into this category. Moderate-duration conflicts, spanning from 91 to 182 days, accounted for 6.5%, reflected in 18 conflict-years. Long-duration conflicts, defined by durations of 182–274 days, constituted 8.2%, with 23 conflict-years observed. The majority of conflict-years, totaling 200, were categorized as very long durations of conflict, persisting for over 274 days within a year, making up 71.7% of the total 279 conflict-years.

These findings align with Garry and Checchi's (2020) study, which noted that prolonged conflicts disrupt essential services, resulting in long-term negative outcomes for the population. Their research highlighted that protracted conflicts have severe, lasting consequences, particularly at the economic level. For instance, according to World Bank data, civil wars delay GDP growth by an average of 30 years. Additionally, national spending patterns are affected, with countries experiencing recent conflicts spending less on health and more on

Table 4.2. Conflict Duration in Selected Asian Countries Between 1950 and 2010 by Country-Year.

Observations	Frequency	Percentage
Total	920	100
No	641	69.7
Yes	279	30.3
Duration of armed conflict		
Short	38	13.6
Moderate	18	6.5
Long	23	8.2
Very long	200	71.7

Note: Number = 920.
Data Source: United Nations Population Division, World Development Indicators by World Bank, UNICEF/WHO Database, Correlates of War Dataset, and UCDP.
A short duration is defined as occurring on 1–25% of conflict days in a year. A moderate duration refers to conflict events happening on 25–50% of the days in a year, while a long duration indicates activity spanning 51–75% of the year. Events classified as very long duration persist on over 75% of the conflict days within a year.

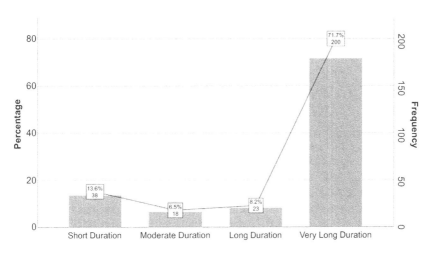

Fig. 4.2. Proportional and Frequency of Conflicts by Duration Categories in Selected Asian Countries From 1950 to 2010. *Note*: Total values are presented for the indicators. The dataset includes $N = 279$ observations across $n = 15$ countries. Conflict duration data is sourced from the PRIO and the Correlates of War Project, covering the period from 1816 to 2010, compiled by Meredith Reid Sarkees. A short duration is defined as occurring on 1–25% of conflict days in a year. A moderate duration refers to conflict events happening on 25–50% of the days in a year, while a long duration indicates activity spanning 51–75% of the year. Events classified as very long duration persist on over 75% of the conflict days within a year.

defense. These economic disruptions contribute to country fragility, increasing the risk of conflict recurrence, as economic instability is linked to the onset of new conflicts.

Overall, from 1950 to 2010, more than half of the country-year observations across the 15 Asian countries were characterized by high-intensity (over 1,000 battle-related deaths) and long-duration conflicts. This highlights the severe and prolonged nature of armed conflicts in this region. High-intensity and long-duration conflicts significantly impact affected areas, leading to widespread disruption of social and healthcare services. The extended periods of instability exacerbate existing inequalities and create an environment where securing basic rights and well-being becomes increasingly challenging. Policinski and Kuzmanovic (2019) have shown that prolonged conflicts exacerbate existing inequalities by creating numerous barriers for vulnerable populations, such as loss of livelihood, food insecurity, and limited access to essential services. These barriers further impact the ability to secure basic rights and well-being. Additionally, the prolonged instability, together with the disruption of essential services, particularly in urban areas, can exacerbate the vulnerability of civilians and degrade essential services, including healthcare, education, and economic opportunities, over time. This degradation perpetuates cycles of poverty and inequality, making it increasingly challenging to restore these services and ensure the well-being of affected populations.

These severe and prolonged conflicts also lead to other critical issues, including widespread displacement and increased instances of GBV, which will be discussed in the next section of this study.

CONFLICT-INDUCED INTERNALLY DISPLACEMENT AND GENDER-BASED VIOLENCE

Aside from the protraction and severity of armed conflicts, several other mechanisms impact the well-being of women and adolescent girls, such as internal displacement and GBV (Black et al., 2014; Kim & Kim, 2014; Kottegoda et al., 2008; McGinn, 2000; O'Heir, 2004; Patel et al., 2012; Rodgers & Rodgers, 2009; Nham Tuyet & Johansson, 2001). This is particularly evident in violent conflicts that feature a large proportion of noncombatant casualties (Holtzman & Nezam, 2004; Kottegoda et al., 2008; Lozano-Gracia et al., 2010; McGinn, 2000). Therefore, this study also includes the number of IDPs and the prevalence and forms of conflict related GBV as part of the comprehensive picture of armed conflicts in this region.

Between 1950 and 2010, IDPs due to conflict were observed in 279 out of 920 (30.3%) conflict-years (see Table 4.3 and Fig. 4.3). The number of IDPs varied significantly, ranging from 1,200 in Burma during the Second Burmese War in 1958 to 3,054,699 in Afghanistan during the Invasion of Afghanistan in 2010. To accommodate this variability, the number of IDPs was categorized into five groups.[4] There were 13 conflict-years with no documented conflict-induced IDPs, accounting for 4.7% of the total 279 conflict-years. There were also 30

Table 4.3. Conflict-Induced Internally Displaced Persons (IDP) in Selected Asian Countries Between 1950 and 2010.

Observations	Frequency	Percentage
Total	920	100
No (0)	641	69.7
Yes (1)	279	30.3
Conflict-year with IDP		
0	13	4.7
1,000–10,000	30	10.8
10,000–100,000	107	38.4
>100,000	129	46.2

Note: Number = 920.

Data Source: World Bank's World Development Indicators (1960–2020), United Nations Commission on Human Rights (1995), Internal Displacement Monitoring Center (2022), Indonesia's Internally Displaced (2000), United Nations' General Principles on Internal Displacement (2000), Relational Displacements of Vietnamese Refugees and the Indigenous Aetas by the Philippine Refugee Processing Center (Le Espiritu & Ruanto-Ramirez, 2020; Ratih, 2000).

conflict-years with 1,000–10,000 IDPs, representing 10.8% of the total. Furthermore, there were 107 conflict-years with 10,000–100,000 IDPs, comprising 38.4% of the total, and 129 conflict-years with over 100,000 IDPs, making up 46.2% of the total.

The findings highlight the high prevalence of IDPs during armed conflicts in this region between 1950 and 2010. Previous studies have shown that conflict-induced displacement severely affects women's health and well-being. For instance, internally displaced women face higher risks of maternal mortality and limited access to reproductive health services compared to those in more stable environments (Black et al., 2014; O'Heir, 2004). The World Health Organization (2019) reported that about 15% of displaced pregnant women encounter life-threatening obstetric complications. Additionally, displaced women are particularly vulnerable to GBV, including rape and intimate partner violence, exacerbated by the collapse of social structures and inadequate access to essential services (McGinn, 2000; Stark et al., 2010; Wirtz et al., 2014). The lack of employment opportunities, social isolation, and inadequate living conditions further contribute to increased domestic violence in displaced settings (Kottegoda et al., 2008; Patel et al., 2012).

Conflict-related GBV was observed in 279 out of 920 (30.3%) country-years (see Table 4.4). The prevalence of conflict-related GBV was categorized based on the relative magnitude of perpetration in a particular country-year.[5]

Reported GBV not likely related to the conflict was present in 95 out of 279 (34.1%) conflict-years, while reported GBV likely related to the conflict was present in 75 out of 279 (26.9%) conflict-years (see Fig. 4.4). Conflicts with numerous and common reported GBV likely related to the conflict were observed in 32 out of 279 (11.5%) conflict-years. Additionally, conflicts with 25–999 reported GBV incidents

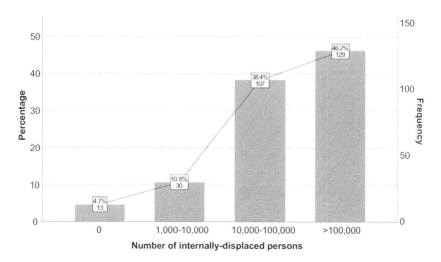

Fig. 4.3.   Proportional and Frequency of Conflict-Induced Internally
Displaced Persons (IDP) in Selected Asian Countries Between 1950 and 2010. *Note*:
Total values are presented for the indicators. The dataset comprises $N = 279$
observations across $n = 15$ countries. Data on conflict-related internally displaced
persons (IDPs) are primarily sourced from the World Bank's World Development
Indicators (1960–2020). For conflicts predating 1960, additional information is
gathered from various reports, including those by the United Nations Commission on
Human Rights (1995), the Internal Displacement Monitoring Center (2022), and
studies such as Indonesia's Internally Displaced (2000) and the United Nations'
General Principles on Internal Displacement (2000). Additional sources include
Relational Displacements of Vietnamese Refugees and the Indigenous Aetas by the
Philippine Refugee Processing Center (Le Espiritu & Ruanto-Ramirez, 2020; Ratih,
2000).

as a means of intimidation were recorded in 48 out of 279 (17.2%) conflict-years,
while conflicts with over 1,000 reported GBV incidents as a means of intimidation
were noted in 29 out of 279 (10.4%) conflict-years.

   Among conflict related GBV incidents between 1950 and 2010, rape was the most
common form, accounting for 144 incidents (51.6%) (see Fig. 4.5). The second most
common form involved incidents reported together with rape, sexual slavery, and
sexual torture, present in 36 out of 279 conflict-years (12.9%). Incidents involving
rape and sexual torture accounted for 30 conflict-years (10.8%). Incidents involving
rape, sexual slavery, sexual mutilation, and sexual torture were reported in 18
conflict-years (6.5%). Incidents involving rape and forced prostitution were documented in 16 conflict-years (5.7%), and incidents involving only sexual torture were
also recorded in 16 conflict-years (5.7%). Incidents involving rape, sexual slavery,
forced prostitution, and sexual torture were present in 13 conflict-years (4.7%).
Furthermore, incidents involving rape, sexual slavery, and forced sterilization/
abortion, as well as incidents involving rape and sexual slavery, were each
reported in three conflict-years (1.1%).

Table 4.4. Frequency and Forms of Conflict-Related Gender-Based Violence in
Selected Asian Countries From 1950 to 2010.

Observations	Frequency	Percentage
Total	920	100
None	641	69.7
Yes	279	30.3
Incident		
Reported, not related with the conflict	95	34.1
Reported, likely related to the conflict	75	26.9
Numerous, common, likely related to the conflict	32	11.5
A count of 25–999 reports, related with GBV, as means of intimidation	48	17.2
Over 1,000 reports, related with GBV, as means of intimidation	29	10.4
Form of gender-based violence		
1	144	51.6
1,2,7	36	12.9
1,7	30	10.8
1,2,6,7	18	6.5
1,3	16	5.7
7	16	5.7
1,2,3,7	13	4.7
1,2,5,7	3	1.1
1,2	3	1.1

Note: Number = 920.
Data Source: SVAC dataset (1989–2019) for most incidents; pre-1989 data from official reports
by various organizations including the United States Institute of Peace, United Nations Human
Rights Office of the High Commissioner, Women International League for Peace and Freedom,
International Institute for Strategic Studies, Geneva Center for Security Sector Governance, and
UN Women.
1 – Rape, 2 – Sexual Slavery, 3 – Forced Prostitution, 4 – Forced Pregnancy, 5 – Forced
Sterilization/Abortion, 6 – Sexual Mutilation, and 7 – Sexual Torture.

Rape has often been used as a weapon of war, intended to terrorize and
demoralize populations. During the Bangladesh War in 1971, an estimated
250,000 to 400,000 women were raped, highlighting the systematic use of sexual
violence to achieve military objectives (Swiss & Giller, 1993). Similarly, the
conflict in Vietnam saw 39% of Vietnamese women aged 11 to 40 being abducted
or raped while fleeing the country by sea in 1985 (Swiss & Giller, 1993). These
acts of violence are not isolated incidents but part of a broader strategy of ethnic
cleansing, aimed at displacing and destroying communities based on ethnic or
national identities. McGinn (2000) noted that the prevalence of GBV is widespread in conflict situations, significantly affecting women's physical and psychological well-being. The use of rape as a weapon of war and ethnic cleansing
demonstrates the severe and targeted nature of violence against women in these
settings, necessitating robust interventions to protect and support affected
populations.

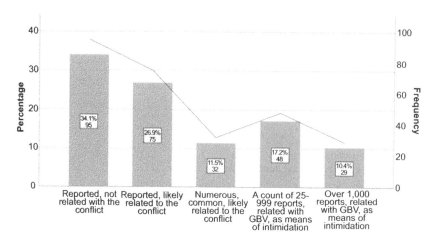

Fig. 4.4.   Proportion and Frequency of Conflict-Related Gender-Based
Violence in Selected Asian Countries From 1950 to 2010. *Note*: Total values are
presented for the indicators. The dataset comprises $N = 279$ observations across $n = 15$
countries. The majority of conflict-related GBV data is sourced from the SVAC dataset,
covering incidents perpetrated by government/state military, pro-government militias,
and rebel/insurgent forces from 1989 to 2019. Pre-1989 data are sourced from official
reports by the United States Institute of Peace, United Nations Human Rights Office of
the High Commissioner, Women International League for Peace and Freedom,
International Institute for Strategic Studies-Conflict-related Sexual Violence, Geneva
Center for Security Sector Governance-SVAC, and UN Women.

Overall, the findings reveal the significant challenges posed by armed conflicts
on populations. The prevalence of IDPs and instances of conflict-related GBV
highlight the severity of the resulting humanitarian crisis. These data findings are
consistent with previous studies and emphasize the urgent need for effective
interventions to safeguard the rights and well-being of affected populations. For
instance, Wirtz et al. (2014) highlighted the prevalence of violence against women
in conflict and displacement settings, finding that displacement due to conflict in
regions like Colombia has led to a high number of IDPs, with millions of people
being forced to leave their homes. This displacement makes them vulnerable to
various forms of violence, including physical, reproductive, and mental health
consequences, further exacerbated by challenges in accessing proper medical care
and support services.

Similarly, Stark et al. (2010) conducted a study in IDP camps in northern
Uganda, highlighting high incidence rates of intimate partner violence, forced sex
by husbands, and rape by perpetrators other than intimate partners. These
findings underscore that women in conflict zones face heightened risks of sexual
violence, exploitation, and abuse. The need for reliable estimates of GBV in such
settings is emphasized due to the challenges in accurately measuring the scope of
the problem.

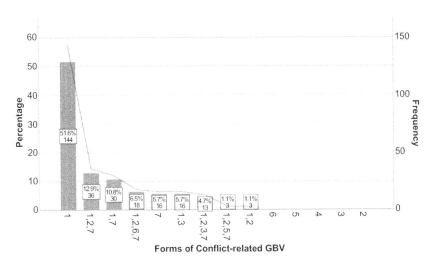

Fig. 4.5. Proportion and Frequency of Conflict-Related Gender-Based Violence in Selected Asian Countries (1950–2010). *Note:* The dataset comprises $N = 279$ observations across $n = 15$ countries. The majority of conflict-related GBV data are sourced from the SVAC dataset, covering incidents perpetrated by government/state military, pro-government militias, and rebel/insurgent forces from 1989 to 2019. Pre-1989 data are sourced from official reports by the United States Institute of Peace, United Nations Human Rights Office of the High Commissioner, Women International League for Peace and Freedom, International Institute for Strategic Studies-Conflict-related Sexual Violence, Geneva Center for Security Sector Governance-SVAC, and UN Women. 1 – Rape, 2 – Sexual Slavery, 3 – Forced Prostitution, 4 – Forced Pregnancy, 5 – Forced Sterilization/Abortion, 6 – Sexual Mutilation, and 7 – Sexual Torture.

The vulnerabilities faced by women and adolescent girls are multifaceted and include increased exposure to GBV, early or forced marriage, limited access to reproductive healthcare, and social stigmatization. These vulnerabilities arise from various factors that are exacerbated in conflict settings. Hutchinson et al. (2016) highlighted that during conflict situations, adolescent girls may be forced into early marriage as a protective strategy or due to limited options available to them in volatile environments. Additionally, Shukla et al. (2023) noted that crisis situations, such as conflicts and social instability, can lead to an increased risk of trafficking among vulnerable populations, including adolescent girls. The disruptions caused by these crises, such as economic instability, loss of resources, and social isolation, create conditions that make individuals more susceptible to trafficking (Rees et al., 2015).

These findings are consistent with previous studies in the literature, underscoring the necessity for targeted interventions that address the specific needs and vulnerabilities of women and girls in conflict-affected regions. Effective interventions should focus on providing comprehensive support, including medical care, psychological support, and legal assistance, to help mitigate the adverse effects of conflict on these vulnerable populations.

CONCLUSION

It is important to note that this study employs descriptive statistical data analysis as a preliminary step to understand the general picture of conflict, displacement, and GBV in Asia from 1950 to 2010. While descriptive statistical data reveal trends and patterns, it does not quantify the extent of impact. Instead, it serves as a foundational exploration, paving the way for future research to investigate causality and the underlying mechanisms.

This study has several limitations. To keep the study manageable, it only addresses conflict, displacement, and conflict-related GBV. In reality, conflicts have other consequences, such as acute exposure to toxins, disrupted social support, extreme stress, and deteriorating economic conditions in the aftermath of conflict. A well-known example is the mass use of hazardous chemical materials as weapons during the 1961–1970 US intervention in Indo-China (the Vietnam War) (Namasivayam et al., 2017). Additionally, there are reports of possible chemical weapon use in Laos against the Hmong tribes (Pita & Romero, 2014), in Kampuchea (Cambodia) during the Vietnamese invasion in 1978, and during the Soviet invasion of Afghanistan in 1979 (Pita & Romero, 2014). These factors will be analyzed in a future study, limiting the ability to explore the holistic picture of armed conflicts.

The study may be prone to selection bias as the study population is based on war incident data from the PRIO and the Correlates of War Project from 1816–2010 by Meredith Reid Sarkees, which only cover Asian countries where nation-state combat has occurred: Afghanistan, Burma, Cambodia, China, India, Indonesia, Laos, Nepal, North Korea, Pakistan, Philippines, South Korea, Sri Lanka, Thailand, and Vietnam. Regions with conflicting territorial disputes, such as Taiwan, Kashmir, and Rakhine (Arakan) state in Burma, are not included in the analyses.

In conclusion, this study contributes to our understanding of the challenges posed by armed conflicts in Asia from 1950 to 2010. It aligns with previous research, highlighting the significant impact of armed conflicts on the region, including their protraction, intensity, displacement of populations, and prevalence of GBV. Notably, the data reveal that more than half of the country-year observations across 15 Asian countries are characterized by high-intensity and long-duration conflicts, emphasizing the severity and prolonged nature of armed conflicts.

This study also illustrates the prevalence of GBV during conflicts, with rape being the most common form. These findings underscore the urgent need for effective interventions to safeguard women and adolescent girls, who are among the most vulnerable during times of social instability.

Moving forward, it is crucial to direct further empirical research towards understanding the long-term impacts of conflict-induced displacement and GBV on individuals, families, and communities in affected regions. Armed conflicts disrupt economies, displace populations, and destroy livelihoods, leading to widespread poverty and making poverty reduction efforts even more challenging in post-war contexts. Additionally, conflicts disrupt food production, distribution, and access, exacerbating food insecurity and malnutrition, thereby hindering efforts to achieve zero hunger.

Armed conflicts disproportionately affect women and girls, exacerbating GBV, displacement, and limiting access to essential services such as healthcare and education. These conflicts exacerbate existing inequalities, reinforcing disparities in access to resources, services, and opportunities, thereby impeding progress towards gender equality.

Given these findings, it is important to address the root causes of armed conflicts and implement targeted interventions to protect the rights and well-being of affected populations, particularly women and girls. By recognizing the potential long-term impacts of unresolved conflicts and investing in sustainable peace initiatives, we can work towards the development of resilient societies in Asia and beyond.

NOTES

1. Battle-related deaths are sourced from the PRIO and the Correlates of War Project, expressed per year and stratified into four groups: 0, 1–25, 26–999, and over 1,000. This aligns with the UCDP's definition of state-based armed conflict.

2. Data on conflict duration were sourced from the PRIO and the Correlates of War Project, covering the period from 1816 to 2010 and compiled by Meredith Reid Sarkees.

3. Conflict duration is measured by the total elapsed time of war, recorded in days within a year and analyzed by country/year observation to ensure compatibility with other data in this study. The duration is categorized based on the proportion of conflict days in a year: a short duration (1–25% of conflict days in a year), moderate duration (25–50% of conflict days in a year), long duration (51–75% of conflict days in a year), and very long duration (over 75% of conflict days in a year).

4. Internally displaced persons (IDPs) are individuals forced to flee their homes due to conflicts, violence, rights violations, or disasters, without crossing international borders. This study records IDPs as the number of people displaced at the year's end, accounting for new displacements, births, returns, resettlements, integration, border crossings, and deaths. IDPs impact health and access to services, particularly for women. IDPs are categorized into five groups: 0, 1–1,000, 1,000–10,000, 10,000–100,000, and over 100,000.

5. Conflict-related GBV is defined according to the International Criminal Court and Elisabeth Wood's Variation of Sexual Violence during War (2009). The forms of GBV are classified into seven categories: (1) Rape, (2) Sexual Slavery, (3) Forced Prostitution, (4) Forced Pregnancy, (5) Forced Sterilization/Abortion, (6) Sexual Mutilation, and (7) Sexual Torture. The prevalence is categorized based on the magnitude of incidents reported in each country-year.

REFERENCES

Allden, K., & Murakami, N. (2014). *Trauma and recovery on war's border: A guide for global health workers.* Dartmouth College Press.

Asia Foundation. (2017). The state of conflict and violence in Asia. https://asiafoundation.org/publication/state-conflict-violence-asia/. Accessed on March 4, 2021.

Black, B. O., Bouanchaud, P. A., Bignall, J. K., Simpson, E., & Gupta, M. (2014). Reproductive health during conflict. *The Obstetrician & Gynecologist, 16*(3), 153–160. https://doi.org/10.1111/tog.12114

Bongaarts, J. (1977). A dynamic model of the reproductive process. *Population Studies, 31*(1), 59–73. https://doi.org/10.1080/00324728.1977.10412747

Brueck, T., & d'Errico, M. (2019). Food security and violent conflict: Introduction to the special issue. *World Development, 117*, 167–171. https://doi.org/10.1016/j.worlddev.2019.01.007

Chukwuma, A., Wong, K. L. M., & Ekhator-Mobayode, U. E. (2021). Disrupted service delivery? The impact of conflict on antenatal care quality in Kenya. *Frontiers in Global Women's Health, 2*, 599731. https://doi.org/10.3389/fgwh.2021.599731

Cohen, D. K., & Nordas, R. (2014). *Sexual violence in armed conflict dataset*. [Data set]. Sexual Violence in Armed Conflict Dataset. http://www.sexualviolencedata.org

Correlates of War Project. (2010). *COW War Data, 1816–2007 (v4.0)* [Data set]. https://correlatesofwar.org/data-sets/

Davis, K., & Blake, J. (1956). Social structure and fertility: An analytic framework. *Economic Development and Cultural Change, 4*(3), 211–235. https://doi.org/10.1086/449714

DeRose, L. F., & Kravdal, O. (2007). Educational reversals and first-birth timing in Sub-Saharan Africa: A dynamic multilevel approach. *Demography, 44*(1), 59–77. https://doi.org/10.1353/dem.2007.0001

Ekzayez, A., Ahmad, Y., Alhaleb, H., & Checchi, F. (2021). The impact of armed conflict on utilisation of health services in North-West Syria: An observational study. *Conflict and Health, 15*(1), 91. https://doi.org/10.1186/s13031-021-00429-7

Garry, S., & Checchi, F. (2020). Armed conflict and public health: Into the 21st century. *Journal of Public Health, 42*(3), e287–e298. https://doi.org/10.1093/pubmed/fdz095

Geneva Center for Security Sector Governance. (2007). Sexual violence in armed conflict: Indonesia. https://dcaf.ch/sites/default/files/publications/documents/sexualviolence_conflict_full.pdf

Ghimire, L. V., & Pun, M. (2006). Health effects of Maoist insurgency in Nepal. *The Lancet (British Edition), 368*(9546), 1494. https://doi.org/10.1016/S0140-6736(06)69634-7

Henry, L. (1972). *On the measurement of human fertility*. Elsevier Pub. Co.

Hobcraft, J. (1996). Fertility in England and wales: A fifty-year perspective. *Population Studies, 50*(3), 485–524.

Holtzman, S., & Nezam, T. (2004). *Living in limbo conflict-induced displacement in europe and central asia*. World Bank.

Hutchinson, A., Waterhouse, P., March-McDonald, J., Neal, S., & Ingham, R. (2016). Understanding early marriage and transactional sex in the context of armed conflict: Protection at a price. *International Perspectives on Sexual and Reproductive Health, 42*(1), 45–49. https://doi.org/10.1363/42e0416

Hyun, M. (2019). *Lao PDR gender-based violence institutional mapping report (Report No: AUS0001484)*. The World Bank. Revised with inputs from the Lao PDR World Bank Team, 2020. https://www.worldbank.org

Internal Displacement Monitoring Center. (2022, April 5). Myanmar country profile. https://www.internal-displacement.org/countries/myanmar

International Institute for Strategic Studies. (2017). Conflict-related sexual violence. In *Armed conflict survey 2017* (pp. 1–10). https://www.iiss.org/publications/armed-conflict-survey/2017/armed-conflict-survey-2017/acs2017-03-essays-2

Iqbal, Z. (2006). Health and human security: The public health impact of violent conflict. *International Studies Quarterly, 50*(3), 631–649. https://doi.org/10.1111/j.1468-2478.2006.00417.x

Iqbal, Z. (2010). *War and the health of nations*. Stanford University Press. https://doi.org/10.1515/9780804773706

Kim, I., & Kim, W. (2014). Post-resettlement challenges and mental health of southeast asian refugees in the United States. *Best Practices in Mental Health, 10*(2), 63–77.

Kottegoda, S., Samuel, K., & Emmanuel, S. (2008). Reproductive health concerns in six conflict-affected areas of Sri Lanka. *Reproductive Health Matters, 16*(31), 75–82. https://doi.org/10.1016/S0968-8080(08)31359-7

Kraehnert, K., Brueck, T., Di Maio, M., & Nistico, R. (2019). The effects of conflict on fertility: Evidence from the genocide in Rwanda. *Demography, 56*(3), 935–968. https://doi.org/10.1007/s13524-019-00780-8

Le Espiritu, Y., & Ruanto-Ramirez, J. A. (2020). The Philippine refugee processing Center: The relational displacements of Vietnamese refugees and the indigenous Aetas. *Verge: Studies in Global Asias, 6*(1), 118+. https://link.gale.com/apps/doc/A623251787/AONE?u=anon~22349c3a&sid=googleScholar&xid=9a15ab02

Lischer, S. K. (2007). Causes and consequences of conflict-induced displacement. *Civil Wars, 9*(2), 142–155. https://doi.org/10.1080/13698240701207302

Lozano-Gracia, N., Piras, G., Ibanez, A., & Hewings, G. (2010). The journey to safety: Conflict-driven migration flows in Colombia. *International Regional Science Review, 33*(2), 157–180. https://doi.org/10.1177/0160017609336998

McGinn, T. (2000). Reproductive health of war-affected populations: What do we know? *International Family Planning Perspectives, 26*(4), 174–180.

Namasivayam, A., Arcos González, P., Castro Delgado, R., & Chi, P. C. (2017). The effect of armed conflict on the utilization of maternal health services in Uganda: A population-based study. *PLoS Currents, 9.* https://doi.org/10.1371/currents.dis.557b987d6519d8c7c96f2006ed3c271a

Nham Tuyet, L., & Johansson, A. (2001). Impact of chemical warfare with agent orange on women's reproductive lives in vietnam: A pilot study. *Reproductive Health Matters, 9*(18), 156–164. https://doi.org/10.1016/S0968-8080(01)90102-8

Office of the United Nations High Commissioner for Human Rights. (2022). Women's human rights and gender-related concerns in situations of conflict and instability. https://www.ohchr.org/en/women/womens-human-rights-and-gender-related-concerns-situations-conflict-and-instability

O'Heir, J. (2004). Pregnancy and childbirth care following conflict and displacement: Care for refugee women in low-resource settings. *Journal of Midwifery & Women's Health, 49*(4), 14–18. https://doi.org/10.1016/j.jmwh.2004.04.031

Patel, S. H., Muyinda, H., Sewankambo, N. K., Oyat, G., Atim, S., & Spittal, P. M. (2012). In the face of war: Examining sexual vulnerabilities of Acholi adolescent girls living in displacement camps in conflict-affected northern Uganda. *BMC International Health and Human Rights, 12*(1), 38. https://doi.org/10.1186/1472-698X-12-38

Pita, R., & Romero, A. (2014). Toxins as weapons: A historical review. *Forensic Science Review, 26*(2), 85–96.

Plumper, T., & Neumayer, E. (2006). The unequal burden of war: The effect of armed conflict on the gender gap in life expectancy. *International Organization, 60*(3), 723–754. https://doi.org/10.1017/S0020818306060231

Policinski, E., & Kuzmanovic, J. (2019). Protracted conflicts: The enduring legacy of endless war. *International Review of the Red Cross, 101*(912), 965–976. https://doi.org/10.1017/S1816383120000399

Price, J. I., & Bohara, A. K. (2013). Maternal health care amid political unrest: The effect of armed conflict on antenatal care utilization in Nepal. *Health Policy and Planning, 28*(3), 309–319. https://doi.org/10.1093/heapol/czs062

PRIO. (2020). *PRIO conflict recurrence database.* [Data set]. Peace Research Institute Oslo. https://www.prio.org/data/31

Ramos Jaraba, N., Quiceno Toro, M., Ochoa Sierra, M., Ruiz Sanchez, L., Garcia Jimenez, M. A., Salazar-Barrientos, M. Y., Bedoya Bedoya, E., Velez Alvarez, G. A., Langer, A., Gausman, J., & Garces-Palacio, I. C. (2020). Health in conflict and post-conflict settings: Reproductive, maternal and child health in Colombia. *Conflict and Health, 14*(1), 1–33. https://doi.org/10.1186/s13031-020-00273-1

Ratih, A. (2000). Indonesia's internally displaced and the United Nations' general principles on internal displacement. *Refugee Survey Quarterly, 19*(2), 84–88. https://doi.org/10.1093/rsq/19.2.84

Rees, S., Thorpe, R., Tol, W., Fonseca, M., & Silove, D. (2015). Testing a cycle of family violence model in conflict-affected, low-income countries: A qualitative study from Timor-Leste. *Social Science & Medicine, 130*, 284–291. https://doi.org/10.1016/j.socscimed.2015.02.013

Rodgers, Y., & Rodgers, Y. (2009). The health status of Cambodia's elderly in a context of gendered violence. *Gender and Development, 17*(3), 453–465. https://doi.org/10.1080/13552070903298469

Sarkees, M. R., & Wayman, F. (2010). *Resort to war: 1816–2007*. CQ Press.

Sheps, M., Menken, J., & Radick, A. (1973). *Mathematical models of conception and birth*. University of Chicago Press.

Shukla, S., Ezebuihe, J. A., & Steinert, J. I. (2023). Association between public health emergencies and sexual and reproductive health, gender-based violence, and early marriage among adolescent girls: A rapid review. *BMC Public Health, 23*(117). https://doi.org/10.1186/s12889-023-15054-7

Stark, L., Roberts, L., Wheaton, W., Acham, A., Boothby, N., & Ager, A. (2010). Measuring violence against women amidst war and displacement in northern Uganda using the "neighborhood method". *Journal of Epidemiology & Community Health, 64*(12), 1056–1061. https://doi.org/10.1136/jech.2009.093799

Swiss, S., & Giller, J. (1993). Rape as a crime of war: A medical perspective. *JAMA, 270*(5), 612–615. https://doi.org/10.1001/jama.1993.03510050078031

The Fund for Peace. (2017). The fragile states index. https://fragilestatesindex.org/country-data/

Tol, W., Kohrt, B., Jordans, M., Thapa, S., Pettigrew, J., Upadhaya, N., & de Jong, J. (2010). Political violence and mental health: A multi-disciplinary review of the literature on Nepal. *Social Science & Medicine, 70*(1), 35–44. https://doi.org/10.1016/j.socscimed.2009.09.037

United Nations. (2007). *World population prospects: The 2006 revision*. United Nations Population Division.

United Nations Commission on Human Rights. (1995, February 2). *Report of the representative of the secretary-general on the human rights of internally displaced persons (E/CN.4/1995/50)*. https://www.refworld.org/docid/45377b710.html

United Nations, Department of Economic and Social Affairs, Population Division. (2002). *World population prospects: The 2002 revision (Volume III)*. https://www.un.org/development/desa/pd/sites/www.un.org.development.desa.pd/files/files/documents/2020/Jan/un_2002_world_population_prospects-2002_revision_volume-iii.pdf

United Nations High Commissioner for Refugees. (1993). *The state of the world's refugees: The challenge of protection*. Penguin Books.

United Nations Human Rights Office of the High Commissioner. (2019). *Report of the detailed findings of the independent international fact-finding mission on Myanmar: Sexual violence*. https://www.ohchr.org/Documents/HRBodies/HRCouncil/FFM-Myanmar/sexualviolence/A_HRC_CRP_4.pdf

United Nations Population Fund. (2007). *State of world population 2007: Unleashing the potential of urban growth*. https://www.unfpa.org/sites/default/files/pub-pdf/695_filename_sowp2007_eng.pdf

United Nations Population Fund (UNFPA). (2022). *Annual report 2022*. UNFPA Publications.

United Nations Security Council. (2017). *Statement by the President of the security council (S/PRST/2017/22)*. https://digitallibrary.un.org/record/1306259

United Nations Women. (2024). *Global database on violence against women*. https://data.unwomen.org/evaw/database

Uppsala Conflict Data Program. (2024). *Uppsala Conflict Data Program (UCDP)*. Department of Peace and Conflict Research, Uppsala University. https://www.uu.se/en/department/peace-and-conflict-research/research/ucdp/

Urdal, H., & Che, C. P. (2013). War and gender inequalities in health: The impact of armed conflict on fertility and maternal mortality. *International Interactions, 39*(4), 489–510. https://doi.org/10.1080/03050629.2013.805133

Wako, E., Elliott, L., De Jesus, S., Zotti, M. E., Swahn, M. H., & Beltrami, J. (2015). Conflict, displacement, and IPV: Findings from two congolese refugee camps in Rwanda. *Violence Against Women, 21*(9), 1087–1101. https://doi.org/10.1177/1077801215590669

Weiner, M. (1996). Bad neighbors, bad neighborhoods: An inquiry into the causes of refugee flows. *International Security, 21*(1), 5–42. http://muse.jhu.edu/journals/international_security/v021/21.1.weiner.html

Wirtz, A. L., Pham, K., Glass, N., Loochkartt, S., Kidane, T., Cuspoca, D. ... & Vu, A. (2014). Gender-based violence in conflict and displacement: Qualitative findings from displaced women in Colombia. *Conflict and Health, 8*(1), 10. https://doi.org/10.1186/1752-1505-8-10

Women's International League for Peace and Freedom. (2014). *Rape and sexual violence by the Burmese Army.* https://www.peacewomen.org/assets/file/Resources/NGO/rape_and_sexual_violence_by_the_burmese_army.pdf

Wood. (2009). Armed groups and sexual violence: When is wartime rape rare?. *Politics & Society,* *37*(1), 131–161. https://doi.org/10.1177/0032329208329755

World Bank. (2024). World development indicators. https://databank.worldbank.org/source/world-development-indicators

World Health Organization. (2019). Maternal mortality: Evidence brief. https://www.who.int/news-room/fact-sheets/detail/maternal-mortality

World Health Organization, Dahlberg, L. L., & Krug, E. G. (2002). *World report on violence and health.* World Health Organization.

Wynn, A., & Wynn, M. (1993). The effects of food shortage on human reproduction. *Nutrition and Health, 9,* 43–52.

Ziegler, B. R., Kansanga, M., Sano, Y., Kangmennaang, J., Kpienbaareh, D., & Luginaah, I. (2020). Antenatal care utilization in the fragile and conflict-affected context of the Democratic Republic of the Congo. *Social Science & Medicine, 262,* 113253. https://doi.org/10.1016/j.socscimed.2020.113253

Ziegler, B. R., Kansanga, M., Sano, Y., Kangmennaang, J., Kpienbaareh, D., & Luginaah, I. (2021). Antenatal care and skilled birth in the fragile and conflict-affected situation of Burundi. *The International Journal of Health Planning and Management, 36*(4), 1081–1106. https://doi.org/10.1002/hpm.3157Appendix

APPENDIX
DEFINITIONS AND DESCRIPTIONS OF VARIABLES

This study has four key variables: (a) battle-related deaths, (b) conflict duration, (c) internally displaced persons (IDPs), and (d) conflict-related GBV. These variables provide a comprehensive understanding of the impacts of armed conflicts in Asia from 1950 to 2010.

BATTLE-RELATED DEATHS

The number of battle-related deaths is used to measure the human destructiveness or intensity of war. The data are sourced from the PRIO and the Correlates of War Project, covering the period from 1816 to 2010 by Meredith Reid Sarkees. In this study, battle-related deaths are expressed as the number of battle-related deaths per year of war. To analyze these deaths, the data are stratified into four groups based on the number of fatalities:

- 0: No battle-related deaths
- 1–25: Minor conflict with low intensity
- 25–999: Significant conflict with medium intensity
- Over 1,000: War with high intensity

This categorization aligns with the UCDP's definition of state-based armed conflict, where a contested incompatibility concerning government and/or territory leads to the use of armed force between two parties, resulting in a minimum of 25 battle-related deaths in a calendar year.

CONFLICT DURATION

The duration of war refers to its total elapsed time, measured in years but analyzed by country/year observation to ensure compatibility with other data in this study. In this study, the duration is measured in days within a year. Conflicts are categorized based on the proportion of conflict days in a year:

- Short Duration: 1–25% of conflict days in a year
- Moderate Duration: 25–50% of conflict days in a year
- Long Duration: 51–75% of conflict days in a year
- Very Long Duration: Over 75% of conflict days within a year

Analyzing the duration of conflicts by country/year observation allows for a more detailed and precise examination of how the length of conflicts within each year impacts various factors, including the intensity of conflict and its effects on civilian populations.

INTERNALLY DISPLACED PERSONS (IDPS)

The variable of IDPs is defined as people or groups of people who have been forced or obliged to flee or to leave their homes or places of habitual residence due to armed conflicts, generalized violence, violations of human rights, or natural or human-made disasters, and who have not crossed an international border. In this study, it is expressed as the number of people living in displacement at the end of each year. This reflects the number of people displaced at the end of the previous year, plus inflows of new cases arriving over the year and births over the year to those displaced, minus outflows that may include returnees, those settled elsewhere, those integrated locally, those traveling across borders, and the deceased.

IDPs are an important variable under the war category because displacement often negatively impacts physical and mental health, particularly for women. Displacement caused by military conflicts limits access to healthcare and essential services, exacerbating vulnerabilities and hardships faced by women. The number of internally displaced persons varies significantly in this study. To manage this variability, the number of internally displaced persons was categorized into five groups:

(1) 0
(2) 1–1,000
(3) 1,000–10,000
(4) 10,000–100,000
(5) Over 100,000

CONFLICT-RELATED GENDER-BASED VIOLENCE (GBV)

Conflict-related GBV is defined according to the International Criminal Court (ICC), encompassing war crimes such as rape, sexual slavery, forced prostitution, forced pregnancy, and forced sterilization or abortion. Additionally, this study includes war-related sexual mutilation and sexual torture, following the example set by Wood (2009).

To integrate existing data effectively, the prevalence of GBV is categorized as follows:

- 0: No incidents of GBV reported
- 1: Incidents reported, not related to the conflict
- 2: Incidents reported, likely related to the conflict
- 3: Reports common, likely related to the conflict
- 4: 25–999 reports, related to GBV used as a means of intimidation
- 5: Over 1,000 reports of such incidents, related to GBV as a means of intimidation

The forms of conflict-related GBV follow the categorization used by the ICC which includes war crimes of rape, sexual slavery, forced prostitution, forced pregnancy, and forced sterilization or abortion, as well as the broader typology of sexual mutilation and sexual torture used by Wood (2009) to better account for war-related GBV. For compatibility and ease of integration with existing data, information about GBV is categorized and presented using both minimal and numerical variables for compatibility:

- 1: Rape
- 2: Sexual Slavery
- 3: Forced Prostitution
- 4: Forced Pregnancy
- 5: Forced Sterilization/Abortion
- 6: Sexual Mutilation
- 7: Sexual Torture

GENDER AND WAR: THE IMPACT OF MILITARY RULE AND WAR ON WOMEN'S LIVES IN BURMA (MYANMAR)

Soe Win

University at Buffalo, State University of New York, USA

ABSTRACT

The Burmese military has been ruling Burma (Myanmar) since Burma's independence from the British in 1948. With increased militarization has come increased ethnic conflicts and the creation of armed ethnic groups. For instance, the Burmese military has been fighting with the Karen armed ethnic group since 1957, making it the longest conflict in the world. The recent coup in 2021 escalated the civil war in Burma. This conflict and war have led to devastation and destruction in ethnic regions, resulting in many ethnic people fleeing to neighboring countries for safety and security. It has also led to increased incidences of gender-based violence and human trafficking. This chapter will examine the history of military rule and ethnic conflicts in Burma. It will explore the impact of war on women's lives including their security, migration, and sustainability. This chapter will also highlight the importance of women's roles in the recent movement against the coup and the importance of women's involvement in social and political movements for peace, democracy, security, and sustainable development.

Keywords: Military; ethnic conflict; gender-based violence; civil war; security; migration; and sustainability

INTRODUCTION TO BURMA

Burma, also known as Myanmar, is a county in Southeast Asia, which is bordered by Thailand and Laos to its east, China to its northeast, and

Scars of War
Research in Political Sociology, Volume 30, 89–108
Copyright © 2025 Soe Win
Published under exclusive licence by Emerald Publishing Limited
ISSN: 0895-9935/doi:10.1108/S0895-993520250000030007

Bangladesh and India to its northwest.[1] The country has a land area of 676,578 square kilometers (261,228 square miles), making the country twice as big as Germany and slightly smaller than the State of Texas. As of July 2021, the population is about 57.1 million and comprising more than 135 ethnic minorities (See Fig. 5.1, World Factbook, 2022).[2] The Irrawaddy River flows through the middle of the country, and it is believed the history of Burma began there. For instance, evidence suggests that the first settlement of Pyu entered from Yunnan and settled around the Irrawaddy valley tens of thousands of years ago. Around the same time, various other groups also entered and inhibited the land, such as the Karen, Mon, Bamar, and Arakanese (Myint-U, 2020).

During the precolonial era, several city-states and kingdoms emerged and dissolved in Burma. For example, the Pyu people created a city-state in the center of the Irrawaddy valley, the Mon near southern coastline, and the Arakanese in the west. The Bamar people also created a settlement in Bagan, located within the Irrawaddy valley.[3] The Bagan Kingdom grew rapidly, and this establishment brought the domination of Burmese culture, language, and religion in the country (Ikeya, 2011; Lang, 2002; Myint-U, 2020).

However, these city-states and kingdoms fell to British colonization after their defeat in the three Anglo–Burmese Wars (1824–1826). The British colonization lasted from 1824 to 1948, and during this era, Burma was known as British Burma (Myint-U, 2020). The British made Burma a province of India in 1886 that was ruled by the Indian government, but it was later given a separate administrative authority until 1937 (Ikeya, 2011). Under British rule, there were two administrations: central Burma (lower and upper Burma) where the British ruled directly, and the surrounding hill region where ethnic minorities ruled themselves (Ikeya, 2011; Lang, 2002; Walton, 2008).[4] The British demolished the precolonial-era kingdom and its culture and changed the policies to those similar to colonial India, introducing Christianity and industrialization. During this period, the British expanded the economy quickly by exploiting oil, gold, timber, and other nature resources. The economy thrived through industrialization and improved infrastructure (e.g. the railway that was built across the country), but exploitation of nature resources and land had been recorded during the colonization (Lang, 2002). Further, the British also replaced Buddhist teaching in school to "modern education" that was based on the British education system (Ikeya, 2017).

By the 1920s, the Burmese nationalist movement surged, which led by Aung San (Bennion, n.d.).[5] At that time, he was seen to be the prominent leader for Burmese independence (Asian Geographic Editorial Team, 2021; Bennion, n.d.). He continued to negotiate with the British officials for Burma's independence which was eventually granted in 1948 (Walton, 2008).

Today, the majority of the Bamar continue to live in lowlands and/or around the Irrawaddy valley, where ethnic minorities remain mostly in the mountain regions. The Bamar also continue to control society, culture, and politics in the country. Burmese is the official language, and Buddhism is the official and most prominent religion (87.9%), followed by Christianity (6.2%), Islam (4.3%), Hinduism (0.5%), and Animism (0.8%). Naypyidaw is the capital and administrative

Fig. 5.1.   Map of Myanmar Adopted From the World Factbook on 6/14/24.

city, whereas Yangon is the largest city and the commercial center of the country (World Factbook, 2022). With it's more than 135 ethnic minorities, Burma is one of the most ethnically diverse countries in the world (Lang, 2002). Although it is rich in natural resources, Burma is one of the poorest countries in Southeast Asia due to many years of dictatorship and military rule (Myint-U, 2020).

The recent coup in 2021 escalated the civil war in Burma. This conflict and war have led to devastation and destruction in ethnic regions, resulting in many ethnic people fleeing to neighboring countries for safety and security. It has also led to increased incidences of gender-based violence and human trafficking. Therefore, there is an urgent need to study the impact of war on women's lives including their security, migration, and sustainability.

First, this chapter will examine the history of the military rule and the ethnic conflicts in Burma. Second, it will explore the impact of military rule on women's lives. Finally, this research will highlight the importance of women's roles in the recent movement against the coup and the importance of women's involvement in social and political movements for peace, democracy, security, and sustainable development.[6]

ETHNIC CONFLICTS AND MILITARY RULE

Discussing ethnic minorities and ethnic conflicts in Burma is complicated. Summarily, the ethnic conflict can be divided into two major segments: the legacy of colonialism and the increased militarization on ethnic people by the Burmese military after the independence. The ethnic conflict is indeed rooted in the legacies of colonialism. According to Hazel J. Lang (2002), ethnicity is a group of people who share the same culture, language, and ancestry. During the precolonial era, indigenous groups were distinguished as *amyo (luumyo)*, translated as ethnicity (e.g. Karen ethnic, Chin ethnic, Mon ethnic, and Bamar ethnic).[7] They cohabited peacefully, although some studies have shown that the Mon, Bamar, and Rakhine Kingdoms competed for power. Despite the conflict, their tolerance for one another and willingness to learn about their distinct cultures and beliefs allowed them to share similar culture and religion among ethnic minorities even today (Ikeya, 2017). For example, Mon and Bamar share similar culture and religion. However, when the British came in, they created a new category of race based on ethnicity and religion, for example, European Christian, Burmese Buddhist, Indian Muslim, or Karen Christian. They insisted that creating this division was for census purposes. However, many scholars argued that this division was used in many colonial practices to draw the line between colonizer and the colonized and to further maintain power over the colonized. This division has caused ethnic people to be aware of their color, identity, ethnicity, and religion, thus resulting in conflicts and mistrust in modern society in Burma (Ikeya, 2017).

Further, the British divided Burma into two administrative regions, where the majority of the Bamar lived in upper and lower Burma (ministerial Burma), and the ethnic minorities resided in the mountain regions (Lang, 2002). From 1886 until 1937, when Burma was under British India, the majority of officials and civil servants were Indian. The British did not train Burmese individuals but rather employed already skilled or knowledgeable Indians in the government offices.

After several riots that killed more than 100 Indians, the British began to give Burma its own administrative power and employ the Bamar within the government (International Crisis Group, 2020). During this time, the majority of ethnic people who lived in hill region were mostly excluded from administrative power and offices. However, this quickly shifted after the Japanese occupation of Burma during World War II.

When World War II broke out, the Bamar leader, Aung San, saw this as a great opportunity to drive out the British from Burma to gain independence. Therefore, they built an allyship with Japan, which allowed Aung San and his 30 soldiers to access military training in Japan. With help from the Japanese soldiers, they successfully expelled the British which led to the Japanese occupation of Burma from 1942 to 1945. Japan then declared Burma an independent state: the State of Burma. However, Aung San and the people of Burma soon learned that the Japanese never actually intended to give Burma its own independence. Eyewitness evidence suggests that the Japanese solders brutally killed and raped Burmese citizens and forced many people into hard labor. In response, Aung San and the 30 other soldiers who received the military training from Japan earlier formed the Anti-Fascist Organization in August 1944.[8] As soon as the Burmese leaders realized the true intent of the Japanese, they called for support from the British and sought to drive out the Japanese from Burma (Bennion, n.d.; Lang, 2002; Walton, 2008). The British, who lost control of Burma from Japan earlier, eagerly agreed to assist the Anti-Fascist Organization. During this time, the British intentionally recruited the majority of ethnic people from mountain regions in order to build a stronger military. The British realized that they needed soldiers that would be loyal to them, as the majority of the Bamar could pose a threat to them anytime, due to increasing nationalist ideology. Aa a result, they began to recruit ethnic people from the hill region, known as "martial races," who had been excluded from the social and politics in the beginning. The British acknowledged that ethnic people were loyal to them and when the missionaries came into Burma, the majority of Bamar people were resistant to Christianity, while many ethnic groups converted to Christianity (Lang, 2002; Steinberg, 2001). British officials mainly recruited ethnic minorities, including the Karen, Chin, and Kachin, to fight against the Japanese alongside the Anti-Fascist Organization.

By 1945, the British (including ethnic fighters) and the Anti-Fascist Organization successfully defeated the Japanese and drove them from Burma, and Burma was once again under British control for several years (from 1945–1948) before gaining independence. During this period, ethnic minorities, mostly the Karen, were trained and employed in economic, educational, and political positions. The relationship between the Karen and the British colonizers was strong. The British even promised the Karen its own independence. However, the Bamar people saw this relationship as the British favoring one ethnic group over the others. They accused the Karen people of not wanting to gain independence from the British and wanting to be slaves to the British (Lang, 2002). This indeed created many conflicts among the Karen and Bamar even today.

Despite this issue and division, the negotiation of Burma's independence continued and occurred with the British officials. The British requested one condition before granting Burma independence: the Bamar people must include the ethnic minority in its political agenda and offer ethnic rights under federalism. Only with this condition, would the British grant Burma its independence. For this reason, Aung San gathered several ethnic minority leaders for a meeting at Panglong, now called the Panglong Agreement (Walton, 2008).

According to Matthew J. Walton, the Panglong Agreement, to some extent, offered ethnic rights and self-determination under a federal union. However, there was a problem of inclusion in the Panglong meeting. The Panglong meeting included several ethnic leaders from Chin, Kachin, and Shan, who signed the agreement, but it excluded other major ethnic people such as the Karen, Karenni, Mon, Arakanese, and Wa. Because these ethnic peoples were excluded from the meeting, it was difficult to determine how much the Panglong Agreement would have changed the current politics, had these ethnic groups been included. However, Walton noted that because the Panglong Agreement met the one condition requested by the British, Burmese independence was grated in 1948. This angered many ethnic minorities, especially the Karen. Walton also pointed out that the Karen believed that they would be given an independent state, a promise made by the British for their loyalty in fighting during the Japanese occupation. This anger led to formation of the Karen National Union (KNU) on February 5, 1957, shortly after Burma gained independence, that would fight against the Burmese military. This would prove to be one of the longest civil wars in the world (Walton, 2008). Overall, the British division of administration, the creation of new races in Burma, the favoring of one ethnic group over others for loyalty, and a failure to offer ethnic rights to autonomy led to distrust and dislike among the Bamar and the ethnic minorities, as well as the formation of ethnic armed groups.

The complexity of the ethnic conflict in Burma can also be observed after the coup in 1962. The coup escalated the ethnic conflicts and civil war due to militarization, economic oppression, political exclusion, and violence and discrimination against ethnic people. As a result, militarization of the ethnic people increased. The Burmese military (formerly known as Anti-Fascist Organization) asserted that they had the right to protect the nation and fight against the armed groups, declaring them terrorist groups and further increased ethnic conflict. In 1947, Burma's first constitution was drafted, which included ethnic rights under federalism. However, this constitution was dissolved in 1962 when the military stated the first coup.

During this time, the country adopted socialism, backed by the military government. Ethnic rights were not granted, and ethnic people were excluded from participating in politics. By this time, more ethnic groups, such as the Shan and Kachin, formed new armed groups in the country. In response, the Burmese military used "the infamous four-cuts strategy," where it cut off the four main sources of support for rebel groups and ethnic people: "Food supplies, funding, intelligence, and recruits to the insurgent" (Lang, 2002, p. 38). The military used these methods against the ethnic minorities by targeting populated areas where many ethnic minorities resided. The military increased its power in ethnic regions by sending tens of thousands of soldiers. These soldiers were underpaid with limited resources (e.g. food, medicine, etc.). The military soldiers targeted many ethnic villagers, accusing them of assisting and providing aide to the armed groups. The soldiers seized villagers' property, including food, clothing, and livestock. They burned the villages, seized the villagers' properties, destroyed their farmlands, and captured anyone suspected of helping the armed groups. The ethnic villagers were brutally beaten and mutilated. Women and girls were raped, abused, and killed. The military adopted area clearance operations, in which everyone living in the targeted regions was to be eliminated (Lang, 2002; Ware & Laovtides, 2019). This led to many ethnic people, like the Karen and Karenni, to flee the neighboring country of Thailand. The military used airstrikes, landmines, and ground attacks to eliminate the ethnic people. These area clearance operations are well evidenced as an ethnic cleansing tactic and a crime against humanity, which result in the majority of innocent ethnic peoples being forced to flee their villages and land. Ware and Laovtides also point out that this brutal response was "a self-fulfilled prophecy" for the Burmese government. The military denied this accusation and claimed that they did not command their soldiers to commit these atrocities and acts, and ultimately, the soldiers were not punished for their wrongful actions. These violent acts, especially rape, were tolerated with impunity (Lang, 2002). Christina Fink argues that the military training directly affected and influenced how these solders treated the civilians and villagers. These soldiers were trained to be superior national protectors. She further argues that these soldiers were trained "to act rather than analyze." They were trained not to ask questions if they were given an order, they must simply follow. This directly affected how the soldiers' treated villagers and civilians. Regardless of the origins of their actions, the military actions evoked a response. The armed groups respond to the brutalization of ethnic people by fighting in resistance (Fink, 2008).

Due to mismanagement of the economy and government corruption, the ethnic people greatly suffered from economic development. Ethnic minorities experienced poverty with a lack of safe water and sanitation and lack of access to education and healthcare services. Because of the militarization, the ethnic people's lands were seized, their property stolen, leading to a limitation of resources. Children, specifically the Karen and Karenni and other ethnic groups, were at the highest risk of poverty. Furthermore, the military used the natural resources belonging to the ethnic people (e.g. timber and gold) for their own benefits. In addition, many minorities were excluded from politics, had limited rights, and had limited access to education, healthcare, and financial institutions (International Crisis Group, 2020). Due to a lack of protection provided by the government and increased violence, trust between the government and ethnic minorities was broken. Many ethnic armed groups believed that the best option was to protest and fight against the military. This came after several failed peace negotiations with the military, in which it refused to grant ethnic rights or autonomy under federalism.

THE IMPACT OF MILITARY RULE ON WOMEN'S LIVES

Historically, women in Burma enjoyed more rights and freedoms than those in their neighboring countries, such as India or China (Ikeya, 2011; Ramusack & Sievers, 1999; Tun et al., 2019). Historian Barbara Ramusack points out that women were equal to men and had relatively high social status and self-autonomy in Southeast Asia prior to the 1500s. This includes Burma. She stated that the Burmese women were involved in economic and agricultural sectors such as trading, selling, and planting (Ramusack & Sievers, 1999). British historian, Lucy Delap, supports this claim and indicates that Burmese women played an especially important role in silk industry, where they were involved in weaving, sewing, and producing of traditional clothes (Delap, 2012).

Further, during this early period, women in Burma were actively involved in rituals and spiritual practices, which was important for Buddhism. They served as patrons to monks (Ramusack & Sievers, 1999). Additionally, Anthony Ried points out that Burma was once ruled by the queen (Shin Sawbu), one of the few female rulers in Southeast Asia (Ried, 1988). During precolonial era, Burmese women married late, and divorce was easy. After the marriage, both men and women took part in public responsibilities, again selling of produce, weaving, and participating in ritual practices. Interestingly, according to Delap, women's equality in Burma was substantial to the point where Burmese men were portrayed as lazy. Some earlier settlers were jealous and claimed that because the men were unresponsive, the women must do all the work claimed (Delap, 2012). These studies indicated that women in Burma enjoyed a wide range of freedom and were treated more justly compared to women in China or India during that time.

Unfortunately, Ramusack revealed that colonization had a profound effect on the lives of both Southeast Asian men and women. These changes included but are not limited to the missionary introduction of the Christian religion to indigenous people, replacing Buddhist teachings with modern education, and the implementation of new colonial rules and policies in the region (Ramusack & Sievers, 1999). In the case of Burma, women in Burma were soon seen as inferior and easy to own by the British colonizers (Afiah et al., 2022). In addition, the rights of women in Burma were further dismantled during the military ruling despite the first Constitution in Burma (Constitution of 1935) that granted women's rights, including the right to participate in politics. Burma also endorsed the Convention on the Elimination of All Forms of Discrimination against Women (CEDAW). However, women experienced increased violence, discrimination, and limited rights under the authoritarian regime, especially after the first coup in Burma in 1962. The first constitution was also dismantled after the coup. Since then, it is accurate to highlight that women's rights issues have not been part of the political agenda for the Burmese government due to the many ethnic conflicts, civil wars, and economic problems in the country. Unsurprisingly, the military government often ignores gender-based violence issues, such as rape and domestic violence (Tun et al., 2019).

By the 2000s, Burma's economy was collapsing due to corruption, international sanctions, and increased funding of the military. During this time, vulnerable populations such as women, children, and ethnic peoples were the hardest hit by economic destruction (Myint-U, 2020). At that time, the United Nations estimated that one in three children in the country were malnourished, and the military government were the ones to blame. They increased spending on the military budget, but they spent less on education and healthcare. During that time, the country was ranked one of the poorest countries in the world with a lack of basic human rights, including freedom of speech, lack of education, and healthcare. Inflation was the highest in the world, where 73% of income was spent on food and basic goods, such as cooking oil, rice, and eggs. All the prices doubled around 2007. Meat became a luxury, and many children died from beriberi, a vitamin B deficiency due to lack of meat, fish, eggs, and diary. In addition, more than 40% of children were taken out of school because their families couldn't afford to send their kids to school. Many children began to work as young as five years old to bring extra income. Child labor persists even today due to poverty, economic disparity, and political instability (Myint-U, 2020).

According to Brenda Belek, ethnic women encounter double the violence and discrimination due to both their sex and ethnicity. She also points out that there are no schools or hospitals in some ethnic regions. The civil war contributes to poverty and food insecurity that forces many ethnic women to migrate away from their communities and leads to disease and high mortality rates (Belak, 2000; Myint-U, 2020). Belek also points out that the government neglects women's development and empowerment through limiting access to education, healthcare, and political participation. She finds that 40% of the country's population is without healthcare access, which affects women more than men. Even in situations where education is available, gender roles in Burma can prevent girls from attending school, and many girls drop out of school to assist their family members or to take care of their younger children (Belak, 2000).

Yasoda Sharma and Chie Noyori Corbett assert that a lack of economic opportunity, poverty, and violence against women all lead to human trafficking. These human traffickers specifically target vulnerable populations such as young girls and ethnic women. Their study shows that ethnic women in Burma are targeted by human traffickers due to ethnic conflicts and the persecution they faced by the Burmese military. These women are then lured and sold into brothels in Thailand, where many of them become sexual assault victims and undocumented aliens. As such, women do not have the agency and power to negotiate safe sex, hence they are at the highest risk of contracting HIV (Sharma & Noyori-Corbett, 2022). Myint-U points out that during 2000s, HIV/AIDS was the high among all women, specifically ethnic women, due to being trafficked into Thailand, which the government tends to ignore, and society then pushes these women further into situations of stigma and violence (Myint-U, 2020).

However, the politics and economic standing seemed to gradually improve after the military finally decided to transition the country to democracy. The military allowed the first election in 2010 although many citizens believed it wasn't a fair election. The military-backed the Union Solidarity and

Development Party (USDP) won the election. Despite the rumors that the election was rigged, the country transitioned itself into democracy, and many citizens experienced democracy, some for the first time in their lives. The second election occurred in 2015, where Aung San Suu Kyi and her party, NLD, won the election. Despite the Rohingya crisis during her leadership, she remained popular among the citizens. The country dramatically transformed into free market economy and saw economic improvement (Myint-U, 2020) (see Fig. 5.2). During the 10 years of democratic transition, women were able to discuss gender-based violence, such as rape and domestic violence. The LGBTQ+ community were able to express their gender identity and their existence was much more visible in society. Economic, communication, and infrastructures improved. The government also invested more in education and the health care system. There was a lack of bribery and corruption during this time. Most importantly, women's participation in politics increased (Win, 2024).

Unfortunately, this reality was destroyed by the recent coup which began on February 1, 2021, when the military arrested democratically elected officials, including President Win Myint and Aung San Suu Kyi. When women realized that their rights could be taken due to this coup, they responded with organizing and participating in the resistance movement, now known as the Spring Revolution.[9] The protests were peaceful. However, after the second week of protests, the military used real guns and began to crackdown on peaceful protestors (Khan, 2021). This coup and the cracking down on peaceful protestors have created profound effects on the people of Burma, especially women and children's lives. For instance, more than 100 people were killed alone on March 27, 2021 (Khan, 2021). During the military crackdown, more than 75 children had been killed, one as young as five years old. Some of them were shot and killed in their neighborhoods when the military opened fire, while others were killed during the protests (The Irrawaddy, 2021). At night, the

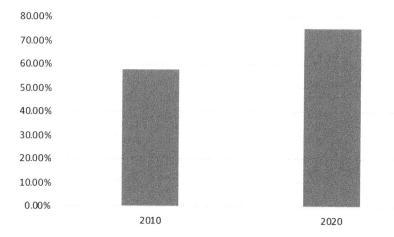

Fig. 5.2.   Population Living Above National Poverty Line.

military went house-to-house to arrest those who participated in the protests. As a result, many individuals were killed or arrested (Beech, 2021).

Since the start of the coup, the independent media have suffered in that their licenses were revoked, and journalists were arrested. According to *Human Rights Watch*, Burma is the second largest country to arrest its journalists, behind China. Since journalists play an important role in spreading the news across the world, the military government perceives this as a threat and accuses the journalists of spreading propaganda. After the second week of protests, the government also shut off communications such as phone lines and internet connections. Social media platforms were blocked and censored. Even though the military government reopened internet access to the civilians later, the communications were closely monitored (Win, 2024).

There has been much evidence to suggest that women are specifically targeted by the military. During the interrogation process, women have been sexually abused, raped, threatened, and beaten. Women have been the easy targets for the military, since rape is a taboo subject in Burmese society. The victims are usually shamed, blamed, and threatened to remain salient (Thangyoojareon, 2023).

Furthermore, the military government has targeted specific ethnic regions. Many ethnic people had been killed by airstrikes in their regions. This is in addition to the countless others who have been forced to flee their villages due to attacks on their villages. For example, thousands of ethnic people have fled to the neighboring countries such as India and Thailand due to airstrikes and bombing of their villages (Olarn & Regan, 2021; Ei & Mar, 2023).

This brutality led the creation of parallel government, the National Unity Government (NUG) and the People Defense Forces (PDF) to response to the military killing against civilians. For instance, these peaceful protestors, both women and men, left their cities, joined the ethnic armed groups in the mountains, trained, and retaliated against the military. Eventually, this led to a fight between the military and the PDF together with the ethnic armed groups (Win, 2024).

The war continues to intensify even today. The fight between the ethnic armed groups (including PDF) and the military has escalated over the last three years. Although the ethnic groups have gained control over many regions in Burma, including major trading routes and major cities, the military government has no plan to surrender (Win, 2024).

Recently, the military announced conscription and has imposed travel restrictions. As a result, millions of people have been displaced internally and along the Thai–Burma border. The United Nations estimated that 18.6 million people in Burma are in need of humanitarian assistance. Hunger has been an increasingly challenging problem, and many children and pregnant women are experiencing malnutrition due to lack of food security. The United Nations has estimated that the 12 million children have experienced interruption in their education due to the coup. Additionally, there is a lack of health care among displaced people. According to PBS news, these causality and destruction are mainly caused by the military due to using heavy airstrike and the bombing of ethnic regions. Airstrikes have been the most used weapon by the military during this war, since ethnic armed groups did not have these advice weapons yet (Ei & Mar, 2023). The military has used this as their advantage to destroy villages and towns that led to the creation of internally displaced or thousands fleeing to neighboring countries.

WOMEN'S PARTICIPATION IN THE RECENT MOVEMENT

As briefly mentioned, around the year 2008 the military government finally agreed to gradually transition the country from dictatorship to democracy. Thant Myint-U, interestingly, points out several reasons that lead to the process of Burma's democratization. The first turning point was the Nargis cyclone on May 2, 2008, which killed thousands and destroyed villages and towns in Delta regions of the country. After this tragedy, it was believed that the military government begun to allow international humanitarian aid and NGOs to come into Burma, which opened the door for the democratization process. Additionally, Myint-U also argues that the military leader, Thein Shwe was planning for his retirement. He implemented a new constitution on May 10, 2008, also known as the 2008 constitution. The true intention of implementing this constitution was unknown. However, the rumor circulated that this constitution would grant power sharing between the military and elected parliament, so that he would not be prosecuted after his resignation or retirement and did not want his family members to be arrested, as he did to his predecessor, General Ne Win. As written in the constitution, the military allowed the first election in 2010, and the second election in 2015, where Aung San Suu Kyi and her party, NLD, won the election. The third election was held on November of 2020, and NLD won again in a landslide victory. Unfortunately, on February 1, 2021, the military staged a coup and announced on military-owned television that it was implementing a 1-year state emergency in the country. The military accused the 2020 election results of being fraudulent and blamed the NLD for failing to investigate. They arrested domestically elected officials, including President Win Myint and Aung San Su Kyi (Win, 2024).

    In response to the coup, women from different backgrounds initiated, organized, and participated in the movement now widely known as the Spring Revolution. They organized the movement at three different level: the ground level, national level, and international level (see Fig. 5.3). At the ground level, many women participated in the grassroot movements, such as participating in daily protests and the Civil Disobedience Movement (CDM). At the national level, more than 120 women's organizations came together within 48 hours and sent letters to government officials, international embassies, and NGOs about their condemnation of the coup. At the international level, many people participated in local protests, signed petitions, and organized fundraising campaigns to support the movement financially. The motivations for participating in the movement depended, in part, on participants' educational background, class, ethnicities, religious background, age, gender, and political background. Some women

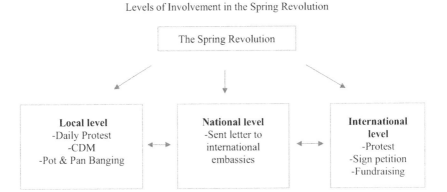

Levels of Involvement in the Spring Revolution

Fig. 5.3.   Involvement in the Spring Revolution at Three Different Levels.

participated in this movement to fight for women's rights while others participated for ethnic rights, to oppose military rule, and to restore democracy. Many
of them are also fighting for basic human rights, such as LGBTQ+ rights, labor
rights, as well as freedom and justice (Win, 2024).

On February 2, 2021, healthcare workers, both male and female, doctors and
nurses, began a strike and refused to work in the government-owned hospitals in
Mandalay. This strike came to be known as the CDM. According to the
Women's Advocacy Coalition-Myanmar (WAC-M), within the CDM, 70% of
participants identify as women. The local non-governmental organization
(NGO), which is the Gender Equality Network, also estimated that between 70
and 80% of the CDM participants were women (Win, 2024).

However, the daily peaceful protests were not organized until February 6,
2021, in Yangon. These daily peaceful protests were organized and started by two
ethnic women in Yangon. However, there is no centralized leadership within the
movement. While these two women may have served as catalysts, the movement
is really characterized by an upswell of women as a whole. These peaceful protests grew in size during the first week, starting in Yangon, where hundreds of
thousands of people participated. More than half of the protestors were women.
The protests quickly spread throughout the country and became the largest
protests in Burma's history, exceeding the participation in the 1988 uprising.
Many students, including young women, men, and the LGBTQ+ community,
who called themselves "Generation Z," also joined these protests. Many of them
were part of the daily protests and accounted for a large number of protesters on
the streets. They came up with creative tactics such as dancing, singing, and
shouting on the streets. The daily protests were creative and innovative. Protesters adopted the three-finger salute from the American *Hunger Games* film as a
sign of resistance while protesting (see Fig. 5.4) (Win, 2024).

During the day, people participated in the daily protests, but at night, they
would bang pots and pans, which usually started at 8 p.m. This banging of pots
and pans was started by women as a symbolic expression of disapproval and

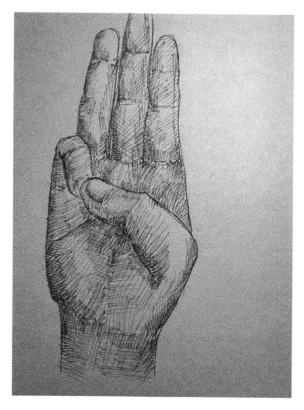

Fig. 5.4.   The Three Fingers Salute Used by Many Protesters as a Sing of
Resistance.

disparagement of the coup. In Burmese culture, banging pots and pans at night is
a way to frighten and chase away the evil spirits. By banding pots and pans, these
protestors were sending a message to the military that they do not want military
rule and dictatorship. Together, women were able to express and relieve their
anger by banging pots and pans (Win, 2024) (see Fig. 5.5).

Protestors also came up with variety of other unique methods during this
movement. On March 8, 2021, on International Women's Day, women came up
with idea to hang women's longyis or sarongs on every street to prevent the police
from coming to their neighbors. In Burmese culture and tradition, going
underneath the women's sarongs brings bad luck. Menstrual blood is considered
unclean and dirty. Men are taught not to go under women's longyi from the time
they are a child. It is believed that men are born with *hpone*, and that men could
lose *hpone* by going underneath women's longyi. *Hpone* is loosely translated as a
man's power, masculinity, or luck. This superstition is so strong in Burmese
culture that most men will never walk underneath women's longyi in order to
maintain their power, luck, or masculinity (*hpone*). Women are using this as an

Fig. 5.5.   How Protestors Bang Pots & Pans at Night.

opportunity to stop the police from coming to their street and to prevent them from arresting protesters (see Fig. 5.6).

However, it must be recognized that participating in the Spring Revolution is risky, especially for those who live in Burma. No one is safe and that many participants have had to hide for their safety. Some participants were fortunate enough to flee the country, however, many became victims of military brutality, either being arrested or killed. Many participants have escalated their protests and have left their cities and joined the ethnic armed groups to fight against the military. As briefly stated earlier, this led to the creation of NUG on April 6, 2021, and the People's Defense Forces (PDF) on May 5, 2021. Many protesters joined the PDF, many of whom were trained by the ethnic armed groups such as the KNU and Kachin Independent Army (KIA) (Strangio, 2021).

On September 7th, 2021, the NUG declared war against the military, stating that the PDF had received enough training and that they were ready to fight. The clashes broke out in many cities and towns such as Yangon, Mandalay, and other ethnic regions. Many cities, including Yangon, saw many blasts and bombings. These clashes have escalated in the last 3 years, which led to civilians fleeing the country.

Fig. 5.6.   Women's Hanging Longyi on the Street.

There has been a lot of destruction devastation, and casualties. Eyewitnesses have reported that the military is solely responsible for the civilian fatalities and displacement. A recent PBS news report claims that the military is accountable for the devastation in this war because they have utilized heavy weapons such as bombing and airstrikes in populated regions.

GENDER, WAR, AND SUSTAINABILITY

One might wonder how war is related to sustainability. There is a strong correlation between war and sustainability because the purpose of war is to destroy the community and/or civilian population which is contradictory to sustainable development goals defined by United Nations. The most used definition of sustainability is from United Nation, which is "meeting the needs of the present without compromising the ability of future generations to meet their own needs." To achieve this goal, the United Nations has adopted 17 sustainable development goals (e.g., no poverty, zero hunger, good health and well-being, quality education, gender equality, clean water and sanitation, etc.).[10] These goals were implemented as a call to the international community to end poverty, to make sure that everyone is able to live with peace and prosperity, and to protect the environment for sustainability.

War has a huge impact on sustainable development goals. War almost always causes food insecurity, economic disruption, environmental impact, inequality, and gender-based violence. During war, food insecurity is a concern (Elder, 2022). The United Nations points out that war and conflicts generate poverty, hunger, and food insecurity. They also state that there is a strong correlation between food insecurity and gender inequality (Justino et al., 2020). As stated above, more than 18.6 million people are in need of humanitarian assistance in Burma. Many people are internally displaced while others are seeking refuge in neighboring countries. Their homeland, villages, and livestock are destroyed by the military, so they have no safe place to live and grow their own food. Access to food has become scarce due to food availability or an increase in food prices. It increases women's responsibility to protect their children from conflict as well as to provide them with food. Studies have shown that when food are limited, women will feed their husband and children first before they will eat the left over, if there is any.

War also accounts for economic disruption. Lack of economic opportunity leads to an increase in migration and the refugee population. Migrants and refugees are not always welcome by destination countries, and hosting refugees is not always sustainable since it depends on humanitarian aid. For instance, Thailand has hosted more than nine refugee camps, and it is usually overcrowded. *Human Rights Watch* (2012) reports physical abuse of refugees by the Thai authorities. Moreover, border crossing can also lead to human trafficking. Several studies have shown that human traffickers specifically targeted women and vulnerable populations. These victims are then sold for prostitution. This is a common problem in Thai–Burma borders. A *Radio Free Asia* reports that there has been an increased in sex work in Burma due to economic hardship.

Additionally, war causes environmental impacts such as land and water pollution. For instance, the military uses airstrike by destroying infrastructure such as buildings and roads. The weapons that they use usually produce toxic and hazardous waste that damages the environment (Elder, 2022).

Moreover, war creates inequality and gender-based violence. As stated above, children are most often taken out of school. They face hunger with lack of safe drinking water and sanitation. The health care system is usually disrupted by war. The military has destroyed 343 hospitals and clinics since they staged the coup. Women also experience increases in gender-based violence. Studies have shown that rape has been used as a war weapon. Rape has been committed by the military as stated earlier. Domestic violence also increases among married couples due to economic hardship from the war (Ei & Mar, 2023).

Therefore, peace and democracy are important for sustainable development in Burma. The underlying issues such as federalism, women's rights, and ethnic rights must be addressed. The people in Burma, including ethnic minorities have been fighting for federal democracy and ethnic rights for many years. The recent coup has opened the door for everyone, including women, ethnic people to unite to fight for peace and democracy. Women understand that their rights are threaten by the military, and as such they organized and participated in the recent movement in response to the military coup. Although the movement is ongoing and there have been much devastation and casualties, participants in the move-ment, including ethnic armed groups believe that they will overthrow the military and restore democracy in the country. They are hopeful for the peace, justice, freedom, and democracy.

CONCLUSION

A survey of the history of Burma provides a solid foundation of understanding of the complexity of Burma's history. However, this is not meant to be an exhaustive analysis of the political, social, cultural, or ethnic history of Burma. These issues are complex, and it is next to impossible to examine them exhaus-tively. Rather, this chapter aims to provide a foundation to better recognize and perceive the complexity of Burma's social, political, and cultural history. The military violence, discrimination, and oppression against citizens, specifically women and ethnic minorities, are highlighted to show how the violence has long been deeply rooted in Burma prehistory, colonization era, and after its independence.

The fight intensifies between the military and the ethnic armed groups after the recent coup in 2021. The war causes many destructions and casualties, including civilians being internally displaced and fleeing into neighboring countries. This led to humanitarian concerns as the military destroyed the villages and towns, including churches, critical infrastructure, including roads, hospitals, etc. As a result, this conflict increases migration, security concerns, and gender-based violence. Most importantly, the war has profound effects on slowing down the sustainable development in Burma, as many citizens face hunger, lack of safe drinking water and sanitation, children being pull out of school, lack of health care, and a safe place to stay.

Historically, prodemocracy movements have failed due to the brutal military crackdowns. This time, the women of Burma have responded to the coup by organizing a counter movement, the Spring Revolution. They organized and participated in the movement to overthrow the military government and to restore democracy. Despite the catastrophe and deprivation, the people of Burma have hope in this movement that they will defeated the military to restore democracy. A true democracy that would provide women's rights, ethnic rights, and basic human rights that is necessary for the future sustainable development.

NOTES

1. Burma is also known as Myanmar. There is no difference in the meaning between Burma or Myanmar. The Burmese government changed the name to Myanmar in 1989. The United States of America still officially uses Burma. In this paper, I will use Burma out of personal preference.

2. There are more than 135 ethnic minorities in Burma. Major ethnic groups include Kachin, Karenni, Karen, Chin, Mon, Bamar, Rakhine, and Shan. They mostly reside in the mountain regions and at the border near Thailand, Indian, China, and Bangladesh.

3. Bamar (known as Burmese) is the largest ethnic group in Burma who control social, political, and economic power in Burma. Majority of the military government is made up of Bamar.

4. The British division of the two administrations were important because this division not only caused the geography divide, but it partially accounted for ethnic divide and tensions. Section "Ethnic Conflicts and Military Rule" will explore more on this issue.

5. Aung San is the father of Aung San Suu Kyi.

6. This paper is an expansion of my doctoral dissertation titled, *Women's Participation in the Spring Revolution: Resistance, Resilience, and Solidarity*, successfully defended on February 1, 2024, at the University at Buffalo. I employed qualitative research method (in-depth interview) and analyzed material from over 100 media outlets (e.g., BBC, CNN, DW News, etc.).

7. The eight largest ethnic groups in Burma are Kachin, Karenni (Kayah), Karen (Kayin), Chin, Mon, Bamar, Rakhine, Shan. https://minorityrights.org/country/myanmarburma/

8. Anti-Fascist Organization is now known as Tatmadaw. Tatmadaw is the official name for Burmese military. It used to be one of the most powerful militaries in Southeast Asia. However, I will use Burmese Military when addressing the Tatmadaw.

9. I discuss the recent coup and women's participation in the Spring Revolution in the following section.

10. The 17 sustainable development goals can be found on United Nations website. https://www.undp.org/sustainable-development-goals/no-poverty

REFERENCES

Afiah, N., Arafah, B., & Abbas, H. (2022). Burmese women portrait under the British imperialism in Orwell's Burmese days. *Journal of Language Teaching and Research*, *13*(1), 213–219.

Asian Geographic Editorial Team. (2021, July 14). The road to independence: Burma (1945–1962). *Asian Geographic Magazines*. https://www.asiangeo.com/articles/the-road-to-independence-burma-1945-1962/

Beech, H. (2021, March 4). 'She Is a Hero': In Myanmar's protests women are on the front lines. *The New York Times*. https://www.nytimes.com/2021/03/04/world/asia/myanmar-protests-women.html?smid=em

Belak, B. (2000). Double jeopardy: Abuse of ethnic women's human rights in Burma. *Cultural Survival Quarterly*, *24*(3), 24–28.

Bennion, J. (n.d.). Burma: A political timeline. https://www.pbs.org/frontlineworld/stories/burma601/timeline.html

Delap, L. (2012). Uneven orientalisms: Burmese women and the feminist imagination. *Gender & History*, *24*(2), 389–410.

Ei, K. K., & Mar, K. (2023, December 31). Women and children suffer amid Myanmar's civil war. *Radio Free Asia (RFA)*. https://www.rfa.org/english/news/myanmar/myanmar-war-women-children-12302023124223.html

Elder, M. (2022). *Environmental and sustainability implications of the Ukraine war for East and South Asia: Sustainability and decarbonisation should be accelerated not paused*. Institute for Global Environmental Strategies.

Fink, C. (2008). Militarization in Burma's ethnic states: Causes and consequences. *Contemporary Politics*, *14*(4), 447–462. https://doi.org/10.1080/13569770802519367

Human Rights Watch. (2012, September 13). Thailand: Refugee policies ad hoc and inadequate. *Human Rights Watch*. https://www.hrw.org/news/2012/09/13/thailand-refugee-policies-ad-hoc-and-inadequate?gad_source=1&gclid=CjwKCAjwi_exBhA8EiwA_kU1MrcBGLBbksqzszwyAKASqbl4NpSSH1vtCh8k0_QvGOfYHwyY7HmmqxoChJkQAvD_BwE

Ikeya, C. (2011). *Refiguring women, colonialism, and modernity in Burma*. University of Hawai'i Press.

International Crisis Group. (2020, August 28). Identity crisis: Ethnicity and conflict in Myanmar. https://www.crisisgroup.org/asia/south-east-asia/myanmar/312-identity-crisis-ethnicity-and-conflict-myanmar

Justino, P., Hagerman, K., Jackson, J., Joshi, I., Sisto, I., & Bradley, A. (2020). Pathways to achieving food security, sustainable peace and gender equality: Evidence from three FAO interventions. *Development Policy Review*, *38*(1), 85–99. https://doi.org/10.1111/dpr.12413

Khan, U. (2021, April 25). The women of Myanmar: 'Our place is in the revolution'. *Al Jazeera*. https://www.aljazeera.com/features/2021/4/25/women-of-myanmar-stand-resilient-against-the-military-coup

Lang, H. J. (2002). *Fear and sanctuary: Burmese refugees in Thailand*. Southeast Asia Program Publications, Southeast Asia Program, Cornell University.

Myint-U, T. (2020). *The hidden history of Burma: Race, capitalism, and the crisis of democracy in the 21st century* (1st ed.). W. W. Norton & Company.

Olarn, K., & Regan, H. (2021, March 30). Thailand pushes back thousands fleeing Myanmar as death toll surpasses 500. *CNN News*. https://www.cnn.com/2021/03/30/asia/thailand-myanmar-refugees-intl-hnk/index.html

Ramusack, B. N., & Sievers, S. (1999). *Women in Asia: Restoring women to history*. Indiana University Press.

Ried, A. (1988). Female roles in pre-colonial Southeast Asia. *Modern Asia Studies*. https://www.jstor.org/stable/312601

Sharma, Y., & Noyori-Corbett, C. (2022). Transnational human trafficking and HIV/AIDS: Women in Asia. *Social Development Issues*, *44*(1), 21–37. https://doi.org/10.3998/sdi.2816

Steinberg, D. I. (2001). *Burma, the state of Myanmar*. Georgetown University Press.

Strangio, S. (2021, May 6). Can Myanmar's new 'people's defense force'. *The Diplomat*. https://thediplomat.com/2021/05/can-myanmars-new-peoples-defense-force-succeed/

Thangyoojareon, T. (2023, February 1). *Two years after the coup, Burma's struggle for democracy continues*. Human Rights Foundation.

The Irrawaddy. (2021, March 31). Here are the children killed by the Myanmar Regime's forces since Feb. 1. *The Irrawaddy*. https://www.irrawaddy.com/news/burma/children-killed-myanmar-regimes-forces-since-feb-1.html?fbclid=IwAR2rbbxQjP00wBB7bAaWJhBoQJ_bhkoOWBqsjcsYNE7VIVEhcKn9mi5irIM

The World Factbook. (2022). Washington, DC: Central intelligence agency. https://www.cia.gov/the-world-factbook/countries/burma/

Tun, A., Ring, L., & Hlaing, S. (2019). Feminism in Burma. https://library.fes.de/pdf-files/bueros/myanmar/15624.pdf

Walton, M. J. (2008). Ethnicity, conflict, and history in Burma: The myths of Panglong. *Asian Survey*, *48*(6), 889–910. https://doi.org/10.1525/as.2008.48.6.889

Ware, A., & Laoutides, C. (2019). *Myanmar's "Rohingya" conflict*. Oxford University Press.

Win, S. (2024). *Women's participation in the spring revolution: Resistance, resilience, and solidarity*. Unpublished doctoral dissertation. University at Buffalo, The State University at New York.

REVISITING THE KASHMIR CONFLICT THROUGH RAHUL PANDITA'S *OUR MOON HAS BLOOD CLOTS*: VIOLENCE, EXODUS AND LOSS

Anupama Vohra and Jasbir Singh

University of Jammu, India

ABSTRACT

Jammu and Kashmir known for its scenic beauty, serene environment and bountifulness has been a witness to turbulent events starting from 1989, when the simmering volcano of infused hatred from across the border against India, and discriminatory practices of the politicians resulted in mistrust; and the demand for azadi *(independence) was made through Kalashnikovs, grenades and bombs, kidnappings, mass demonstrations and other means of groundbreaking violence. To declare Kashmir an Islamic state, the militants spread fear amongst Kashmiri Pandits (KPs), the original Hindu inhabitants of Kashmir, through newspaper advertisements and pamphlets ordering them to leave Kashmir or face death. KPs initially resisted exodus. They looked for every possible way to avoid abandoning the place where their families had roots and their ancestors were consigned to flame. The present research paper will examine Rahul Pandita's narrative* Our Moon Has Blood Clots *to underscore the violence of KPs being thrown out of their homes, dangling between the status of 'migrant KP', 'refugee KP', 'displaced KP' to 'reckon with the loss and gain of place, we (may) discover through the force of interpretation, forms of absence – of pain, of fear, of guilt, of desire' (Kapur 47) to highlight the psyche of KPs in terms of resistance and survival, trauma and victimhood, struggle and survival.*

Scars of War
Research in Political Sociology, Volume 30, 109–119
Copyright © 2025 Anupama Vohra and Jasbir Singh
Published under exclusive licence by Emerald Publishing Limited
ISSN: 0895-9935/doi:10.1108/S0895-993520250000030008

Keywords: conflict; Kashmiri Pandits; violence; gender; loss; exodus; cross-border terrorism

INTRODUCTION

Conflicts between and among groups, societies, kingdoms and countries have been an integral part of human evolution since the beginning of civilization. According to *Oxford Advanced Learner's Dictionary* conflict means 'a situation in which people, groups or countries are involved in a serious disagreement or argument' (Dictionary, 2020, p. 319), which often results in war(s), leading to *beginning and end, continuing wars, multiple wars, simmering conflicts,* playing havoc with people, economy, environment, health, development, progression, etc. Conflicts are global, prevalent and persistent with multiple '[...] conflict-configurations and-coalitions, with their own dynamic and their own logic' (Dennen, 2005, p. 1) spreading violence and destruction as '[...] each kind of social unit, having its own range of size, structure, and institutions, will also have its own modes of interaction and thus its own patterns of conflict with other social units' (Fink, 1968, p. 417).

THE HISTORY OF JAMMU AND KASHMIR

The erstwhile state of Jammu and Kashmir came into existence under Maharaja Gulab Singh in 1846 AD[1] The three regions of the state namely Jammu, Kashmir and Ladakh presented a synthesis of diverse geographical, economic, social, cultural, ethnic, religious and linguistic strands. Besides, each region has had its peculiar contribution towards the development of Jammu and Kashmir.

In the annals of history, Jammu and Kashmir finds crucial references in important documents and studies. The historical and scenic beauty references of Kashmir are documented in Kalhana's *Rajatarangini*:

> Such is Kashmir, the country which may be conquered by the force of spiritual merit but not by armed force; where the inhabitants in consequence fear more the next world; where there are hot baths in winter, comfortable landing places on the river-banks, where the rivers being free from aquatic animals are without peril; where, realizing that the land created by his father is unable to bear heat, the hot-rayed sun honours it by bearing himself with softness even in summer. Learning, high dwelling houses, saffron, iced water, grapes and the like-what is a commonplace there, is difficult to secure in paradise. (Kalhana, 1935, p. 12)

Whereas the references about Jammu 'By and by people of every caste thronged there and it became a flourishing town' (*Kalhana*, 1935, p. 18) are found in *Rajdarshini*: 'For the ancient annals of Jammu territories prior to the thirteenth century *Rajdarshani* is the only existing book of history, and this fact in itself is enough to establish it as a priceless composition in the traditional classical style' (1935, p. viii). Besides, the archaeological excavations in Jammu trace its history to the Harrapan civilisation. And the cultural history of Ladakh can be traced to the Upper Indus Valley area.

Jammu and Kashmir was founded by the British rulers on the ruins of the Sikh Empire following the first Anglo-Sikh war fought after the death of Maharaja Ranjit Singh. The British imposed an indemnity (of Rs. 75 lakh) on the Sikh rulers which the later refused to pay and instead offered the territories of Jammu, Kashmir and Ladakh, which were then a part of the Sikh domain to the Britishers. The British rulers secured the indemnity from Raja Gulab Singh of Jammu, who was a feudatory of the Sikh Darbar, and transferred to him the territories, the Sikh rulers had offered them.

Jammu, Kashmir and Ladakh became a single political entity only after the Treaty of Amritsar signed by Maharaja Gulab Singh with the British Government on March 16, 1846. Jammu and Kashmir, being a native state governed by a local ruler, was allowed to retain the existing system of political control, economic and social arrangements, etc. but was subject to the paramountcy of the British crown. In less than four decades, after Gulab Singh, his grandson Maharaja Partap Singh was unceremoniously removed from the throne for misgovernment by the British and the Dogra state was taken over and integrated into the flanks of the British colony. However, in 1921, Maharaja Partap Singh was reinstated but a new state Council was formed under the supervision of the British Resident to run the state.

The partition of India by the British in 1947 had envisaged the division of the British Indian provinces into two dominions – India and Pakistan; besides, it was expected that the princely states ruled by native rulers would accede to either of the two dominions by signing an Instrument of Accession. Keeping in view the geographic and political considerations, the ruler of Jammu and Kashmir, Maharaja Hari Singh showed interest in retaining the independent character of his state. He did not want to accede to either of the two dominions, that is India or Pakistan. However, immediately after independence, the *Kabaili* (tribal) invasion in October 1947, instigated and supported by the newly created Pakistan, changed the scenario. Maharaja Hari Singh agreed to join India to save the lives of the people from the brutality of *Kabailis* (tribals) by signing the Instrument of Accession with India on October 26, 1947. It was accepted by the Governor General of India on October 27, 1947, and on the same day, Indian troops landed at Srinagar to contain the onslaught of tribal invaders into the state from across the border.

The invasion of Kashmir by *Kabailis* (tribals) at the behest of newly created Pakistan, and the resultant mismanagement and vested interests by successive governments in the state, the appeasement policy of the centre and the support to secessionists both from within the country and across the border; inflow of arms, money and training of Kashmiri Muslim youth in camps along the LoC and Pakistan occupied Kashmir (PoK); spread of hatred for minority and miniscule communities, and 'India is enemy' instigated slogans from across the border, over a period of time, flared the simmering volcano of crisis to erupt into mass scale violence in Kashmir in 1989.[2]

KASHMIRI PANDITS AND POST-1990 KASHMIRI PANDIT LITERATURE

KPs are Hindus who hail from Kashmir and 'belong to the same caste of Sarasvat Brahmanas known as Pandits' (Duschinski, 2008, p. 41). They form a unique religious and cultural minority in Kashmir. Other minorities in Kashmir include Hindus, Sikhs, Christians, Buddhists and Jains. However, KPs were the largest, non-Muslim, religious minority in Kashmir before 1990.

The beginning of a new conflict in Kashmir in the 1990s has had an adverse effect on the lives of KPs; being forced to leave their homes to flee to other parts of the country has traumatized them. It has shown adverse effects on the personal and public lives of the members of this community who were displaced, had to abandon their homes and have become 'displaced in their own country' dangling between the status of 'migrant Kashmiri Pandit,' 'refugee Kashmiri Pandit,' 'displaced Kashmiri Pandit' to '[…] reckon with the loss and gain of place, we (may) discover through the force of interpretation, forms of absence – of pain, of fear, of guilt, of desire' (Kapur, 2007, p. 47) to highlight the psyche of KPs in terms of resistance, struggle, trauma, victimhood and survival.[3]

This period gave a new premise to Kashmiri literature. A novel phase of Kashmiri literature began to emerge not just in the Kashmiri language but in Urdu, Hindi and English by Kashmiri Pandit writers from Jagati township and Purkhoo camp, also from across India and abroad wherever the community has migrated or settled.[4] Kashmiri literature written after the exodus of Kashmiri Pandits from Kashmir is dominated by young Kashmiri Pandit writers who prefer writing in English language. These writers personal experiences are emblematic of the turmoil in Kashmir – the horrific situation that led to their exodus; the atrocious suffering and killings of the KPs, their scattered status within the country and abroad, the loss of homeland, etc. Consequently, the post 1990 Kashmiri Pandit literature speaks of violence, exodus and the permanent loss of homeland, that is Kashmir, which the Kashmiri Pandit generations now symbolically carry in their hearts.

KASHMIRI PANDIT EXODUS THROUGH THE LENS OF *OUR MOON HAS BLOOD CLOTS*[5]

Bomb blasts, curfew, strikes and cross firing became a part of Kashmir's everyday life: 'There were reportedly between January 1 and January 19, 1990, 319 violent acts – 21 armed attacks, 114 bomb blasts, 112 arsons, and 72 incidents of mob violence' (Jagmohan, 1991, p. 76). The militants spread fear amongst KPs through loudspeakers, newspaper advertisements and pamphlets ordering them to leave Kashmir or face death. KPs initially resisted extradition. They looked for every possible way to avoid abandoning the place where their families had roots and their ancestors were consigned to flame. The torture, rapes and killings of the members of their community forced them to move outside the region. Militants riding on motorcycles shot at officers, officials, security forces and KPs turning

Kashmir into a cauldron. Young zealous Muslim gunrunners who had returned after training from across the border opposed anything Indian: KPs, other minorities, security forces, etc. They used mosques and religious slogans to give the movement an Islamic cloak: Kashmir is an Islamic society with no place for others.

Memory is a means of 'passing on,' of sharing a social past, and an inescapably inter-subjective act. As W. J. T. Mitchell remarks, 'Memory is an inter subjective phenomenon, a practice not only of recollection of a past by a subject, but of recollection for another subject' (Mitchell, 1994, p. 17). Besides, acts of remembering extend beyond the acknowledgement of collective sites of memory, historical documents and oral traditions to activate its potential for reshaping future of, and for, other subjects. Rahul Pandita in *Our Moon Has Blood Clots* (2013) engages traumatic remembering around the Kashmiri Pandit exodus. He narrates everyday life of inequality, suffering and humiliation along the narratives of self, family, relations and community that illuminate the dark side of oppression, subversion and treachery.

Rahul Pandita at the age of 14 years had to leave his ancestral house 'the house we left forever to become refugees and court suffering and homelessness' (Pandita, 2013, p. 217) in Kashmir in 1990. Twenty-three years later, he relives the trauma of his exodus in *Our Moon Has Blood Clots* 'We have been in exile for more than two decades. Kashmir is a memory, an overdose of nostalgia. But beyond this, there is nothing. Many among us have moved on. For most of us, Kashmir means a calendar hanging in our parents' bedroom, or a mutton dish cooked in the traditional way on Shivratri, or a cousin's marriage that the elders insist must be solemnized in Jammu' (Pandita, 2013, pp. 209–210). Rahul Pandita's personal journey into the core of darkness – the horrific past – intertwined with the tragedies of many known/unknown KP victims of militants' guns who did not survive to speak for themselves, underscores in the public space the somewhat forgotten narrative of the KPs for 'social change' (Nance, 2006, p. 12).

Our Moon Has Blood Clots from a childhood narrative of Rahul Pandita grows into a poignant narrative of pain, loss and survival. Rahul Pandita, a growing up child, witnessed violence in Kashmir in the late 1980s and early 1990s. He begins the narrative with a brief survey of Kashmiri Pandit culture and tradition: '[...] my ancestors took to the pursuit of knowledge. It is thus that Kashmir became the primeval home of the Brahmins, or *Brahmans* – those who are conscious' (Pandita, 2013, p. 12) to underscore that the origin of Kashmiri Pandit clan and their history is a permanent part of Kashmir. The joyful memories of his house constructed in Kashmir '[...] my father had exhausted his entire Provident Fund; whatever little jewellery my mother possessed was also sold to help finance the construction' (Pandita, 2013, p. 21); his room's '[...] wooden shelves [were] lined with books' (Pandita, 2013, p. 28); kitchen garden, childhood friendships, school days, visits to cinema hall and gardens, the caring elders, family feasts and rituals on ceremonial occasions dot the narrative.

The realization that inter-community relations between the Kashmiri Muslims and KPs in Kashmir had never been peaceful on the whole starts from his early days in school when his friends tore the cover of the school magazine because it featured an image 'of the goddess Saraswati' (Pandita, 2013, p. 30). Moreover, his friends '[. . .] would all hurl abuses when the national anthem was sung during the school assembly and kicked those of us who sang it' (Pandita, 2013, p. 30); at home when he overhears Rehman the milkman telling his mother 'Why are you wasting your money like this? [. . .] Tomorrow, if not today, this house will belong to us' (Pandita, 2013, p. 62) moves Rahul Pandita to realize that things were changing in Kashmir. The majority community on the provocation of militants and separatist leaders had become intolerant toward KPs and left no stone unturned 'to frighten us into exile' (Pandita, 2013, p. 78).

Rahul Pandita in *Our Moon Has Blood Clots* highlights that in the late 1980's there were visible signs of horrendous days ahead in Kashmir: '[. . .] a group of young men racing up and down the stairs [. . .] hordes of men doing physical exercises' (Pandita, 2013, p. 63) who, it was later believed, were among those who had returned from arms training camps across the border. A Pandit woman 'Prabhawati of Chadoora tehsil' was 'the first Pandit casualty' in a blast in March 1989. A known political activist Tika Lal Taploo was shot in his home, and his 'funeral procession was pelted with stones' (Pandita, 2013, p. 65). Retired High Court judge Neelkanth Ganjoo was '[. . .] waylaid by three men on Hari Singh Street, in the heart of Srinagar, and shot at close range' (Pandita, 2013, p. 74) in November 1989. What was the fault of Ganjoo? As District Court judge, Ganjoo had in August 1968 sentenced to death J&K Liberation Front (JKLF) founder and leader Maqbool Bhat for the murder of police inspector Amar Chand in 1966. The killings of Taploo and Ganjoo were to hype the control of the militants in the public space and also to instill fear in the minds of the judiciary, bureaucracy, police and to coerce KPs to leave Kashmir. Earlier in June '[. . .] pamphlets were distributed in Srinagar [. . .]. Pandit women were asked to put a tilak on their foreheads for identification' (Pandita, 2013, p. 64). Rahul Pandita underscores how Kashmir was charged with terrorizing slogans which became a routine:

> *Zalzala aaya hai kufr ke maidaan mein,*
> *Lo mujahid aa gaye maidaaan mein*
> An earthquake has occurred in the realm of the infidels,
> The mujahids have come out to fight. (Pandita, 2013, p. 66)

January 19, 1990 was a horrific night when neighbours turned against neighbours, friends against friends and humanity disappeared in Kashmir. Rahul Pandita recalls 'Father was waking me up. "Something is happening," he said. I could hear it – there were people out on the streets. They were talking loudly. Some major activity was underfoot. Were they setting our locality on fire?' (Pandita, 2013, pp. 75–76) Groups of Kashmiri Muslims were out on the streets, demanding freedom from India and kicking out of KPs from Kashmir:

> *Hum kya chaaaate:azadiiii!*
> *Eiy zalimon, eiy kafiron, Kashmir humara chhod do.*
> What do we want- Freedom!
> O tyrants, O infidels, leave our Kashmir. (Pandita, 2013, p. 76)

In this atmosphere of fear and threat, KPs began to feel an increasing sense of vulnerability and insecurity. Rahul Pandita further recollects the horrifying night of January 19, 1990: 'I remember Ma began to tremble like a leaf when we heard it. *"Assi gacchi panu'nuy Pakistan, batav rostuy, batenein saan."* The crowd wanted to turn Kashmir into Pakistan, without the Pandit men, but with their women' (Pandita, 2013, p. 77). The rest of the night his mother sat 'with a long knife. It was her father's. "If they come, I will kill her," she looked at my sister. And then I will kill myself. And you see what you two need to do"' (Pandita, 2013, p. 77). His mother's panic was justified because at the time of the *Kabaili* (tribals) attack she as a young girl had heard incidents of how: 'The tribesmen converted Baramulla's cinema hall into a rape house. Hundreds of women were taken there and raped. some of them were later abducted and taken to Rawalpindi and Peshawar and sold like cattle' (Pandita, 2013, pp. 183–184). His mother preferred violent death for herself and her daughter rather than submitting to the other community. Rahul Pandita's mother's decision underscores that sexual violence is a weapon used by perpetrators during conflict/war to humiliate the other to break the morale, especially of the men by sexually abusing their women.

Besides, the laughter of the boys outside Rahul Pandita's house on that dreadful night: '"Let's distribute these houses," one of them shouts. "Akram, which one do you want?" he asks. "I would settle for this house any day," he points to a house. "Bastard," shoots back another, "how you wish you could occupy this house with their daughter!" There is a peel of laughter. They make obscene gestures with their fists and Akram pretends as if he is raping the girl [. . .]' (Pandita, 2013, p. 90) contextualizes Rahul Pandita's sense of fright, distress and disgust. These boys were his friends and lived in the neighbourhood. But their offensive intentions at this young age were exposed along with Rahul Pandita's sense of unsafety in Kashmir as the basic trust between the two communities was lost: 'The imagery of these events often crystallizes around a moment of betrayal, and it is this breach of trust which gives the intrusive images their intense emotional power' (Herman, 1992, p. 55). This antagonistic conversation among the boys led to 'intense fear, helplessness, loss of control and threat of annihilation engulfed' (Herman, 1992, p. 33) Rahul Pandita and his father. His father who till now was resisting the pressure to move out decided: 'It's over [. . .]. We cannot live here anymore' (Pandita, 2013, p. 92) as he was worried about the safety of his family. In this context, Bhan states 'The night of January 19, 1990 will remain the most unforgettable one in memory of every Kashmiri Pandit child who had attained the age of consciousness of surroundings, and grown-up men and women. That night stands singled out as the harbinger of the terrible catastrophe which before long engulfed the panic – stricken unfortunate community' (2003, p. 43).

January 19, 1990 for KPs marked the loss of homeland. The militants in order to spread terror and to expedite the exodus of KPs started targeting selective KPs, paramilitary forces and central government officials working in Kashmir. Rahul Pandita gives a comprehensive list of the KPs who became the targets of the militants' mad frenzy. In this context, P. L. Kaul remarks this was not the handiwork '[…] of some misguided Muslim youth alone, but an assault by a large section of the Muslims on the entire Hindu community of Kashmir' (Kaul, 1996, p. 15). In one such incident B. K. Ganju, a 'thirty-six-year-old telecommunications officer' whose '[…] name was on a "hit list" in a neighbourhood mosque' decided to leave Srinagar with his wife. However, early morning militants came looking for him. His wife 'urged him to hide in the attic, in a drum partially filled with rice' (Pandita, 2013, p. 115). Unable to find him, they left. In downtown, Srinagar houses are built quite close to each other. A Muslim lady from the neighbourhood who had seen Ganju hiding in the drum prompted the men who '[…] went directly to the attic and shot B. K. Ganju dead inside that drum.' As they were coming down, Mrs. Ganju asked them to kill her as well. '"No, someone should be left to wail over his dead body," they replied' (Pandita, 2013, p. 116). This incident shows the death of humanity as women too became perpetrators in the killing spree of KPs.

Another victim of the militants' brutality was the Kashmiri Pandit poet and scholar Sarvanand Kaul Premi who 'was secular to the core – in his prayer room, he kept a rare manuscript of the Koran. After his retirement, he had taught for free for three months a year in two schools, one run by an Islamic and the other a Hindu educational society' (Pandita, 2013, p. 116). His relatives urged him to leave Kashmir, but he was 'confident that nobody would touch him. He had spent his whole life with his Muslim neighbours, he said. They will protect me, he told his relatives.' (Pandita, 2013, p. 116). Sarvanand Kaul Premi was right in his belief. The creative writers cannot be contained within the boundaries of religion, caste, etc., as they belong to the world and their religion is humanity. But he was wrong those prompted militants took no heed of these considerations. He and his son were taken away by three armed men, one night, who barged into Premi's house. They ordered the family to assemble in one room. '"Bring all your valuables here", one of them told a family member. These were brought-jewellery, cash, heirloom pashmina shawls. Then the men ordered all the women to hand over whatever ornaments they were wearing. This was complied with as well. The valuables were packed into a big suitcase which Premi was ordered to carry' (Pandita, 2013, pp. 116–117).

The family desperately waited, but they never returned. Their bodies were found '[…] hanging from a tree a day later. The men had *hammered* nails between their eyebrows, where the tilak [sandalwood mark] is applied. Their limbs were broken and their bodies ravaged with cigarette burns. They had been shot as well' (Pandita, 2013, p. 117).

Another victim of militants' ghastly violence was Lassa Koul Director, Doordarshan Kashmir. He was shot dead when he had gone to visit his handicapped father in Bemina. The information about his intended visit was 'leaked to the militants by one of his colleagues' (Pandita, 2013, p. 84), which exposes the malicious intentions of the majority community to expedite the exodus of minority community by creating distress amongst them. Naveen Sapru, the 37-year-old telecom department employee was shot dead by militants in Habba Kadal market where he had gone to collect his coat:

while on the tailor's hanger remained hung
his warm coat.
Passing as it did through scissors and thread –needle
in the tailor's hand, till the previous day
it was merely a person's coat
that suddenly was turned into a Hindu's coat. (Pandita, 2013, p. 84)

And Rahul Pandita through the story of Satish Tickoo, who was killed by
Farooq Ahmad Dar alias Bitta Karate, reminds how justice always eluded the
KPs, for even a self-proclaimed killer of KPs could not be convicted due to the
apathy of the public prosecution: 'The court is aware of the fact that the alle-
gations levelled against the accused are of serious nature and carry a punishment
of death sentence or life imprisonment but the fact is that the prosecution has
shown total disinterest in arguing the case, which is in complete violation of
Article 21 of the Constitution' (Pandita, 2013, p. 82).

Besides, a number of Kashmiri Pandit women fell victim to the nefarious
intentions of the militants joined by the common people Sarla Bhat, a Kashmiri
Pandit nurse from the Soura Medical College Hospital in Srinagar was
gang-raped and then beaten to death. JKLF admitted the crime, accusing her of
informing the police about the presence of militants in the hospital. Girja Tikoo,
another Kashmiri Pandit laboratory assistant at a government school, was
kidnapped: 'Four men had taken turns to rape her in a moving taxi. As they were
conversing with each other, Girja recognized the voice of one of the men who
went by the name Aziz. "Aziz, chhetey chukha? Aziz, are you here as well?" she
asked. Aziz got worried. He knew that Girja had recognized him. So, in a final
act of barbarism, they took her to a wood-processing unit and cut her alive on a
mechanical saw' (Pandita, 2013, p. 118). Babli Raina, a Kashmiri Pandit teacher,
was gang raped in her house in the presence of her family and then killed. In
another glaring incident, militants demanded food and shelter from the family of
a Kashmiri Pandit truck driver Sohan Lal. The family obeyed, but the militants
raped his daughter. When he and his wife tried to stop them, the militants shot
him dead and even raped his wife who later died in the hospital.

Also, militants assassinated 23 members of Kashmiri Pandit family in
Wandhama village in Kashmir 'when the gun shots were being fired, the people of
the village increased the volume of the loudspeaker in the mosque to muffle the
sound of gunfire' (Pandita, 2013, p. 231), which speaks of the treachery of the
neighbours as well. Even the Sikh population was not spared. The killings of 40
Sikhs in Chittisinghpura and the massacre of 24 KPs in Nadimarg, followed by
many more such reported/unreported cases of the killings of ordinary persons
contributed to an atmosphere of shock and insecurity among the KPs. Rahul
Pandita's cousin Ravi too was pulled out of a bus along with two KPs and shot
while on his way to Gool, the place of his posting. He left behind old parents, a
young wife and an infant son. Rahul Pandita's *Our Moon Has Blood Clots* is not
only his narrative but the narrative of every single Kashmiri Pandit who
encountered terror in Kashmir. Innocent people were assaulted '[. . .] the Pandits
were hounded on the streets and killed brutally. Killings of the Hindu minority
had turned into an orgy; a kind of bloodlust. By April 1990, the mask was

completely off. It was not only the armed terrorist who took pride in such killings-the common man on the streets participated in some of these heinous murders' (Pandita, 2013, p. 115) and rapes.

Our Moon Has Blood Clots attempts to break the silence in the socio-political discourse over the exodus of KPs as in the discourse regarding Kashmir conflict the human rights abuses and victimization of the Kashmiri Muslims are argued without reference to KPs who too are the victims of human rights abuses: 'Throughout 1990, Pandits are picked up selectively and put to death. They are killed because Kashmir needs to be cleansed of them. And if the one chosen is not to be found, a proxy suffices. It is all about numbers. It is all about how many are killed. It is known that if one among them is killed, a thousand will flee' (Pandita, 2013, p. 72). Due to geo-politics, the issue of Kashmiri Pandit exodus took a back stage.

To understand the brutal politics of Pakistan and the changing mindset of Kashmiri Muslims who did not hesitate to erase a minority community from their homeland, Rahul Pandita's narrative gives insights into the simmering fissures of hatred ignited from across the border which led to not only the exodus of KPs but also the loss of older generation due to the severe heat of the plains, and the generations born thereafter devoid of any idea or connectivity with their home-land except through books, parental discussions leading to an important question – what is Kashmir in reality? Where do the KPs stand today? Thrown out from home and hearth as 'refugees in 1990, our [Kashmiri Pandit] lives became restricted to eight-by-eight feet rooms' (Pandita, 2013, p. 50). Symbolic references to their plight have left a deep anguish and feelings of bitterness among the community, The feeling of being made forced migrants, displaced community, strangers in their own homeland, victims of exile, forced to face not only the painful reality of the killings of their near and dear ones by militants but also of losing the link with their homeland 'is a wound that never heals' (Crapanzano, 2011, p. 2).

NOTES

1. The present status of Jammu and Kashmir is of Union Territory after the Jammu and Kashmir Reorganisation Act 2019 passed on 9 August 2019, wherein the state was reorganized into two Union Territories namely Union Territory of Jammu and Kashmir and Union Territory of Ladakh. Jammu and Kashmir is referred to as state as the time period taken is from 1989 to 2011 with some references to the attack in 1947 immediately after the partition of India.

2. The present research paper refers to the time period of 1989–2011, underscoring the trauma and turmoil of the exodus of Kashmiri Pandits from their homeland Kashmir.

3. The status of KPs is unclear. KPs do not fall under the category of migrants as their movement from Kashmir is not voluntary. Similarly, they cannot be refugees in their own country. Hence, they are variously referred to as displaced KP, forced KP migrants, internally displaced migrants KP.

4. Jagati township and Purkhoo camp are the places where Kashmiri Pandit families have been resettled after their exodus from Kashmir. The governments at the centre and in Jammu and Kashmir from time to time have initiated various financial and educational aids for these KP families.

5. *Our Moon Has Blood Clots* was published in 2013. As the present paper is looking at the varied aspects of conflict in Kashmir through the lens of this text, the time period selected is from 1980s to 2011.

REFERENCES

Bhan, K. L. (2003). *Paradise lost: The seven exoduses of Kashmiri Pandits*. Kashmiri News Network.

Crapanzano, V. H. (2011). *The wound that never heals*. University of Chicago Press.

Dennen, J. M. G. V., & Falger, V. S. E. (Eds.). (2005). Introduction: On conflict. In *The sociobiology of conflict* (pp. 1–19). Chapman & Hall.

Duschinski, H. (2008). "Survival is now our politics": Kashmiri Hindu community identity and the politics of homeland. *International Journal of Hindu Studies, 12*(1), 41–64. https://doi.org/10.1007/s11407-008-9054-z

Fink, C. F. (1968). Some conceptual difficulties in the theory of social conflict. *Journal of Conflict Resolution, XII*(4), 412–460. Sage Publication.

Herman, J. L. (1992). *Trauma and recovery*. Basic Books.

Jagmohan. (1991). *My frozen turbulence in Kashmir*. Allied Publishers Pvt. Ltd.

Kalhana (1935). *Rajatarangini: The saga of the kings of Kasmir* (transl. by Pandit R.S.). Moti Lal Banarsi Das.

Kapur, S. P. (2007). *Dangerous deterrent: Nuclear proliferation and conflict in South Asia*. Stanford University Press.

Kaul, P. (1996). *Kashmir: Trail and travail*. Suman Publication.

Mitchell, W. J. T. (1994). *Picture theory: Essays on verbal and visual representation*. University of Chicago Press.

Nance, K. A. (2006). *Can literature promote justice? Trauma narrative and social action in Latin American Testimonio*. Vanderbilt University Press.

Oxford Advanced Learner's Dictionary - 10th Edition. (2020). Oxford University Press.

Pandita, R. (2013). *Our moon has blood clots*. Penguin Random House.

WOMEN REFUGEES IN ITALY DURING THE RUSSIAN–UKRAINIAN CONFLICT[1]

Maria Anita Stefanelli[a] and Cecilia Cinti[b]

[a]Roma Tre University, Italy
[b]Independent Scholar, Italy

ABSTRACT

The essay presents a forced move from Ukraine to Italy at the time of the 24/02/2022 Russian invasion of Ukraine. It focuses on a woman with her child who left their home to reach Italy. Ukrainian-born people in Italy in 2022 reached 223,000 residents; yet, with the ongoing war, at least 100,000 Ukrainian citizens, mostly with refugee status, entered the country. An account follows the journey of mother and child towards San Marino, a state within the state, but their target had to change because only a limited number of migrants could stay. They left for Emilia where, with some difficulty, a relatively stable residence was found a few kilometres from the beach. They managed to spend the summer months there before relocating to town for the little one to find cognitive and social protection attending maternity school. The mother explained, in an interview, her need to protect her little one and find support for them two. She had to learn ways of socialising, avoiding the sense of loss trying and conceiving of how to explore and practice art. Beauty amid war, besides colouring our personal feelings, can help recreating an atmosphere of recollection and intimacy drawing attention to images, sound, movement and all the ways of stimulation for body and mind to raise emotions, symbolisation and well-being. Final aims were the embodiment of aesthetics to recreate oneself and the achievement of a state of resilience.

Keywords: Ukrainian refugees; war; school; psychological distance; child protection; beauty and art

Scars of War
Research in Political Sociology, Volume 30, 121–136
Copyright © 2025 Maria Anita Stefanelli and Cecilia Cinti
Published under exclusive licence by Emerald Publishing Limited
ISSN: 0895-9935/doi:10.1108/S0895-993520250000030009

INTRODUCTION

Official figures of the European Commission supported by the European Institute for Statistics (Eurostat), press releases by UNICEF, agencies like ICRC (International Committee of the Red Cross) or IRC (International rescue Committee), journalistic reports or media in general (documentaries, websites, TV debates and discussions, among others) inform us every day about people that leave their homes owing to some unpredicted events in their country or region, sometimes in a hurry, other times as a consequence of an abrupt change in one's life: a call to arms of a family member, intolerance of new political arrangements, natural calamities, repeated attacks of some sort, a family call from elsewhere and violation of human rights.

A situation may also develop nearer to us that presents a case which we happen to experience. This is the beginning of a case study, i.e., a detailed study of a specific subject, a situation involving one person or more, an event or organisation or a phenomenon or other case taking place in a specific real-world context which is being studied applying wider reading or theory. An interview is often a preliminary circumstance that leads to a case study.

Based on an interview conducted in the summer of 2022, a case study concerning a mother-with-child's move from Ukraine to Poland and finally to Italy is presented after some demographic and contextual figures dating to the beginning of the war. The mother's psychological distance from her past and a potential future, her being in touch with herself, the protection and security of the child, the mother's experience of beauty and art and the future ahead of them are the themes to be discussed. The mother's future perspective, expressed at the time concerned, however, is far from being definitive.

OVERVIEW: UKRAINIANS WHO LEFT FOR POLAND AND ITALY

Within the official portal for European data, we learn that, by the end of the year 2020, Italy has hosted a community of at least 223,000 Ukrainian-born people, plus the approximately 100,000 Ukrainian citizens with refugee status who entered the country after 24, February, 2022 (Mancino, 2022). In Poland, the EU country nearest to the Ukrainian north-western border that counted 499,000 Ukrainian citizens before the war, Ukrainian nationality is the third most represented non-EU citizen who hold a valid residence permit obtained from the police after the established Moroccan and Turkish migrants (AgenSIR, 2022). While the last two have remained stable or have decreased since 2013, residence permits for Ukrainian nationals increased steadily, with a growth of more than 50% up to 2020 (Mancino, 2022). In Italy, Lombardy (with 29,000), Emilia Romagna (with 22,000), Lazio (with 16,000) and Campania (with 19,000) listed geographically are the regions where, from April 29 to July 8, 2022, most Ukrainians settled, often with a temporary job.

Women with children range as the first gender to have settled in Italy or to have left their country for Italy planning to go back in the future. Since 2014, during the ongoing international conflict between Russia and Ukraine, most Ukrainian mothers have progressively been alerted to leave their homes and find a safer place for themselves and their children across borders. The Covid-19 pandemic emergency with its travel restrictions had an impact on most migrants; yet flows from Ukraine became more severe after the special military operation announced in winter 2022 by the Russian President. The event stimulated even more female adults to take shelter, alone or with children, further away from disruption of their life. Many of them joined Ukrainian relatives, forming part of a pre-existing community abroad. In the case of Italy, large cities like Milan, Rome and Naples attracted migrants and refugees as places for wider opportunities in respect of smaller cities or towns. The choice of Lombardy sounded like an optimal response to job demands; Emilia Romagna, with its traditional appeal for its organisational apparatus in vital needs, among which healthcare and schooling beside the attractiveness of the Adriatic coastal amenities, became sought-after; Campania, usually popular for milder weather and her reputation of sympathetic people, did act as a magnetic field; Lazio for its central position as the region of the capital city and a provisioner for all Christian denominations responded to the call for diverse facilities and devotional demands.

Compared with other European countries, Italy places itself among the last in Europe for job offers. A year after the beginning of conflict, more than 600,000 Ukrainians, mostly female, had found a job in Europe. Italy ranks under 0.5% for Ukrainian Refugees' labor force among the EU countries, with Poland ranging first with a figure 2.5% (Prestigiacomo, 2023). Thanks to Ukrainian refugees, Poland added 2.7% to the size of the labour force (mostly male adults), while Italy could count only 0.2% (Prestigiacomo, 2023). It is also to be noticed that the share of adult women in Poland and Italy is between 85 and 90% and the share of minors under 40%. In March 2023, Save the Children stated that, as from the previous year, in response to a request for help from Lviv, they organised together with CIR (Italian Council for Refugees [Centro Italiano Rifugiati]), a safe transfer of Ukrainian children and adolescents from Poland to Italy (Save the Children Italia, 2023).

Unless there was a definite place where people had been invited to join a family of relatives or friends, most immigrants – whether refugees or asylum seekers – would have approached an organisation providing them with a stable residence. Caritas, for instance, has the commitment to promote a human rights-based approach to ensure that every person affected by armed conflicts and violence feels safe, protected, welcomed and respected.[2] Despite many who would offer help, very often people – mostly female, with children and without a job – may be forced to change from one arrangement to another before finding a suitable accommodation for the time being.

It is not surprising that difficulties for parents or a single parent with a child or children are not always overcome. Despite the favourable situation for job seeking in Poland, for instance, parents started noticing a negative change in their children's behaviour since their arrival from Ukraine. By the end of the summer

2023 (we need to speak of what happens day by day, since the situation is so fluid), obstacles were identified in the field of education for Ukrainian children living temporarily in Poland. A survey by IRC (Polish Education System), in a communiqué concerning Warsaw, came to the following conclusion: 'Social isolation, lack of language proficiency, and the effects of trauma and displacement still constitute significant barriers for Ukrainian children trying to integrate into the Polish education system' (IRC, 2023). The choice for parents who desired the best for their children was either returning to a country devastated by bombs or migrating to a different country in the hope of finding a job to support the family – both solutions subject to disagreements within the family or to less economically or socially favourable situations.

A YOUNG MOTHER-WITH-BABY'S JOURNEY FROM ZAPORIZHZHIA TO POLAND AND ITALY

In cases of a pandemic or conflicts of some kind, the people's choice is between 'stay and resist' or 'leave and find protection.' The focus, in the case study that follows, is on one adult woman and her child of the 4.07 million Ukrainian citizens who left their country after Russia attacked Ukraine to find temporary protection in the EU (Eurostat, 2023).

Protection for her son was the main reason for the young woman to leave her hometown, owing to the political, diplomatic and military conflict between her native country and Russia, to go abroad. Subsistence, education, care and welfare for the child, more parental responsibility for the child and need for protection are a must in time of war. Being a woman with a child would multiply problems and provoke risk of personal violence, dis-respect for women and, in extreme, but not improbable, cases, fatal submission to male physical power.

Three million Ukrainian children suddenly needed more protection, assistance and security. When lucky enough to be in the family, in the present war, many children were deprived of school and their friends, their life was disrupted and they had to experience having to run, in order to protect themselves, to underground bunkers where they spent, at first, a few hours, then several hours, then days, weeks and later the cold months of the winter season. Many of them have been separated from their families, transferred to areas under the foreign nation's control, and for many there was no hope of going back to their parents – that is, in case their parents might still be alive. About the process concerning children who would be made members of new families, called *abduction*, IRC (International Committee of the Red Cross) has republished an article where a UNESCO study on children and warfare is quoted that attests to the crucial need of preserving family unity in conflicts. When amidst bombing and explosion a child might not even be 'conscious of his peril if he keeps near him his protector who, in his child's heart, incarnates security, and if, at the same time, he can clasp in his arms some familiar object' (Plattner, 1984, p. 144).

For those who could remain in Ukraine with their parents there were daily bombardments, bodily and mental injuries, lack of food, lack of water, no education, little playing, hospitalisation only sometime, and continual life risk. *No way for children to grow up. 500 days of war in Ukraine* is the title of an article written for UNICEF where one reads of 182,000 children under five who, for not attending kindergarten or pre-school, would be deprived of adequate cognitive and social development (2023). It is not surprising that a mother with a little boy would be looking for a safer way to live, if momentarily, waiting for the end of war.

In conflict, protection is a need for many people, whether fragile or too old to be able to cope. On June 30, 2023, Ukrainians under temporary protection were 98% of the total number of those sharing the same destiny in Europe, a fact that forces one to respond to the struggle or struggles that life demands. Our narrative concerns the above-mentioned mother (of almost half of temporary protection women beneficiaries) and child (of the slightly over one third of temporary protection minors beneficiaries) respectively, whom EU enabled with temporary protection. To be precise, the percentage was: 46.6% of all women and 34.4% of all children, while adult men included 19%, i.e. less than a fifth of the total temporary protection male beneficiaries.

The two potential refugees, who had managed to reach Poland in an over-crowded bus from the town of Zaporizhzhia where they lived, had left in the father's car without hesitation for an implausible adventure towards the south of Europe. The couple is exemplary of a way to cope in actual life with unexpected life trials. They would become two of around one fifth of all Ukrainian refugees in Italy, while one quarter of them would be hosted by Poland (Prestigiacomo, 2023). The Ukrainian diaspora in Italy, from April 29 to July 8, 2022, is repre-sented with shapes of different sizes: highest (20,000 requests) in Lombardy, lower (15,000 requests) in Emilia-Romagna, lower still (10,000) in Venetia, Latium and Campania, lowest (5,000) elsewhere.[3]

The first station of mother and child who had left, after a few days' stay for the mother to make an optimal resolution, Poland for Italy, was *The Republic of San Marino*, a state within the Republic, where the mother's mother had emigrated years before.

A brief account of the small independent state – just over 24 square miles – enclaved by the Romagna area in the central Italian peninsula is necessary to appreciate the effort made by the Republic to help refugees and wish to facilitate peace keeping. The – officially – *Most Serene Republic of San Marino* is approximately six kilometres from Rimini and the Adriatic coast. The Republic stayed neutral in both World War I and II. A state who has developed a close relationship with Moscow, San Marino welcomed the earliest people fleeing the conflict as early as March 2022, offering accommodation, healthcare and eco-nomic support. Among the 414 Ukrainians who had San Marino as target, the woman and her baby arrived, seeking refuge. Eventually, parents with school-children who enrolled at school and grown-up youngsters at university – a quarter of the total number – remained, while other guests had to leave. The number of temporary residents dropped to 116 by the beginning of summer. San Marino confirmed her neutrality in the Russia–Ukraine conflict, granted asylum or temporary residence permit to Ukrainians, and offered to play host to the Vatican future diplomatic talks.

There is no statistics for people who left Poland for Italy after leaving home because of war, yet the young woman with her baby in our narrative did so. Even if she had already experienced being jobless back home and received her parents' help, her choice did not depend on an easier way to find a job, but, more conceivably, on the assistance she would receive in Italy from her mother and grandmother with her son still in the toddler's stage, and protection from the state. Unable to settle much longer than a few weeks in the small republic, mother and baby boy had to leave San Marino, and so they did.

With a little luck, they were able to join the Caritas program for the province of Ferrara in the Emilia-Romagna region, who helped them with a home in a Holiday Village for summer tourists on the Adriatic coast, south of the river Po delta, for a temporary stay. With conditions having changed after the summer, and hospitality in the Holiday Village being less palatable (especially with a small child in a place unfit for the winter), mother and child, with the end of the holiday season, were unable to remain. They were given the possibility to go back to Ferrara to live in a hospice. The proposal was not attractive since no job prospect would materialise. Once again, mother and child had to rely on help from relatives' friends and newly acquired friends to find a place to stay nearby. With the Covid-19 virus having become much less contagious or lethal during the summer, the mother managed to find shelter with a family. The question of finding a job, then, appeared more likely to the mother. She set out to enrol her child in the nursery school and contacted the Youth Information Centre of the area to secure a part-time job. Back home she had started teaching masterclasses to adults wishing to learn how to draw and paint. She had also used her free time to learn how to start a nail business with the little financial help she had received from her parents. Nail art was useful to start earning a little money so she could recapture faith in a less bitter fate for herself and her baby. With school for the son, and a small job for the mother, life appeared suitable for mother and child who fled from a conflict-affected area where bomb or missile attack, human rights violation and high risks of psychological damage were becoming more predictable than a foreseeable better future. Six months had passed since the beginning of the war, yet there was no cease fire, no peaceful truce, not even diplomatic talk definition produced. Personal, far from happy, consequences would ensue.

AN INTERVIEW WITH A FEMALE REFUGEE'S MAIN PROBLEM/S

An interview was organised with the mother – whose first six months of unrest had passed – to test one of the main problems that was seemingly becoming more pressing with the passing of time: the physical distancing – from loved ones, friends, home, context, work, habits and the natural environment – and the psychological distancing – in terms of the temporal, spatial, social and hypothetical dimension. The main object was to evaluate the causes of the family's steps towards moving abroad and the consequences for their well-being.

The planned departure of the two had materialised too quickly. Leaving Ukraine had been, for mother and child, a matter of hours. For the child's sake – protecting him, ensuring food for him, granting peace around him – they had to leave with a hurried planning. A brief talk by the mother in response to a question posed during an unofficial interview will throw some light on the way in which the mother faced the demanding situation, and what compensation she could rely on to confront her personal involvement in it.

Q. Is physical distancing for you also mental alienation? Can you find space for self-representation as a woman? Can your own writing or your art – drawing, painting, and writing for yourself besides practising the art of nail painting on others – help you to overcome the unknowns you encountered on the path that took you away from your origins to experience an uprooting that you hope will be only temporary?

The reply brings together the physical and psychological distance being experienced:

A. Being away from home is obviously difficult not only *physically,* but also *mentally.* It is as if *a part of yourself* had remained *there* – meaning your home, your homeland, your environment, your hopes, and even your own identity – as if you were unable to break off and leave your previous life behind, or just disregard what was and is happening *there.*[4] You are experiencing a continuous *split* within yourself: on the one hand, you are physically in Italy with daily problems to face, such as securing accommodation and finding a job that allows some economic independence, learning a language, standing up to bureaucracy and communicating in a language that is not your mother tongue. On the other hand, with your mind and your heart, you are in your own mother country, thinking about your relatives who stayed back, of your own house that might be *reduced to debris* in a minute or two and of the *future* that you are scared even to just imagine. It would have been impossible for those of us who have left, to remain, and this for obvious reasons; yet we are refused the ability to fully live our own reality since *our worries* and *our hopes* take us away, take us back home. It is an excruciating situation. I am not just talking of a physical place that is now lost, of course, but also of my *home*, my *relatives*, my *job*, the *people* that you know and that you love, my *feelings*, my *dreams*! In these circumstances, I find help when I compare my life with that of *other women* who go through the same difficulties as I do: they fully *understand* my attitude. So, we manage to exchange suggestions on how to deal with everyday problems, we talk about our homeland, we try to figure out the physical and mental conditions of our people who have been left behind to fight [...] That is why I try to keep myself *busy*. It helps me to do what I always liked to do even before the war burst out: drawing, nail art (which I have been able to practise here during Halloween's three days festivities), listening to music, cooking, watching movies, walking and even reading about *psychology*. Art – drawing and painting, but also nail art – helps me, because it embodies the *beauty* that helps us to overcome the difficulties of everyday life and because it represents us both as individuals and as human beings. As I experience it, besides expressing our personal feelings, art also represents the *culture of a people*. Unfortunately, since I have been here, in Italy, I have not yet found a way to recreate the *scenario* for drawing, that is, my study where I used to hold workshops, with the necessary tools (canvas, easel, palette, brushes, pencils and other technical instruments for drawing and graphics), where I could recreate that atmosphere, that *recollection* and that *intimacy* that might allow me to *rediscover myself* and to express myself. Back in Ukraine I often draw at night, when all is silent, my baby asleep and my mind able to find concentration and get in contact with my own self[...] All that I have mentioned and that I experience every day help me to learn new things, like getting to know aspects of the local culture, visiting *unfamiliar* places, exhibitions, museums and galleries, even cooking new dishes. I am a person who deeply needs to experience *something new*.

ANALYSING THE PROBLEM/S

As is known from the cognitive sciences, people do experience concretely what happens 'here and now', but they can also imagine, or experience abstractly, what would happen at some distance from themselves, in the future, in the past or even, through the mind, what may or may not happen, dream of a realisable or unrealisable event or fear an atrocious one to come. Concrete distances tend to be seen as psychologically closer, while abstract ones are felt as further away from your everyday life.

Differently from many Europeans' psychological anticipations of what would happen, however, the Russian President's worldwide announcement of a 'special military operation in Ukraine' surely led many Ukrainians to anticipate at least some of the weight and losses the conflict would bring with itself, making their immediate future more present and unsafety a reality. A conflict with Russia had already been experienced by Ukrainians in 2014, so what had been conceived mentally during the passing of time turned increasingly realistic at the announcement.

Here it is useful to make a distinction between the perception of time at the social level and time as described by the natural scientist. The 'world of common sense as the scene of all social relationships and actions,' envisioned by Edmund Husserl, as A. Gurwitsch (1962) contends, is identified in the 'life-world,' the construct that the social scientist deals with and that is in contrast with the idealised constructs of the physical sciences characterised by the absence of precedent or underlying constructs studied by the natural scientist. The 'life-world,' or 'world of common sense,' is perceived in concrete terms, given the biographical 'pre-interpretation' and 'preconceptions' that characterise the data, facts and events we all live through (p. 70). The psychological distance in time is related, as

Trope and Liberman (2010) explain to the 'level of mental construal': when high, it is abstract and coherent, when low, it is concrete and detailed. The farther the psychological distance in time is, then, from our interviewee's direct experience – as it does, with reference to the future, regarding the feeble hope of going back home and the factual need to survive with her child in the meantime – the higher and more abstract is the level of construal. In other words, because it is impossible to experience the past or the future, the mother's mental constructions become a useful instrument to transcend the immediate situation, a time when she professes her need to *read about psychology*, evidently to come to terms with her own 'self' and the 'here and now,' as per the construal level theory (Trope & Liberman, 2010).

Moving from concrete to abstract representation of an object entails retaining certain features of the object that are relevant to one's goals and omit fewer specific ones. The case of the mother's claim of wanting to experience the *beauty of art* concretely is intended to overcome the difficulties because the pleasure it gives – 'here and now' – would make her life more tolerable. The claim, however, also entails the 'abstract' fact of *representing* herself and her child as *individuals* and *human beings* entitled to live their *own culture* (the *culture of the people*, as she says). Such abstract ideas are due to the psychological distance that separates them from a potential future and concern the human dignity that the war is obfuscating as value to be recovered. In the context of conflict, art can become a tool of resistance against hegemonic power and can provide individuals who feel alienated and disconnected from the context in which they have chosen to live temporarily with a way to express their perspectives. With its ability to create connections, art can provide, as Frederic Jameson's analysis of the complexities of modern aesthetics (1991) indirectly suggests throughout his elaborate discussion of the radical cultural break after the turn of the 1950s into the early 1960s, a sense of belonging and empowerment in the context of social conflict.

At the time of the interview, the summer had gone, the school term had started with the child in kindergarten and a small job was some concrete, though small, help. The mother feels a split within herself, divided as she is between the 'here and now' where a part of herself is in the present, and another part that is simultaneously 'there,' at home. She feels 'in limbo,' as Callagham puts it speaking of refugees and asylum seekers, 'suspended between the danger from which they flee and the safety which they seek' (Callagham, in Dokter, ed., 1998, p. 25). The anxiety derives from dealing with what is new in the country of arrival, the steps to follow in order to face the difficulties and the use of a foreign language, on the one side; the worries about what is happening at home to the people you love, and the possible loss of everything there which allows refugees very little 'chance to relax,' on the other (p. 27). Even identity may be perceived as something you cannot hold because 'facing a foreign society with different customs, norms, values, behaviours, rhythms, and relationships to time and space is actually a strike at one's cultural identity' (Frigessi-Castelnuovo & Risso, 1986, in Dieterich-Hartwell & Koch, 2017, online). A *strike* is something that hurts; *nostalgia* links the Greek word *nostos* (returning home) with *algos* (pain) – together, the lexicon refers to the pain of return, while *homesickness* defines the distance from home as a *pathology:* what the refugee needs, then, is some *therapist* treatment. As our protagonist tells us, some relief can come from the community when other refugees are available who may understand the other's pain. It is something though it is not enough.

Art and *beauty* come to rescue, both as a recollection, and in response to a present need; both as an expression and recreation of oneself, and as the experience of the local culture; both as personal activity and as admirers of the work of others. That creative arts can work as help and therapy for patients with serious mental problems such as loss of memory and even senile dementia or Alzheimer disease is well known. The *World Wide Web*, on the other end, can help enrich the heritage of individual users and lead to an accrued social interaction. MOMA in New York, among others, have launched a three-year public program focused on histories of migration between displacement and shelter.[5] The use of creative arts for the treatment of refugees' mental disquiet has been established in medical literature drawing attention to images, sound, movement, dance, performance and all the ways in which body and mind are stimulated to raise emotions, symbolisation, and well-being – all senses which can naturally fight nostalgia and homesickness (Dieterich-Hartwell & Koch, 2017). Disorientation and sense of loss among refugees cause stress and the need for protection. Art, instead, can lead one to recover memories that can be integrated into a story with its symbols and visual links. The aesthetic experience of creating a new though small world with one's treasured past offers the stability and protection that a home can give and provides shelter, restoration and integration. A sense of wholeness develops through one's cognition in place of a 'pieced together *sense of self*' or a 'patchwork identity,' as some refugees feel when they refer to 'a feeling that the body is not part of the self' (Callagham, 1998, p. 29). As Dieterich-Hartwell and Koch put it, 'Aesthetic pleasure can be experienced like a protective cloak, shielding oneself from the aversive environmental conditions, bringing back a feeling of wholeness,' (online), an issue methodologically supported by Koch's theory of embodied aesthetics that includes art perception and active artmaking (Koch, 2017, pp. 85–91). As conclusion to their report, the authors' statement sounds encouraging:

> For those who struggle in a state of limbo and feel like the old is no longer accessible, yet the new seems so far away, the creative arts may provide a temporary home. In the hands of a skilled *therapist*, this place of art-making through visual art, music, drama or dance and movement, can not only represent a safe container (safe space) that encourages authenticity and familiarity – a journey on which clients can integrate different pieces of their identity through self-expression and aesthetic creation – but also *build a bridge* to the new environment (enactive transitional space), so that the host country can become a home country. (Dieterich-Hartwell & Koch, 2017, online)

EVALUATING SOLUTIONS TO THE PROBLEMS

That creative arts, in this case the visual arts, practised by those who suffer for having left home forcedly, or approached individually to experience something new and widen one's knowledge of the local culture to overcome the feeling of being far away from loved ones, home, habits and all that has temporarily been lost, are useful as a method of finding some stability in a new situation when an improvement of the situation is potentially conceivable. When, instead, the perspective offers no hope of a rapid end to some conflict, peace between two opponents is unlikely, and a resolution of the war implausible, questions come, in cases as the present one, to the adult of the two. Will the little boy who depends on his parent, in that perspective, be able to overcome the difficulties at the social level in a new community (playground, school and new friends)? Will he learn the new language quickly? Will the mother be able to help him to overcome any unforeseen problem or embarrassment that could arise? And the like. Additionally: would the *intimacy* needed to recreate the scenario for drawing or painting as the mother used to when at home be realisable? The realistic picture of their life is that of a mother and child in *perpetual transience*.

The theoretical solution to their problem with a therapist to assist in *building a bridge* between home and the new country that could be perceived, confidently, as a second home, though conceivably feasible, sounds impracticable for economic reasons and the obvious difficulty of finding the right person in a restricted environment, with the added difficulty of the foreign language needed to handle the situation.

Better chances would be offered by a collective program designed specifically for the situation of Ukrainian refugee parents in Italy. A study within the program 'Envisioning the Future: Ten Keys to Resilience' has been conceived 'to (i) describe the adaptation challenges and the resources of refugee parents and, indirectly, of their children and (ii) investigate the impact of neuropsych-pedagogical training on their wellbeing' (Paoletti et al., 2023). This research report article addresses the 80% women and children of the 7.8 million people who have left Ukraine in the previous year. Anxiety, psychological distress and trauma impacted negatively on most parents, while children were affected in parallel with the increasing age. Through an interview, the people's difficulties and their personal resources to adapt to them were identified. Training them with a series of steps identifiable with resilience activities capable of fortifying parents by focusing on their ability to be parents appeared a useful step. The complex set of educational issues proved appropriate to turn challenging events into opportunities for self-improvement. The program also included strategies for implementing the well-being of parents who showed a loss of the ability in caring for their children, and recovering their solicitousness and concern so that a sense of security and more positive thoughts could grow out of the experience.

THE WAY OUT

The interview reveals, at one point, the difference between the mother's situation and that of the two generations of women preceding her – something that pinpoints a way out of the impasse. Hence, the following question and answer:

Q. As far as your personal situation is concerned, three generations have suffered departure from their country to migrate to Italy. As a daughter and a grand-daughter, you have inherited, as a third generation, the political and cultural dynamics of leaving home. Might your situation as – unlike them – a fully educated person with work experience help in overcoming the personal change that you are suffering from having left home?

A. Every day I hope to return to Ukraine. I really like *our* Ukraine, I would like to live there, but, unfortunately, we do not know *when* this war will end. There are many things that need to be improved in our country, but there are also a lot of very modern things such as technological apparatus, schooling, and the new way of life.

My grandmother and my mom also live in Italy, but they do not share the same desire. This depends on the reasons that brought us here. My grandmother has lived in San Marino for 25 years: obviously, she is not here because of the war. She loves Ukraine of course, but her life in our country was exceedingly difficult, first during the Soviets, because she did not share the communist ideology, then because of the *economic* and *political* situation that arose in Ukraine after the collapse of the USSR. That is why my grandmother left Ukraine to find *work in Italy* and improve her living conditions. Now, over the years, our country has improved a lot and many people of my generation like to live in Ukraine. She, instead, does not think about her coming back. Her life is here now.

For my mom, the reasons were decidedly economic more than political. She came to Italy almost three years ago, shortly after my baby was born, to look for work, hoping that we would be able to join her in a family reunion. Over time, I realised that I would not have wished to join her in Italy and, if the war had not broken out, most likely I would not be here now. However, the responsibility towards my son, the will to protect him from the *dangers of war* led me to leave my country, like mom and grandma did, and come to Italy, where I knew I could count on them who have friends and contacts. Unlike them, however, I imagine my *future in Ukraine* because there are no reasons that keep me here, at least not for the moment.

As I said, I experience a partial loss of identity here, and sometimes I *do not recognise myself*. For example, I am an easy-and-outgoing person. I like making jokes, but I still cannot make jokes in Italian, as I do in my own native language, or in English for that matter. In Italy few people speak English […] So, I cannot express myself as I would like to […] It is very limiting! That is why I always think about how it would have been at home, with my friends. I really like Italy, the people here, but it is still not my home.

Being at the intersection of the authoritative governmental policy of the past and the critical feminist theory of the present, today's children of the former Soviet Union have left behind them the ideology of gender inequality and are ready to build their lives accordingly. As our acquaintance says in a later exchange, she is not in the same situation as her grandmother, who, not having a job of her own, had to put up with her husband's alcoholism and aggressiveness that characterised the habits of many men of previous generations. Today's Ukrainian women who are, instead, quite competitive, both professionally and emotionally, and do not depend on a man for a living, feel free in their thought that includes *democracy*, respect for *human rights* and approach to *gender* or *transgender*, as the activists in the past decades and centuries have been able to posit; then, rounding off her argument, our interviewee adds

> They have made their heirs ready for the sacrifice to enforce their ideas and the rights they believe in. They, in turn, must be thankful for this to the activists who, in the past decades and centuries, have fought for human rights to be respected. If we can live with such *freedom of thought* and approach today, we certainly owe it to them.

SURVIVING AND LOOKING INTO THE FUTURE

Being far away from your home physically can mean a mental estrangement, in such a way that symptoms typical of dissociative identity disorder can occur (Spiegel, 2023). A person suffering from such pathology can completely forget activities performed within a brief time or even longer periods. One feels like one has lost part of one's life or can become dissociated from her own self and, therefore, from memories, perceptions, identity, thoughts, emotions, body and behavior. The woman may feel disconnected from the world around her. As a result, her sense of identity, memory and/or consciousness are fragmented. Amnesia, the disjunction of identity states, the feeling of being cut off from one's thinking processes, together with the need to escape from the present situation – all those conditions may be consequences of severe stress such as having suffered or witnessed physical abuse, having faced a traumatic event or detachment from the surrounding environment, having been knocked over by the sudden death of a loved one, or by an incipient war. Although women are more likely to be stressed by a traumatic event in terms of intensity or duration of the problem than men, a pronounced gender difference arises with women seeking social support as a coping style, consisting in recurring to their social context for a response.

LOOKING FOR FREEDOM

With peoples' mobility having gone global for reasons like starvation, poverty, violence, conflict and war, art production might seem to be devoid of any use and thus it tends to be forgotten about till a new epoch might come and change things. Even if the whereabouts of artists and their work in a period of war might seem quite unimportant and their products or performances far from being an object of desire, what is true is that a new direction is being conceived for art by cultural policy makers when disasters of some sort have struck the lives of those involved. The cultural heritage in some places has been reduced to a ground zero, but this does not mean that a rebirth is not possible. Cultural Policy Yearbook 2019 entitled *Forced Migration and Cultural Production*, for instance, has 23 chapters that discuss initiatives to save the cultural heritage with constructing policies of waiting, reconnecting and moving identities against the fixed gaze. There are also ways for broken promises and stolen dreams to be at least partially recaptured, relocating cultural initiatives, giving impulse to interactive art projects, regaining control over public spaces, as is the case for a 'creation of Syria' to empower Syrian artists in exile (Ünsal & Ertürk, 2019). All that, to recapture control of the *beauty* that is lavishly flowing from art works. *Art and beauty* as a whole is something our interviewee is yearning while trying to obtain tidbits that she can easily find at hand both when she practises the art or arts that she was involved in at home and when she makes efforts to approach and learn the culture of the new people she has joined during her forced visit caused by the war. Beauty is a requirement for most members of humankind, whether arising from persons or objects, sensory manifestations or high art. Women are culturally linked with the expression of beauty in more intense ways than men are. Most women desire beauty for their own physical appearance and for their progeny; most of them attempt in whatever ways to fill their own world with it; for most of them beauty is a necessity.

Art and beauty and what is new are far-fetched in tough times, yet their appeal is there. Art usually arises through the artist's tools and the artist's practice along with the intimacy allowing the subject to communicate with oneself. Learning what is available in a new context helps one to continue being alive and surviving while forgetting the fact of having been obliged to leave home, work, loved ones, friends, old habits – in a word, most of what one used to have. Thinking about returning home can help to overcome the distance, both physical and mental, that separates one from one's homeland. Having a child makes you think about your child's education, if there is a future for him; and if there is, the question is: when?

Our interviewee's familiar experience includes a grandmother living in San Marino for 25 years, after the collapse of the USSR, when economic difficulties made it difficult to raise children in Ukraine with an arrogant heavy drinker as companion and a mother forced to emigrate for a job opportunity. The present situation, instead, is ideological. Unlike them, the contemporary woman who has left because of the war foresees her future in Ukraine, for herself and her son. She thinks of the civil liberties in Ukraine and is thankful to activists who have taught the respect for *human rights* and *freedom in sexuality* for all, including homosexual and transsexual individuals. Freethinking – that she shares – is not unpopular in the country.

CONCLUSION

The final judgement of the mother whose unfortunate destiny is, at the moment, still problematic stresses the absurdity of a perspective that might justify the madness of what is happening. In her own words – with which it is fair to conclude – the Russians are determined to destroy the Ukrainians' *national identity*. It is not a problem of an out-of-date regime. That is born with the people who oppress them, she thinks. She is happy that Ukrainians have gradually reached *democracy*. When they feel that something is wrong, they carry out protest actions. They sacrifice themselves to support their ideas and enforce the rights they believe in. It is a question of self-interest. They do not accept that other people exercise their power over them. The only way for them to resist is to have as many weapons as possible. She does all that is possible not to do what their enemies want them to do, so she even really struggles to find what she needs in a supermarket in order not to buy what is produced by the enemy. She does not want to help the people who are devastating her country. Not everybody is ready, like herself, to give up a product if they want it because it would give an economic advantage to the opposite side: she strongly believes in the triggering of a new balance. In her opinion, Russia should divide into many Republics, so power would not be in the hands of one country; on the contrary, people could earn *independence* and *freedom*.

NOTES

1. Stefanelli and Cinti planned the case-study presented together. The former wrote the introduction, analysed and discussed the interviewee's replies; the latter's delicate job consisted in meeting with the interviewee, organizing the interview, conducting it, and discussing main points; she then polished it, wrote it, and translated it into English.

2. *Caritas Internationalis* is a confederation of over 160 Catholic relief, development and social service organisations operating in over 200 countries and territories worldwide.

3. The image, 'Requests for Temporary Protection in Italy' is from ISTAT (Istituto Nazionale di Statistica), Protezione civile [Civil Protection], 29 July 2022; see Lowenthal, 2022.

4. Italics is used for words or phrases that are specific to the delicate situation of the two people.

5. MOMA (Museum of Modern Arts, New York City): Insecurities: Tracing Displacement and Shelter October 1, 2016–January 22, 2017.

REFERENCES

AgenSIR. (2022, April 07). Eurostat: dati pre-guerra, ucraini titolari di un permesso di soggiorno nell'Ue - 499,000 in Polonia, 223,000 in Italia [Pre-war data, Ukrainians with residency permit in Eu – 499,000 in Poland, 223,000 in Italy]. *SIR (Servizio Informazione Religiosa [Religious Information Service])*. https://www.agensir.it/quotidiano/2022/4/7/eurostat-dati-pre-guerra-ucraini-titolari-di-un-permesso-di-soggiorno-nellue-499mila-in-polonia-223mila-in-italia/

Callagham, K. (1998). In limbo: Movement psychotherapy with refugees and asylum seekers. In D. Dokter (Ed.), *Arts therapists, refugees and migrants: Reaching across borders*. Jessica Kingsley Publishers.

Dieterich-Hartwell, R., & Koch, S. C. (2017). Creative arts therapies as temporary home for refugees: Insights from literature and practice. *Behavorial Sciences*, 7(4), 69. https://www.ncbi.nlm.nih.gov/pmc/articles/PMC5746678/

Dokter, D. (Ed.). (1998). *Arts therapists, refugees and migrants: Reaching across borders*. Jessica Kingsley Publishers.

Eurostat. (2023, August 9). 30 June 2023: 4.07 million with temporary protection. *Eurostat*. https://ec.europa.eu/eurostat/web/products-eurostat-news/w/ddn-20230809-1

Frigessi-Castelnuovo, D., & Risso, M. (1986). *Emigration und Nostalgia*. Cooperative Books.

Gurwitsch, A. (1962, Spring). The common sense world as social reality. A discourse on Alfred Schultz. *Social Research*, 29(1), 50–72.

IRC (International Rescue Committee). (2023, August 25). Back to school: Ukrainian children in Poland still face unique challenges. *Reliefweb*. https://reliefweb.int/report/poland/back-school-ukrainian-children-poland-still-face-unique-challenges-irc-survey-reveals#:~:text=Warsaw%2C%20Poland%2C%20August%2025%2C,International%20Rescue%20Committee%20(IRC)

Jameson, F. (1991). *Postmodernism, or, the cultural logic of late capitalism*. Duke U.P.

Koch, S. C. (2017). Arts and health: Active factors and a theory framework of embodied aesthetics. *The Arts in Psychotherapy*, 54, 85–91.

Lowenthal, H. (2022, January 29). Ukrainian diaspora in Italy. https://data.europa.eu/en/publications/datastories/ukrainian-diaspora-italy

Mancino, D. (2022, July 29). Ukrainian diaspora in Italy. data.europa.eu. *European Data*. https://data.europa.eu/en/publications/datastories/ukrainian-diaspora-italy

Paoletti, P., Perasso, G. S., Lillo, C., Serantoni, G., Maculan, A., Vianello, F., & Di Giuseppe, T. (2023, March 15). Envisioning the future for families running away from war: Challenges and resources of Ukrainian parents in Italy. *Frontiers in Psychology*, 14. https://www.frontiersin.org/articles/10.3389/fpsyg.2023.1122264/full

Plattner, D. (1984, June 30). Protection of children in international humanitarian law. *International Review of the Red Cross*, N° 240, 140–152. Republished in ICRC (International Committee of the Red Cross). (2024). https://www.icrc.org/en/doc/resources/documents/article/other/57jmat.htm

Prestigiacomo, C. (2023, February 23). Che fine hanno fatto i rifugiati ucraini? [Whatever happened to Ukrainian refugees?] *Europa Today*. https://europa.today.it/fake-fact/rifugiati-ucraini-lavoro-europa.html

Save the Children Italia. (2023, Febraury 23). Un anno di guerra in Ucraina: aiuti a bambini e famiglie [One Year's War in Ukraine: Aids for Children and Families]. *Children*. https://www.google.com/search?q=https%3A%2F%2Fwww.savethechildren.it%2Fblog-notizie%2Fun-anno-di-guerra-ucraina-gli-aiuti-bambini-e-famiglie

Spiegel, D. (2023). Panoramica sui disturbi dissociativi [A Survey of dissociative disorders]. https://www.msdmanuals.com/it-it/professionale/disturbi-psichiatrici/disturbi-dissociativi/panoramica-sui-disturbi-dissociativi

Trope, Y., & Liberman, N. (2010). Construal-level theory of psychological distance. *Psychology Review*, 117, 440–463. https://www.ncbi.nlm.nih.gov/pmc/articles/PMC3152826/

UNICEF – Europe and Central Asia. (2023, July 7). No way for children to grow up. https://www.unicef.org/eca/stories/no-way-children-grow

Ünsal, D., & Ertürk, N. (Eds.). (2019). Forced migration and cultural production. *Iletisim*. Istanbul Bllgi University, Cultural Policy Yearbook, 2019. https://iletisim.com.tr/dergiler/kultur-politikasi-yillik/5/sayi-2-cultural-policy-yearbook-2019/10044/forced-migration-and-cultural-production/11826

WOMEN AND WAR: PEDAGOGIES OF CARE

Agnieszka Chwieduk[1] and Izabela Skórzyńska[2]

Adam Mickiewicz University, Poznań, Poland

ABSTRACT

The aim of the authors' text is to consider the ethics of care *in the context of academic performative didactics, to which the authors dedicated the book* Performative Didactics for Humanists. A Matter of Coincidences *published in 2021 would describe, despite the different academic disciplines the authors represent (history and anthropology), as practicing care. As part of (teachers') history teaching, it was work with migration memory consisting in performative processing of migration narratives into the form of a joint undertaking of university and primary school students, which was their performative reading. In the case of (engaged) anthropology, the efforts were based on volunteering, as an activity for the benefit of people migrating and detained against their will in Secure Centers for Foreigners (SOdC). In both cases, taught in a performative way, the students were confronted with the unpredictable effect of their actions (the teaching axis) while their emotional, cognitive and creative resources were mobilized. Most importantly, achievement thereof was a reward in itself. The relevant context in which the authors consider care as a subject of study is the war in Ukraine and its impact on women's lives. In the authors' opinion, "ethics of care and justice" require reconsideration and social practice through education.*

Keywords: Women; war; ethics of justice and care; academic teaching; performative didactics; pedagogies of care

[1]https://orcid.org/0000-0003-2750-413X
[2]https://orcid.org/0000-0002-2549-8592

Scars of War
Research in Political Sociology, Volume 30, 137–149
Copyright © 2025 Agnieszka Chwieduk and Izabela Skórzyńska
Published under exclusive licence by Emerald Publishing Limited
ISSN: 0895-9935/doi:10.1108/S0895-993520250000030010

INTRODUCTION

The aim of our text is to consider *the ethics of care* in the context of academic performative didactics as conceptualized in our book *Performative Didactics for Humanists. A Matter of Coincidences* (Chwieduk & Skórzyńska, 2021, p. 227). When discussing performance in academic teaching, we resorted to examples that we would describe, despite the different academic disciplines we represent (history and anthropology), as practicing care.

What we refer to as academic performances, for over two years – as part of historical studies for future teachers – revolved around migration memory consisting in the performative processing of autobiographical narratives, including research, reading, selection and critical analysis of ego-documents and visual sources, work by engaging in a dialogue, also writing scripts and preparing multimedia visual settings (inspired by the documentary theater) for future storytelling sessions with primary school pupils. The culmination of the project was performative reading of autobiographical migration narratives with the audience involved in the process. In the case of anthropology, at the center of the teaching efforts were students volunteering to act for the benefit of migrants and people detained in Secure Centers for Foreigners (SOdC), implemented and documented in accordance with the Action Research Methodology (Chwieduk & Skórzyńska, 2021, pp. 77–178).

In both didactic performances, the students were confronted with the unpredictable effect of their actions (the teaching axis) while their emotional, cognitive and creative resources were mobilized, which determined their specific solutions to a specific social reality. Importantly, their achievement was a gratification in itself, and the effects of this work triggered off a change in academic curricula, enriching them with new activities, including workshops and field research. In this way, together with our students we made an attempt at putting to a test performative didactics and its care potential, in response to the full-scale war in Ukraine (2022); it turned out to be of special importance, cognitively and socially alike.

Why?

To answer this question, a statement needs to be made that the experience of war makes relevant two coexisting ethics which happen to have different social gravitas: the *ethics of justice* and the *ethics of care* (Czyżowska, 2004, pp. 119–120).[1] The former reflects the male perspective of the world order *si vis pacem, para bellum* (Publius Tarutenius Paternus), the latter is, by necessity, a response to the former, related to the female experience of the world, albeit tailored to the male dimensions. As a result, the desire for justice has a strong cultural background: education, the defense system and adoption of a patriotic attitude. As such, it somehow predisposes people to *being in an armed conflict*. Care is a different story: although perceived as absolutely necessary, it does not enjoy immediate public support. This type of attitude is systemically neglected and – especially in the case of conflicts – rests on the shoulders of women. They then fulfill the social expectations of care for those who are not on the "front-line" and to help others. Moreover, women are in a sense forced to do this in brutal wartime conditions, even though it is in this context of care that they fall victim to the *ethics of justice*, often taking the form of ethnocide combined with mass rape and torture.

War: Memory and Care

The starting point for our considerations is the power of the war experience as indicated above with the issue of care revealed. However, in Poland and we know it today, this experience is almost exclusively mediated in the history and memory of the war, where especially the memory is of a heroic, patriotic and martyrdom nature and, as such, it strongly emphasizes the *ethics of justice*. On the other hand, over the last 20 years, in addition to this war narrative, alternatives appeared in the Polish public space, including the memory of everyday life of war and its unsung heroes: women, children, immigrants, refugees, prisoners and the sick. This memory reversal, gaining in strength, strongly corresponds with the agitation within academic humanities (not only in the theoretical and research sense as engaged humanities but also in the didactic and social sense) as a question about practicing care in everyday life. To some extent, it is an appeal, especially of young Poles, to include ordinary Polish men and women into a shared *imaginarium*. It can be safely assumed that this memory reversal is a valuable source of shaping social imagination and sensitivity which proves their worth in the face of social crises such as war and migration. It becomes even more important in the context of the war in Ukraine and the mass flow of Ukrainians not speaking Polish, looking for housing, work and support in Poland, first as war immigrants, and after 2022, as refugees. Eurostat data for October 2023 indicate that the total number of Ukrainians in Poland at that time amounted to nearly 957,000 (Information Bulletin of the Eastern Studium, 2023). According to a report by the National Bank of Poland, among the nearly one million Ukrainians staying in Poland in the fall of 2023, "the majority were women – about 68% (in the group of pre-war immigrants they represented 55%, and in the group of refugees – 78%) (NBP, 2023). More than half of them are aged 27–44; 48% of the pre-war migrants and 29% of refugees stay in Poland with a spouse/partner, and over 40% of the refugees and 30% of pre-war migrants live [...] with underage children. The majority of Ukrainian citizens staying in Poland with children send them to Polish schools and kindergartens" (NBP, 2023, pp. 10–11).

Many Poles deeply empathize with Ukrainian citizens who came to Poland, actively engaging in broadly defined assistance for the refugees. In March 2022, 68% of Poles (more women than men) provided such help. In the following months, the number of people helping dropped yet remained at the level of 50% (CPOS, 2022). It was only in January 2023 when the number of people helping Ukrainians began to decline; in a Centre for Public Opinion Research (CPOS) study, it was interpreted as Poles' reaction to the very high inflation rate rather than a change in their attitude towards Ukrainians (CPOS, 2023). However, a subsequent CPOS survey from April 2023 (CPOS, 2023) revealed that only 41% of Poles were involved in helping Ukrainians, for the number only to drop to 28% in November (CPOS, 2023). Moreover, many respondents, especially young women, began to boldly express their fears of a further inflow of Ukrainian refugees to Poland, which, apart from the obstinately high inflation, indicates three other reasons for concern (CPOS, 2023). The first is related to the well-established systemic assistance, with the state and local governments as the main actors. Another concern is related to the tiredness of long-term helping to Ukrainians, accompanied by a fear of the living conditions of Polish families deteriorating, especially among women. This is not surprising because at the beginning of the full-scale war, women helped refugees more than men while women and children prevail among the refugees from Ukraine. They are said to be competing against Poles for jobs and places for their children in nurseries, kindergartens and schools (CPOS, 2023). But, as Krzysztof Krakowski from Collegio Carlo Alberto in Turin suggests, there is also a third reason for the reluctance of young Polish women towards Ukrainian women, namely competition on the bridal market. This is amplified by a belief among Polish men that "Ukrainian women are better than Polish women, they have lower expectations and are better candidates for wives." It was the men who emphasized the "competition" theme more (Krakowski, in Theus, 2023, p. 2). So, the issue of the attitudes towards Ukrainian refugees also connects with the family order of young Polish women's concerns about their own matrimonial future, while Polish men effectively toy with these concerns.

Meanwhile, with the developments on the front unfavorable for Ukraine, since December 2023, a war attitude in Europe is gaining in strength, expressed in NATO's and national armies concentrating in the event of a Russian attack. Therefore, the formula *si vis pacem para bellum* has become valid again, negotiated in the context of a key question for the continent: in the face of Russia's escalated military actions in Ukraine, should we help the latter more or increase our own defense capabilities? In this context, the fate of the Ukrainian population and the costs we all bear as a result of the war have lost their topicality.

In a long-term struggle, refugees have begun to lose against the so-called "self-interest" of everyday practice related to the *ethics of justice*, self-justified in the face of Polish women's fears of failure in their personal lives and the fears of most Poles about the state's security in the face of a potential new armed conflict with Russia. Yet again, the practices of caring have proven too weak.

Is there any way to remedy this? Can academic teaching be one way of changing it?

Pedagogies of Care: The Conceptualization

As we mentioned in the introduction, what we refer to as the practice of care connects with engaged didactics with its primary task of contributing to social change. In our case, it is a matter of collective practices of the *ethics of care* in response to the crisis of war.

First, we assume that ethics are judgments of a normative nature, relating to generally recognized principles that underlie social practice. They are therefore different from those referred to as moral judgments that are descriptive in nature (Kojder, 2006, pp. 13–15).[2] Maria Ossowska provided a distinction between ethics and morality: "Ethics do not care about harming or favoring oneself. They only steps in when the interests of others come into play" (Ossowska, 1966, p. 22).

Therefore, and second, we reject the approach of Lawrence Kohlberg, author "of the theory of human moral development, with justice as the central virtue, defined as a universal category assigned to morality" (Kohlberg, 1984, in Czyżowska, 2004, pp. 119–120). However, we agree with the feminist argumentation of Carol Gilligan who believes that the *ethics of justice* takes into account almost exclusively the male perspective of the moral assessment of reality, impairing "the specifics of women's moral reasoning" (Czyżowska, 2004, p. 120; Gilligan, 1982). Explaining in a new way the specificity of gendered *ethics of justice and care* in decision-making and problem-solving by women and men, Gilligan sees it as follows:

> [...] for centuries to the voices of men and the theories of development that their experience informs, so we have come more recently to notice not only the silence of women but the difficulty in hearing what they say when they speak. Yet in the different voice of women lies the truth of an 'ethic' of care, the tie between relationship and responsibility, and the origins of aggression in the failure of connection. The failure to see the different reality of women's lives and to hear the differences in their voices stems in part from the assumption that there is a single mode of social experience and interpretation. By positing instead two different modes we arrive at a more complex rendition of human experience which sees the truth of separation and attachment in the lives of women and men, and recognizes how these truths are carried by different modes of language and thought. (Gilligan, 1982, pp. 173–174)

Third, we consider the thought of Richard Rorty expressed in his essay *The Ethics of Principles and the Ethics of Sensitivity* to be significant for us. The voice of this philosopher-pragmatist is important because he proposes a specific "ethnography of contemporary Western democracies" founded, among other things, on the role of universities, especially humanities and social sciences, which act as areopagi of the critique of reality. Thus, he draws attention to the most important function of these institutions, shaping specific ethical attitudes. Rorty's thought is still a relevant project with which intellectuals reflecting on the contemporary (neoliberal) democratic society can identify. Rorty speaks as if in their voice:

> In democratic societies like ours, colleges and universities play a unique role. They make money by promising to give students high-income qualifications and research that will enable society to produce more goods and services at less cost. The face of these institutions shown to sponsors, state legislative bodies, and the nation, in general is essentially commercial. Colleges and universities suggest that they have a "good" that society needs, and on that basis they ask for financial support. However, what they do not usually admit is that their function is often to create anxiety in students, make them doubt the way they were raised, and force them to ask unanswered questions. [...]. Lecturers are not satisfied until their students, after finishing classes, become discouraged with the society in which they live and have doubts about the moral principles in which they were brought up. (Rorty, 2002, p. 51)

What is worth noting and what corresponds to our attempt to conceptualize the *ethics of care* in the context of university teaching (Rorty, 2002, p. 51) is accepting the fact that contemporary Western democracies are an entity in which, in principle, representatives of different, axio-normative systems must coexist.

This entails the need not only to negotiate their boundaries but also to transcend them in order to make such coexistence as satisfying as possible. In this context, Rorty himself rejects the *ethics of principles* derived from the belief in the existence of one universal (transcendent) truth, in favor of the *ethics of sensitivity*, as a principle resulting from an opposite belief: the existence of many equivalent truths and, let us add, ethics – since the truth is always entangled in some ethical order. It is impossible to ignore the fact that in the face of a war conflict, the principle of equal truths/ethics works poorly or does not work at all [. . .] In this respect, we would be closer to Rorty's thought where, suffering can be pictured as a consequence of sanctifying, once and for all, the established principles and institutions or making them essential as revealed truths and therefore superior and necessary: "What counts in moral progress is not the strength of insisting on established customs, institutions or principles, but the readiness to ask the question: who suffers because of the existence of such institutions or the application of these rules?" (Rorty, 2002, p. 62).

And, even, who suffers from it and how?

Fourth, and summarizing our considerations, the thought of the "ethics of sensitivity" understood in this way, transmitted by the institutions of the academy, inspires a question about the *ethics of justice* and *ethics of care* defined long before Rorty. First, we assume that the *ethics of justice* in times of danger is expressed by the formula *si vis pacem para bellum*. It reflects the traditionally male point of view on matters of conflict and war, which seems to confirm the belief of some Poles as expressed in subsequent CPOS surveys, more often men. Considering the end of the war in Ukraine, they focus on the uncompromising nature of the government in Kiev until its final victory (CPOS, November 2023). Consistently, men are also more likely to support Ukrainian refugees in Poland, although their involvement, especially in everyday assistance, is less intense than that of women, and their expectations towards the state and the system that should provide such assistance are greater (CPOS, 2003). In both cases, men bear less responsibility for the fate of immigrants from the war-torn country, understanding war as a pursuit of justice in the legal and ethical sense. It is different for women, who more often refer to the *ethics of care* and responsibility in their assessments and actions in conflict situations, which also means that they consider the consequences of a prolonged armed conflict in a more complex and non-obvious way.

By the *ethics of care*, we understand an attitude of informed support, which is reproducible, especially through academic teaching, and which is positively valorized – that is, recognized as socially important in the axio-normative interpretation of conduct. Political conflicts that arise and develop into wars are fought primarily in the field of *ethics of justice*, including international law, from treaties on the inviolability of borders and cooperation, through defense treaties, to humanitarian law. Conflicts are therefore resolved by great diplomacy and armies, while guilt and punishment are administered by courts martial and tribunals of justice. Anything else, including the fate of the civilian population and their everyday life in war-torn and migration areas, takes place in the perspective of the *ethics of care* and largely rests on the shoulders of women, regardless of their attitude to the problem – this is because of social coercion and existential, and then physical, lack of men engaged in fighting on the front.

We do not mean to play down for the importance of military preparation – in which women are also engaged – to defend the sovereignty of states and regions, targets of potential or effective armed attacks. However, it is equally important in such difficult circumstances to develop knowledge, skills and competences towards the *ethics of care*. The example of the war in Ukraine and the Polish experience of war migration shows the importance of this issue now and in the future, for the refugees and Poles alike. Care, as a moral attitude, would not, however, be exclusively the domain of women operating in a simplified scheme of men go to war to defend, women left at home and thus take care of them. Society's internalization of the *ethics of care* means a realization that women are situationally burdened with it. It is also about making room in the masculinized discourse for the voice of women expressing the need to take care of themselves (the odium of ethnocide related to the crime of rape). In our opinion, the *ethics of care* understood in this way involves learning a certain sensitivity that strengthens the role of women: different yet equally difficult, in relation to that assigned to men. In times of danger, women not only help them survive, they also become victims of brutal violence. Therefore, care is, apart from deep sensitivity and everyday empathy, also a kind of art of action and survival tactics in the concept of "coping" with daily hardships – in a thoughtful, well-organized way, supported by a number of skills, with a belief that "[…] the more numerous and the greater the social threats, the more important it becomes to care for people who are both at risk and who pose a threat to themselves or others" (Żywczok, 2018, p. 107). Assuming, as did Ryszard Nycz, that "[…] the basic function of the humanities still consists in forming critical self-knowledge as well as sensitivity and causative creativity of individuals and communities" (Nycz, 2017, p. 19), we return to the question if it is possible to learn care in the field of humanities understood in this way?

CARING: CAN IT BE TAUGHT/LEARNED?

In seeking the answer to the above question, although our recipe may turn out to be more universal, we look at care from two different perspectives of university education: future history teachers, and committed anthropologists.

History and Care

In the first case, the education of future history teachers, the determinant of their studies is the academic discipline of history, and then their professional preparation for the teaching profession. In the field of history as a discipline, the ethics of care are dealt with in a theoretical and research sense by approaches to knowledge about the past generally referred to as "the new humanities." The curricula of historical academic studies therefore draw on the critical potential of the humanities involved "[…] in social, political, economic, cultural matters […], of a critical and emancipatory nature towards modern assumptions of neutrality and autonomy" (Nycz, 2017, p. 23).[3] At the same time, it is not an attempt to replace traditionally defined academic history, but only to enrich it, often through the students' choice of specific courses, with the history of gender along with reflection on its social effectiveness, and the ethical responsibility of historians for what and how is presented and understood in history, which particularly concerns future teachers. In our opinion, the broad category of gender history includes key issues for academic teaching such as "[…] femininity and masculinity, physical, mental and economic violence, discrimination, sexism, racism, xenophobia, homophobia, marginalization, minority, foreignness, stereotype, prejudice, subjectivity, human rights, women's rights, emancipation, equal treatment, equality, feminism, diversity" (Chmura-Rutkowska, 2016, p. 15). Therefore, we translate the slogan of performative didactics into preparing future history teachers for their profession, so that they have the ability to transform school history into their students' agoras, civic forums with cooperation and dialogue characteristic of them. Only such school teaching creates a real field for talking about the *ethics of justice* and *ethics of care* as social practices, including educational ones among children and adolescents, drawing on the past in response to the challenges of the present and expectations for the future. At the cognitive level, it is a critical approach to school historical knowledge as a derivative of academic discourses related to social history with its problems of social inequalities, symbolic and physical violence, and manipulation of history taught at school by politicians, well recognized by professional historians and teachers. It turns out that at the executive level, the ability to critically analyze and interpret historical sources, or more broadly, sources of historical knowledge, developed in cooperation where criticism and cooperation are goals in themselves, is of importance. At the competence level, the aim is to develop in-depth historical awareness in connection with the values of historical sensitivity. In this respect, the *ethics of care* have a chance to emerge from the shadow of the *ethics of justice*.

How much of a burning issue this is becoming is shown by the experience of the war in Ukraine described above and the issue of Ukrainian wartime refugees in Poland. Interpreted from the perspective of the *ethics of justice*, the common history of Poland and Ukraine is beset with obstacles in the form of sometimes very bloody ethnic and national conflicts, the memory of which is eagerly fueled by nationalists in Poland. From the perspective of the *ethics of care*, these conflicts primarily mean the refugees' suffering from violence, which is supported by the common history of forced Polish and Ukrainian immigrants. It belongs as much to the past as to the present, with the key question of who and how would alleviate this suffering.

One example is avoidance of paying lip service. Here, recent graduates of AMU history teacher studies faced the challenge of the influx of Ukrainian children to Polish schools in 2022. Overnight, they faced the shock of the language and psychological barrier of Ukrainian students traumatized by the war in the face of the national interpretation of Polish–Ukrainian history in Polish history curricula, where Ukrainians are presented quite one-sidedly and in a bad light, as, among others, the perpetrators the Volhynia massacre committed on Poles in the Eastern Borderlands (1943–1944) (Balcer, 2023, p. 13; Skórzyńska, 2024, pp. 21–58).[4] Balancing this just history of Polish victims of the massacre in the context of the colonial policy of the Second Polish Republic towards Ukrainians, but above all in the context of the real problem of the presence of Ukrainians in Poland and Polish schools, requires from teachers not only reinterpretation of Polish–Ukrainian history for the sake of their Polish and Ukrainian students but also re-education of the school environment, including the parents of students who, due to historical resentments, criticize the formation of intercultural classes. In a study by the Batory Foundation, entitled "Polish historical memory and policy towards Ukraine and Ukrainians," Adam Balcer writes,

> Polls show that after 1989, the attitude of Poles towards Ukrainians improved gradually yet significantly. However, before 2022, Ukrainians were rather at the bottom of the list of nations liked by Poles […] Just a few years ago, in one study, as many as 40% of Poles declared their dislike for Ukrainians, slightly less than for Russians. Just before the war in 2022, the attitude towards Ukrainians was as follows: 40% - sympathy, 35% - indifference and 25% - reluctance. The full-scale Russian aggression has led to a situation where, in surveys from the beginning of 2023, for the first time, just over half of Poles declared sympathy for Ukrainians. However, 17% still felt reluctance towards them, and over 30% felt indifference. (Balcer, 2023, p. 13)

Ultimately, the *ethics of care* supported by a renewed reflection on the past, and by imagination, turns out to be all the more valuable of "using imagination of situations and events that involve" (Koziołek, 2008, p. 3) historical actors, in this case immigrants and refugees whose testimonies are the subject of the performance. Together with the *ethics of justice*, it is a living source of coping with the challenges of everyday life.

Anthropology and Care

The anthropological capital of knowledge shows that care is an area of research and scientific pursuits of anthropologists within the subdiscipline of anthropology of care (Open Encyclopedia of Anthropology/*Care*), in analogy with pedagogy of care and its theoretical and didactic implementations in the idea of "the new humanities," and the engaged university. Essentially, the following common determinants of care-ism are important here: care is about practices related to the cultural understanding of several areas of social life: health (illness), both autonomously studied as cultural phenomena, and analyzed as part of broadly defined exclusion; the relationship between human beings and non-humans embedded in an ecological perspective; the relationship of migrants and (non-) migrants in the context of universal mobility; as an ethical challenge to engaged anthropology, in relation to situations of victimization and violence in which the researchers (anthropologists providing assistance) are also involved. This last area is most similar to how we understand care as a subject of performative teaching.

Care presented as an ethical challenge to history, anthropology, pedagogy and didactics, contains an encouragement to adopt the *primum non nocere* attitude – if

an anthropologist does not know or understand the axio-normative and ontological system of a specific community (entity), her/his attitude towards them, be
it as a volunteer or a researcher respecting Others as autonomous and different
entities (nomenclature of partnership in research), is doomed to failure. In
principle, it may simply harm rather than help, even when helpers strive to be
communicative at the level of indigenous languages. Therefore, aware of the
pitfalls of caring, we will first define it as the humanitarian law, presiding above
the cultural context, but strictly dependent on it.

> Care is a universal ethical and pragmatic category, as it belongs to the field of humanitarian
> work in general, regardless of specific national, cultural, religious, and political references. It is
> related to the issue of the essence and vocation of man and a specific system of values. Caring
> for someone or something protects against threats and contributes to the development of
> specific goods, regardless of whether it is undertaken by people or the formal and legal
> system. It directs a person towards what he aspires to, what he desires and is looking for, so
> it is the source of the dynamics of human action and the sense of meaning in life. (Theiss, 2012,
> p. 15 in Żywczok, 2018, pp. 106–107)

Moreover, we will interpret it as an area of social neglect (in social discourse,
volunteering as a manifestation of care, although strongly desired, turns out to be
depreciated, for example in many areas related to education), despite the fact
that, as such, it is a force for the survival of groups. Therefore, it can be
considered a kind of superior law, although forcing the negotiation of its
meaning, depending on the specific axio-normative systems of the addressees:

> Man, in the course of phylo- and ontogenetic development, improved the ability to manifest
> caring for himself and others. Thanks to, among others, acts of care, activated positive
> emotions and feelings such as empathy, kindness, sympathy, tenderness, generosity, while
> minimizing negative emotions and feelings, e.g. anger, anger, hostility, envy, etc. (Żywczok,
> 2018, p. 107)

But [. . .] care also develops in the pragmatic field. Knowing the needs of war
victims and helping them, we fulfill our own needs, including adequate knowledge
and skills to help others without harming ourselves. The need for care is therefore
associated with specific skills and values which, developed in times of peace, bring
about specific effects in times of threat and war.

CONCLUSIONS

One of our female students has decided to join the defense service after the
Russian attack on Ukraine. When asked why she was doing it, she replied: "If
war comes, what do I know, what can I do to protect myself and others? I want to
prepare myself." Another girl, currently a doctoral student, completed a migration project during her master's studies, in which, together with her colleagues,
she analyzed migration and refugee narratives (as covered above), and based
them on a performative educational project intended for primary school students.
In the same order of learning, acting for the benefit of others, students and future
anthropologists became volunteers in SOdC, learning about their living

conditions and their needs, which also applies to women and children experiencing armed conflicts.

Many people studying and practicing preparation for a professional role as part of higher education, participate in volunteer projects and work in aid organizations. In the face of the war in Ukraine, they provided and continue to provide assistance to migrants and refugees, recognizing in the process their own attitudes, knowledge, competences and skills acquired during studies and tested in social life. Therefore, many people develop the capital acquired at universities, shaping their own professionalism which includes helping others. To the question if caring for others can be learned, the answer seems simple. Yes, it can be learned. First as a "mental attitude of the subject" rather than a specific action, although "taking care or concern" refer to human actions. In turn, caring belongs to caring traits/dispositions and is not synonymous with action, although it announces it. Moreover, "[...] care is an attitude directed not only at a given entity, but also generalized to the world/cosmos." In other words, "care, help and support," are activities in the literal sense of the word, however, "[...] addressed to specific people in need and bringing tangible results" (Żywczok, 2018, p. 115). Is it possible to reconcile the mental predisposition of caring with the action of helping in academic teaching, which is artificial by definition (the art of teaching)?

Therefore, in our teaching work with students, we look for a *modus vivendi* between the *ethics of care* and reflected aid action, convinced of the possible perform of the art of teaching towards the agency of our students, future anthropologists and history teachers. In the theoretical field, we are helped by an assumption made within the performative reversal, that thinking and feeling are not separate from action, but are its specific form, in this case a type of didactic performance that takes place in circumstances close to, although not identical to, social reality. There, to act means to transform reality by practicing social sensitivity in the spectrum of, "ethics of justice and care" treated together, as a feminist perspective of the core of women and men with social crises, which certainly include the war in Ukraine and Ukrainian refugees in Poland.

NOTES

1. The issue of *ethics of care and justice* was once taken up by Lawrence Kohlberg and discussed by feminist authors, among them, Carol Gilligan and Dorota Czyżowska, what we write next.

2. "The ethical judgment which states that 'helping others in need is the duty of every person' is not identical with the moral judgment which states that people generally believe that a person who helps others in need does good" (Kojder, 2006, p. 15) and "Today, ethics are defined as the totality of reflections on morality, on ethical doctrines and moral views, on values, norms and ethical assessments" (Kojder, 2006, p. 13).

3. In our own environment, the humanities at the University of Adam Mickiewicz, the "new humanities" manifests itself in a critical approach to the history of women and the history of gender, which is reflected in three other texts included in this issue: by Weronika Halaburda and Katarzyna Witek-Dryjańska.

4. The Volhynia massacre took place in July and August 1943. The perpetrator was the Ukrainian Insurgent Army (UPA). The massacre was exceptionally brutal and targeted primarily at women and children. Other victims of the massacres included several hundred

Armenians, Jews, Russians, Czechs, Georgians, and also Ukrainians who refused to cooperate with the UPA, who were part of Polish families and also warned Poles against their compatriots.

REFERENCES

Balcer, A. (2023). Polska pamięć historyczna i polityka wobec Ukrainy i Ukraińców [Polish historical memory and policy towards Ukraine and Ukrainians]. Fundacja Batorego.

Chmura-Rutkowska, I. (2016). Metodologia badań [Research methodology]. In I. Chmura-Rutkowska, M. Duda, M. Mazurek, A. Sołtysiak-Łuczak (Eds.), *Gender w podręcznikach. Projekt badawczy. Raport* [Gender in textbooks. Research Report] Vol. 1. Fundacja Feminoteka.

Chwieduk, A., & Skórzyńska, I. (2021). *Dydaktyka performatywna dla humanistów. Kwestia przypadków* [Performative didactics for humanists. A matter of coincidences]. Wydawnictwo Nauka i Innowacje.

Czyżowska, D. (2004). Płeć a etyka troski i etyka sprawiedliwości [Gender and the ethics of care and the ethics of justice]. *Psychologia Rozwojowa*, 9(1), 119–120.

Gilligan, C. (1982). *In a different voice. Psychological theory and women's development.* Harvard University Press.

Kohlberg, L. (1984). *The psychology of moral development.* Harper & Row.

Kojder, A. (2006). Etyka - przedmiot i stanowiska oraz rozwój myśli etycznej [Ethics - subject and positions as well as the development of ethical thought]. In H. Izdebski & P. Skuczyński (Eds.), *Etyka zawodów prawniczych. Etyka prawnicza* [Ethics of the legal profession. Legal ethics]. Wydawnictwo Prawnicze LexisNexis.

Koziołek, R. (2008, January 15). Przeszłość w działaniu. O *zwrocie performatywnym*, literaturze i literaturoznawstwie rozmawiają Krzysztof Uniłowski, Ryszard Koziołek, Paweł Tomczok i Piotr Bogalecki [The past in action. Krzysztof Uniłowski, Ryszard Koziołek, Paweł Tomczok and Piotr Bogalecki talk about the performative turn in literature and literary studies]. *Art. Papier*, 2(98). no pagination. http://artpapier.com/index.php?page=artykul&wydanie=52&artykul=1134. Accessed on September 11, 2024.

Nycz, R. (2017). Nowa humanistyka w Polsce: kilka bardzo subiektywnych obserwacji, koniektur, refutacji [New humanities in Poland:Somevery subjective observations, conjectures, refutations]. *Teksty Drugie*, 1, 18–40.

Ossowska, M. (1966). Pojęcie moralności [The concept of morality]. *Etyka*, 1, 19–29.

Rorty, R. (2002). Etyka zasad a etyka wrażliwości [Ethics of principles and ethics of sensitivity]. *Teksty Drugie*, 1–2, 51–63.

Skórzyńska, I. (2024). Critical potential of the historical description of the Black Sea Region in Polish history textbooks. *Historia Slavorum Occidentis*, 4, 21–58.

Theiss, W. (2012). *Troska i nadzieja. Działalność społeczno-wychowawcza ks. Henryka Szumana na Pomorzu w latach 1908–1939* [Care and hope. Social and educational activities of Fr. Henryk Szuman in Pomerania in 1908–1939]. Wydawnictwo Adam Marszałek.

Theus, J. (2023, November 4). *Młode kobiety tracą serce do ukraińskiej obecności. Powód? Chodzi o rynek matrymonialny* [Young women are losing heart towards the Ukrainian presence. Reason? It's about the matrimonial market]. Oko Press. https://oko.press/ukraincy-w-polsce-sondaz-ipsos

Żywczok, A. (2018). Troska, zatroskanie, troskliwość – niespecyficzne przedmioty badań pedagogiki ogólnej [Care, concern, thoughtfulness – non-specific subjects of research in pedagogy]. *Forum Pedagogiczne*, 1, 105–118.

REPORTS

Biuletyn Informacyjny Studium Wschodnie [Information Bulletin of the Eastern Studium]. (2023, December 12). *Po ponad pół roku znowu rośnie liczba ukraińskich uchodźców w Polsce* [After more than half a year, the number of Ukrainian refugees in Poland is growing again]. Warsaw.

https://studium.uw.edu.pl/po-ponad-pol-roku-znowu-rosnie-liczba-ukrainskich-uchodzcow-w-polsce/

CPOS [Centre for Public Opinion Research]. (2022, March). *Polacy wobec rosyjskiej inwazji na Ukrainę* [CPOS research announcement, Poles towards the invasion of Ukraine] (no. 38). https://www.cbos.pl/SPISKOM.POL/2022/K_038_22.PDF

CPOS [Centre for Public Opinion Research]. (2022, August). *Polacy wobec wojny na Ukrainie i ukraińskich uchodźców* [Poles towards the war in Ukraine and Ukrainian refugees] (no. 101). https://www.cbos.pl/SPISKOM.POL/2022/K_101_22.PDF

CPOS [Centre for Public Opinion Research]. (2022, October). *Polacy o wojnie na Ukrainie* [Poles about war in Ukraine] (no. 123). https://www.cbos.pl/SPISKOM.POL/2022/K_123_22.PDF

CPOS [Centre for Public Opinion Research]. (2023, January). *Polacy wobec wojny na Ukrainie i ukraińskich uchodźców* [Poles towards the war in Ukraine and Ukrainian refugees] (no. 12). https://www.cbos.pl/SPISKOM.POL/2023/K_012_23.PDF

CPOS [Centre for Public Opinion Research]. (2023, April). *Polacy wobec wojny na Ukrainie* [Poles towards the war in Ukraine] (no. 41). https://www.cbos.pl/SPISKOM.POL/2023/K_041_23.PDF

CPOS [Centre for Public Opinion Research]. (2023, November). *O wojnie na Ukrainie i scenariuszach jej Rozwoju* [Research report About the war in Ukraine and its development scenarios] (no. 142). https://www.cbos.pl/SPISKOM.POL/2023/K_142_23.PDF

NBP [National Bank of Poland]. (2023). *Sytuacja życiowa i ekonomiczna migrantów z Ukrainy w Polsce w 2023 roku* [Living and economic situation of Ukrainian migrants in Poland in 2023]. Dudek B., Panuciak A., Strzelecki P. (eds.). Warsaw. https://nbp.pl/wp-content/uploads/2024/01/raport_migranci_z-Ukrainy_2023.pdf

THINGS IN WOMEN'S HANDS: RECLAIMING DOMESTIC SPACE AFTER THE WAR

Katarzyna Witek-Dryjańska

Adam Mickiewicz University, Poznań, Poland

ABSTRACT

The aim of this work is to present the results of qualitative research on the diaries of women living in the "Recovered Territories (RT)" after World War II in Poland. In particular, the diaries of the first settlers of the "RT" have been subjected to analysis. These women, between 1945 and 1956, were creating, organizing, and domesticating the new and unfamiliar space of the "RT." The fundamental questions guiding my considerations concern how women coped with domestic and material space in their new places of residence, including dealing with their foreignness, the abundance of some items and the lack of others, essential for daily life, and the relationships between space, objects, and people in the process of domestication.

Keywords: Recovered territories; repatriation; women; domestic space; everyday life; postwar period

INTRODUCTION

The Polish "Recovered Territories (RT)" in the early years after World War II were areas of great migratory and resettlement movements, where a new post-migration society was forming. Mostly, it was the incoming Poles from various regions who took over and gradually adapted to these lands, while the previous inhabitants – Germans – either fled or were displaced. Besides them, the "RT" also housed autochthons (Masurians, Silesians, and Kashubians), Ukrainians, Lemkos, Boykos, Greeks, and soldiers of the Red Army. All of this took place in an atmosphere of postwar trauma, loss, and surrounded by ruins and destruction from all sides.

Scars of War
Research in Political Sociology, Volume 30, 151–170
Copyright © 2025 Katarzyna Witek-Dryjańska
Published under exclusive licence by Emerald Publishing Limited
ISSN: 0895-9935/doi:10.1108/S0895-993520250000030011

Women played a significant role in the rebuilding and integration of these lands, which is why my considerations focus on how they coped with the material and social space of the "RT" from 1945 to 1949, precisely during the period of deep postwar crisis in these lands, mainly resulting from the almost complete population exchange and destruction caused by wartime and postwar actions.

Arriving in these areas, women had to leave behind their old lives and homes. After the trauma of wartime experiences, often difficult and prolonged journeys, they arrived in unfamiliar places, usually greeted by rubble and ruins. Despite such difficult conditions and experiences, they tried to create, organize, and domesticate the new space, encountering numerous difficulties along the way. Apart from the few who received well-maintained and fully equipped apartments, women, along with their families, typically found destroyed and plundered houses with piles of garbage and feces on the floors, lacking necessities for life. Wanting to acquire them to ensure decent living conditions for their families, they had to face an ethical dilemma of whether to participate in "looting," i.e. to seize the remaining German property in the absence of its owners.

Women sought to start a new life in these lands, to create a home – a safe and personal place – for themselves and their families. However, to achieve this goal, they had to undertake many difficult and demanding tasks. Specifically, I am interested in: How did women perceive domestic and material space in their new places of residence? How have they dealt with their foreignness, the abundance of some items and the lack of others essential for daily life? What relationships did they form in terms of space–things–people in the process of domestication?

The "RT" are the areas annexed to Poland in 1945 under decisions made at the Yalta and Potsdam conferences. They included territories located east of the Oder and Lusatian Neisse rivers, which prior to 1939 belonged to the Third Reich and the Free City of Danzig. From September 1945, Polish authorities began to take control over them although this did not include areas under the jurisdiction of the Red Army (Fic, 2020, pp. 11–27).

The term "RT" is not straightforward and is still widely debated among historians. This term carries numerous connotations and propaganda implications. Communist authorities emphasized this name, indicating that these territories returned to Poland after years of German bondage as *ancient Piast lands*, justifying their takeover.[1] This designation was so prevalent that after World War II, the term "RT" appeared in the official names of the most important state institutions to which these lands belonged, such as the Ministry of "RT" or the Official of the General Plenipotentiary for the "RT." Over time, this area began to be referred to as the "Western Lands" or the "Western and Northern Lands," attempting to move away from the propagandistic and hence false designation. Today, the term "RT" is still used, but quotation marks are used in its notation – a convention I also adopt – to emphasize its ambiguity (Jasiński, 2006; Osękowski, 2006; Tyszkiewicz, 2018).

The deep crisis of the "RT" after World War II was caused by many factors. One of them was the almost complete population exchange. It was mainly caused, on the one hand, by the escape, expulsion and displacement of Germans, and on the other hand, by the settlement of Polish population flowing in from various areas due to the wartime situation. Poles arrived from central Poland, the Eastern Borderlands annexed by the USSR, from forced labor in the Third Reich, and from other countries as re-emigrants. In addition to Germans and incoming Poles, autochthons should also be mentioned, including Kashubians, Masurians, Silesians, ethnic groups like Lemkos and Boykos, Ukrainians resettled as part of the "Vistula" operation in 1947, the surviving Jewish population after the Holocaust and Greek communist partisans with their families who arrived after the civil war in the years 1948–1949 (Chrisidu-Budnik, 2021, pp. 291–301). This population differed from each other in many ways, including ethnic and national origin, religion, culture, tradition, wartime experiences, attitude towards the newly inhabited lands and Poland's postwar political reality, as well as education level and proficiency in the Polish language (Fic, 2020, pp. 11–27; Osękowski, 2006).

Another important factor contributing to the crisis of the "RT" was wartime and postwar destruction. During the war, the Germans fiercely defended these territories, leading to significant destruction during the frontline actions. Equally, if not more, damaging was the passing Red Army, plundering and devastating the existing German property during and after the war, either by transporting it deep into the USSR or by destroying and setting it on fire. Further devastation and looting were also caused by numerous "looters" seizing abandoned property and enriching themselves by selling it. As settlers arrived in the "RT," they found ruins, debris and rubble in many places.

A third factor exacerbating the crisis and destruction was the sense of temporariness among the settlers. They did not believe they would stay in the new areas due to the lack of legal sanctioning of the new Polish–German border. They feared the return and takeover of the received farms by the German population, often neglecting the received property, not investing in it, and allowing it to deteriorate, awaiting a return to their old homes. This often applied to the population displaced from the Polish Eastern Borderlands. This feeling was also linked to the fact that new residents had to deal with different architecture of towns and villages, interior decoration of apartments and agricultural equipment. They were surrounded by an unfamiliar landscape, different names of towns, rivers, or streets. The local agriculture of the land was also different, requiring different management and cultivation (Mazur, 1997, p. i).

WOMEN IN THE "RECOVERED TERRITORIES": CULTURAL DOMESTICATION OF SPACE

Although the issue of the "RT" is extremely rich, it rarely presented the history of these areas from the perspective of women. Much has been written about their integration, social and political problems, often overlooking the importance of women's actions, reducing them primarily to the role of mothers and wives, rarely acknowledging their entrepreneurial and inventive everyday heroines. This approach has been changing in recent years with the development of gender studies (Bieńkowska, 2011, pp. 26–44; Helios & Jedlecka, 2018).

Czesław Osękowski wrote about the involvement of women in the settlement and integration of the "RT," indicating that they influenced these processes as political activists, scholars, journalists, civil servants, teachers, and mothers. Among the areas of women's impact on the integration of the "RT," the researcher pointed out neighborhood and family contacts, influence on their own children, schools where the majority of the staff were female teachers, as well as social organizations such as the Women's League, the Union of Military Settlers, or the Rural Housewives' Circle (Osękowski, 2006).

Izabela Skórzyńska wrote about the ethics of care and justice in women's narrative strategies, indicating how the attributed *ethics of care* to women and *ethics of justice* to men organized the experiences and language describing their relations with Germans and autochthons in the "RT." She argued that this division of care for women and justice for men is an artificial division burdened with stereotypical thinking about women's ethics in conditions of economic, social, and personal crises (Skórzyńska, 2018, pp. 355–390).

Women constituted 53% of the settlers in the "RT" in 1948 (over 276,000 more than men) (Osękowski, 1989, pp. 111–119). They arrived in the "RT" from various parts of Poland and Europe, at different ages, with different wartime and life experiences. Sometimes, they sought a new place to start a better life, while in other cases, they were forced to do so by changes in borders caused by political arrangements. They arrived with their entire families, alone, or as single mothers with children.

> Women's activity in the "RT" included, among other things, cultural domestication of space over time. This process, as Beata Halicka writes, "[...] occurs collectively in situations of total or partial population exchange and new settlement in a given area, as well as individually in the context of migration" (Halicka, 2022, pp. 184–189). It consists, following Thomas Serrier, "[...] in an individual or collective process of spatial imagination and building a mental relationship to a given space". (Serrier, 2007, pp. 15–24 in Halicka, 2022, p. 185)

New settlers arriving in the "RT" had to confront a culturally different region, significantly different from what they were accustomed to. For many inhabitants, as Beata Halicka states, this change could manifest as *cultural shock*. These individuals, torn from their previous places of residence, abandoning their homes, forced to sever their social relationships and ties, thrown into new realities and spaces, had great difficulty adjusting and establishing contact with the new environment, often found at a higher level of development, as was the case with settlers from the Eastern Borderlands. All of this was exacerbated by the depopulation of the areas, wartime destruction and uncertainty about the future. The incoming population had to learn anew to establish relationships and build a relationship with the space they encountered, that is, to culturally adapt it by modifying elements of their own culture or abandoning it under the influence of both internal (individual) factors and external (imposed by authorities/state) factors. The author provides two categories of possible attitudes towards the domestication of space by settlers: *appropriating domestication* (rejecting and historicizing) and *accepting domestication* (managing, creative, and combining them with heritagisation) (Halicka, 2022, pp. 185–187).

Małgorzata Praczyk presents a different perspective on the domestication of space in the "RT." In her research, she focuses on two aspects. The first is related to "[...] the issue of being on the road, associated with fear of the future and the fact of constantly being in a liminal phase of transition and dealing with objects" (Praczyk, 2017, p. 79). The second aspect concerns "[...] what happens to a person who settles permanently in a new spatial context, where they are forced to domesticate a new, unfamiliar space." (Praczyk, 2017, pp. 80–82). The author draws attention to the rarely discussed issue of trauma resulting from the constant necessity of movement and the perspective of abandoning and acquiring new things. She emphasizes the necessity of confronting new residents with encountered objects, non-human entities, which, as she emphasizes, have their agency and are important in the context of human experience (Praczyk, 2017, pp. 77–90). Based on the diaries of the first settlers of the "RT" and research by ethnologists from Poznań in the Nadodrze region, the researcher presents a division of spaces being domesticated by new residents into private and public, urban and rural. Furthermore, she points out the practices that these residents applied to the settled areas and the things found there, including destruction, exchange, domestication, and ignoring. (Praczyk, 2017, pp. 77–90)

SPACE AND THINGS ON "RECOVERED TERRITORIES"

Małgorzata Roeske discusses the notion of space in the context of "RT," particularly focusing on two aspects: the attic and the basement. She divides space into private and public realms and introduces the concept of *sub territory* (Korosec-Serfaty, 1984, pp. 303–321 in Roeske, 2018, p. 20), referring to the division of domestic space into specialized areas with different functions, such as bedrooms or bathrooms. Roeske examines these spaces from an ethnographic perspective, analyzing them in terms of transcendence, folk beliefs, associated mystery, time, memory, cosmic and functional space, as well as childhood imagery (Roeske, 2018). The researcher explores various scholars' approaches to the issue of space and its contents, high-lighting Martin Heidegger's view, which sees space as the relationship between humans and the surrounding world. According to Heidegger, space is produced during human existence, creating a reciprocal relationship. Humans, through their existence-in-the-world, create reality, and the world is the world only to the extent that it remains in relation to human existence (Roeske, 2018, p. 38). Roeske emphasizes that space establishes a relationship not only with humans but also with the objects within it, which, according to Roeske, based on Heidegger's arguments, give "[...] dimension to a place through the relationship it maintains with humans" (Roeske, 2018, p. 40). This perspective aligns with the trend known as the *turn to things* or *material turn*, where objects are depicted as agents of actions.

Agata Zborowska explores the role of objects in the context of their agency and migration, particularly focusing on the *abandonment* of things in the "RT" (Zborowska, 2022, pp. 573–588; 2023, pp. 578–602). Zborowska analyzes the diaries of the first pioneers, legal acts, and materials from the Film Chronicle, aiming at understanding how the looting of German property in the "RT" was perceived by those involved in these practices in the early postwar years and how objects were perceived in a migratory situation. She points out that objects undergo displacement not only due to physical space but also in legal, social, and ontological spheres. In the "RT," where stability was lacking and semi-regulated practices of both seizing and acquiring items existed, objects underwent many redefinitions. They changed their functions and meanings, closely linked to the prevalent looting practices in these areas. Zborowska analyzes the concept of *looting* in the "RT," indicating that it involved the definitive deprivation of former owners' (Germans) property rights, enabling the establishment of a new relationship with objects by Polish settlers. This was strongly associated with the language used by Polish authorities, who, in their official discourse, sought to erase relations with German-owned items (Zborowska, 2023, pp. 1–5). In their narrative, objects existed in a state of complete freedom from any social relations. In such a context, internal resistance to looting by new settlers was weaker than to ordinary theft because these items were removed from the social context of relationships. Additionally, among the Polish population, there was a strong perception of German property as compensation for the wartime losses caused by the German side. Significant in this context was the escalating official discourse of Polish authorities regarding German property in the "RT," using two terms: "left behind" and "abandoned." The former term suggests that the property was less free, as someone could return for it, while the latter implies that it was completely liberated from its German owners (Zborowska, 2023, pp. 584–586).

Agata Zborowska delves into the issue of hospitality and hostility of objects in the migratory experience in her article "Between Hospitality and Hostility: The Experience of Migration Through Things." First, the researcher points out that not only do people undergo displacement during the migration process but also the belongings they carry with them, find in their new home, purchase or steal. Second, she proposes the concept of "hospitality of things" regarding German property left in the "RT," which was transformed and utilized by the propaganda of Polish authorities. These items were presented as objects that "wait," "long," and "expect" new Polish owners. The experience of "hospitable things" arises in radically inhospitable situations in interpersonal relationships. Such an approach in these circumstances served as a defensive mechanism for Polish settlers when taking over German property, in which creating an emotional bond with the objects was crucial. However, a necessary condition for full appropriation and domestication was the absence of their former owners – Germans. The presence of owners hindered this process and portrayed the objects as inhospitable (Zborowska, 2022, pp. 574–575).

MEMORIES OF THE FIRST WOMEN SETTLERS

As part of qualitative research, I analyzed 52 memoirs written by the first female settlers in the "RT," which were submitted to the Western Institute (hereinafter referred to as WI) as part of a competition announced in December 1956. The competition encouraged new settlers from various social groups to submit memories from the years 1945–1956. The competition closed in May 1957, during which 227 memoirs were collected, of which 205 met the competition criteria. Thirty-four memoirs, primarily from social activists and activists, were distinguished and published. The remaining, mostly unpublished memoirs are located in the Archive of Western and Northern Lands at WI. They were digitized between 2013 and 2017 as part of the Institute's project under the National

Humanities Development Program. Among the authors of the memoirs are farmers, teachers, and civil servants. The length of the submitted works varies, with most ranging from a few to several dozen pages and being transcribed for competition purposes. There are also a few longer works, several hundred pages long, which are part of the authors' personal diaries. These sources are auto-biographical and narrative in nature. People and things are depicted in specific actions and relationships. These memoirs, as biographical material (ego-documents), provide a fuller insight into the postwar situation prevailing in the "RT," including the perspective of perceiving and domesticating the unknown, former German space, with a crucial role played by things.

METHODOLOGY AND RESEARCH METHODS

In my research, I rely on the biographical method as one of the qualitative research methods. It involves the analysis of personal documents such as the memoir narratives of women, the first settlers of the "RT" (Bukraba-Rylska, 2021–2022, pp. 10–34; Piorunek, 2016, pp. 7–16). These memoirs were created as part of a competition announced by the Western Institute, which is part of the long tradition of memoir writing in Polish sociology. This tradition was initiated by Florian Znaniecki, who organized the world's first scientific competition for biography – *The Worker's Own Life Story* (Kubera, 2015, p. 48). The form of the researched sources and the competitive way of obtaining them may raise questions about the authenticity of the elicited narratives. However, as pointed out by Ingeborg Helling, "Categories of truth and falsehood are not very useful in biographical research. Because the construction of meaning depends on time, interests, and the interactive situation, the same person can provide a variety of different biographies at different times and for different listeners" (Helling, 1990 in Kubera, 2015, p. 47). Therefore, the researcher does not need to confront the author's subjective assessment with data presented in other sources, especially when it comes to diaries as sources providing information that other sources do not contain, such as sociopsychological conditioning, allowing to perceive the values of individual units, enabling a deeper dive into the researched problem, and examining closely the relationships, motives, attitudes, and behaviors of the subjects (Kubera, 2015, p. 46). Thanks to them, I can examine the relationships between things, people and spaces based on data not contained in quantitative sources.

In my research, I operate with two important concepts. The first one – *space* – probably comes from the Proto-Slavic word *persterti*, meaning to spread out, extend, or lay out. I understand this concept broadly as: an unlimited three-dimensional area in which all physical phenomena occur; a part of such an area bounded by some limits; also: a place occupied by an object; an extensive, empty surface without clearly defined, visible boundaries; the distance between something and something else. The second important concept is "thing," which I understand as anything that can be the subject of sensory perception, has spatial properties, persists in time, and to which we attribute independent existence. Two connections are emphasized here: a material element of the surrounding world; an object that belongs to someone.[2]

My research is related to the topic of materiality, agency of things and the relationality of non-human entities, as discussed by Bruno Latour in the "sociology of associations," directing my attention to the relationships between diverse actors that make up and break down what is called society (Latour, 2010, pp. 231–232). Latour indicates that society emerges as a result of connections and interactions of actors forming a network. It is created not only by humans but also by non-human actors. The author points out that objects and things are part of the world inhabited by humans, but they remain in traditional history and sociology as a one-way connection between human and object. However, reality is different, and the networks of human and non-human actors make the latter mediators (endowing them with subjectivity, which means agency and effectiveness). An actor is therefore "[...] any entity that has succeeded in modifying another" and it does not have to be a living entity (Latour, 2009, pp. 163–192; Latour, 2010; Pałęcka, 2014, pp. 6–16).

Latour's concept fits into a new research trend known as the "turn to things" or "turn to materiality" (Domańska, 2008, pp. 27–59). In the literature, this trend is presented in a radical way. Convincing to me is the moderate position represented by Ewa Domańska and Björn Olsen, who write that "[...] in the mutual relations between humans and things, it is not about rejecting them or putting them on an equal footing" and advocate for "[...] a more balanced vision of reality, which [...] would depict its creation in terms of constantly evolving connections between humans and non-humans" (Domańska & Olsen, 2008, p. 91).

Hence, my questions arise: how do the authors perceive residential space in their memoirs on the "RT?" What actions do they take to familiarize themselves with it? What things do they encounter in new places? How do these things influence their perception of space? What activities do they undertake to familiarize themselves with new spaces?

To answer such questions, I conducted an in-depth analysis of two memoirs of the first settlers in the "RT."

The first one, Helena, was a repatriate from the Eastern Borderlands. She was born in Lviv and arrived in Złotów with her family, her husband – a teacher, and their 16-year-old son. Like her husband, Helena was a teacher, and upon arrival, she was involved in preparing the Złotów boarding school for future students attending the local Pedagogical Lyceum. Her memoir spans hundreds of pages and contains a wealth of detailed material related to postwar life in Złotów.

The second memoir was written by Krystyna, who arrived in the "RT" in 1947, a few years after the end of the war. She moved with her husband and children to Szczecin. The narrator mainly focused on household matters and her large group of children. In her several dozen pages long memoir, she extensively described the spaces of the successive apartments and houses she lived in.

The in-depth analysis of these two *memoirs* allows us to capture numerous spaces presented by the authors. Among them are the spaces of apartment/house, yard, garden, farm, workplace and hospital. These spaces will also appear in the memoirs of other first settlers from the collections of the Institute of Western Affairs. However, I chose the above two due to the quantity and quality of the spaces described. The diversity of descriptions in just these two personal documents would allow for a broader book publication, but I focused my work on the residential space and the things within it.

Considering the relatively short time elapsed since the memoirs were written, depicting events, people and places, I decided to anonymize the names of the authors and the surnames of other individuals mentioned in memoires. I did this by leaving only the first name and initial of the surname. I made corrections to the spelling and punctuation of the quoted excerpts, while preserving their original wording.

WOMEN PRETEND THE SPACE[...]

The analysis of the presented memoirs reveals how through their actions and activities, the authors of the memoirs created relational networks of connections with new spaces and things, in accordance with Bruno Latour's actor network theory, thereby familiarizing themselves with what was new and unknown to them.

The first stage of relationship-building began even before arriving in the "RT" and was present in the imaginations of the narrators. The first author, Helena, like many other settlers who arrived in the "RT," expressed doubts and fears about the new place in her statements: "We were traveling unknown to anyone, into the unknown" (Helena,1957, p. 5). The author's family was not only forced to leave their previous home but also to sever existing ties and relationships. Traveling into the unknown, they did not know what to expect and what situation they would encounter upon arrival. However, the author had a clearly defined goal, which was to create a new home for herself and her family. A place where her son could develop, her husband could teach, and she could work. She had certain expectations regarding the new space, which guided her actions and aspirations.

The second author, Krystyna, was very pleased upon receiving information from her husband that they would have to move due to his transfer to another workplace. She quickly began to dream about the new apartment, describing this situation as "liberation." She couldn't wait to move. As she wrote herself: "I'm so happy. I would move even this year if it were possible" (Krystyna, 1957, p. 5).The narrator was very positively disposed towards the "RT" despite warnings reaching her, and as she stated: "[...] now it is the year 1947 – the plunder is over, but as our friends claim, the Wild West still continues, where, to the scandal of the local society, we intend to move out" (Krystyna, 1957, p. 3).

Similarly to Helena, Krystyna had specific expectations regarding the new home. In her imagination, she already created the size and appearance of the apartment. Although she hadn't seen it yet, she was certain that Szczecin and its surroundings would become their new home. Thus, the women were already forming the first connections with the new space, transferring their expectations, imaginations, and desires onto it.

FIRST CONTACT WITH SPACE AND LIVING IN IT

The next stage of building relationships and connections with the new spaces involves the first real contact with them and the initial actions aimed at making them into a home space. Helena, along with her family, guided by previously set guidelines, found a single-story house in Złotów, containing two three-room apartments. In addition to the aforementioned plans and intentions, Helena also considered practical aspects, such as the possibility of bringing her extended family to the second apartment in the future. This would allow her to partially recreate the old relationships severed by the forced resettlement. The first contact with the new home was not pleasant for the protagonist and her family. Inside, they saw a huge amount of garbage and dirt:

> We started cleaning up. The garbage filled some rooms halfway up the walls. The bathtub in the bathroom was full to the brim with filth. We cleaned for a week, and I washed [...] washed [...] washed. My son and husband took out the trash. When the apartment was relatively clean, we felt a homely atmosphere. (Helena, 1957, p. 5)

The space encountered by the family was daunting. Piles of garbage and excrement transformed the house into a dump. However, the desire to have their own sanctuary, the need to create a safe place for themselves and their loved ones prevailed, providing the family with motivation for intense action. They began with thorough cleaning. They removed the obstructive and pervasive trash, cleaned the bathtub full of feces, and washed away all impurities. Cleaning took them a whole week and required a lot of effort, but through these actions, they began to interact with the existing space, gradually entering into relationships with it and with the things found there, such as garbage, which resisted them, disgusted them, required effort, and did not fit into the vision of home space. Thanks to these efforts, the previously contaminated rooms now became a space that, through further acclimating actions, could become a home for the author and her family.

The second narrator, Krystyna, couldn't immediately confront the space of the new apartment. However, this did not prevent her from taking further action to bring about this encounter. The apartment was located in a block on the first floor. The presence of the former owner prevented them from moving in immediately, as she was to vacate it shortly. Krystyna's husband was the first to move in, occupying one room and preparing everything for her arrival with the children. Despite being pregnant at the time, Krystyna was undeterred and visited to see her dream apartment. Although she couldn't fully explore it due to the presence of the previous tenant, she sought other ways to get to know the space. Visiting neighbors served as an opportunity for her to see the layout of the rooms in full. As she emphasized, "The apartment of these neighbors interested me especially because we are supposed to receive an identical one on the first floor" (Krystyna, 1957, p. 4). Through her actions, the narrator tried to give her previous imaginings of the new apartment a real picture. She did this by confronting them with the actual space, albeit not yet complete, based on the substitute provided by the neighbors' apartment. Krystyna's network of connections with the new apartment gradually began to develop, driven on one hand by her imagination and the changes proposed in them, and on the other by the presence of her husband and the bonds she shared with him, which also resonated with her vision of the ideal new home.

After six months, the narrator finally moved into the new place. Initially, along with her husband and two children, they took over one room because the previous owner, despite promises, had not yet vacated. However, the narrator emphasized, "I didn't mind it: I was finally home and I was together with Bronek. Both of us had endured the separation for almost six months" (Krystyna, 1957, p. 6).

TAMING AND SPACE

Domesticating the space meant making it feel like home, a safe and familiar environment for the arriving new families. To achieve this, the first step taken by the women in the analyzed memoirs was to organize the space. They removed items that didn't belong in a domestic setting, such as garbage and other foreign bodies, and then began to introduce new objects brought from their previous homes, utilizing what was already available or found on-site, and transforming existing items, giving them new functions and uses. In the strategies employed by women to familiarize themselves with the new space, objects became essential companions. On one hand, they supported and facilitated this process, while on the other, they resisted and hindered it.

The first things Helena encountered in her new home were garbage and impurities. Along with her entire family, she had to spend a week sorting, removing, and scrubbing the soiled surfaces. Once the spaces of both apartments in the occupied house were organized, they needed to be domesticated. To make them feel more familiar and safer, Helena and her family prepared a communal dinner:

> The first dinner in their own dining room, at a table taken from the backyard, consisted of fresh potatoes, fried eggs, and sour milk. Acquiring these supplies was not easy at the time. In the city, such items were not sold. There were no shops yet, and food was not sold because the Polish currency was not yet in circulation. Products had to be obtained by traveling far to the countryside. It was easier to get them there than to buy them. In many villages, Polish money was viewed as a novelty. (Helena, 1957, p. 13)

A table was needed for this, which they found in the backyard. One might get the impression that it stood there waiting to be used, as depicted by Agata Zborowska as "guest items" (Zborowska, 2022, p. 578). Helena did not describe the circumstances of how it ended up there, but through their actions, they restored it to its rightful place and reactivated its former functions, serving as an object for dining, gatherings, and celebrations. They had dinner at it, which made this item even more tightly woven into the network of connections and contributed to further deepening the domestic space. Especially since the meal they prepared seemed exceptional to them, given the effort put not so much into its preparation as into obtaining the products described. In the economic and social conditions surrounding them in "RT," acquiring food often posed many problems and required resourcefulness and being cunning.

Meanwhile, Krystyna and her family were forced to share the space with other subtenants, which prevented her from fully enjoying it and hindered the process of familiarization. She did not feel comfortable in it. She grew impatient with the previous tenant's delays but tried not to intrude into her living space, so she avoided using the kitchen and installed an electric stove in her room to cook freely there. In addition to the owner and the narrator's family, one of the rooms was also inhabited by a resettled person from Vilnius, who lived with them for some time after the owner moved out, thus preventing the narrator from feeling completely "at home." The space of her dream apartment was therefore divided into different zones, from private to shared and foreign areas. Full domestication was not possible, something that caused frustration in the narrator. Unlike Helena, Krystyna had limited space to act. However, she tried to subdue it to herself. She did not encounter garbage and dirt in it. However, she faced other obstacles, such as the presence of roommates. In her descriptions of the living space, Krystyna placed great emphasis on cleanliness and aesthetics. It was clearly by then that she finally obtained the two rooms previously occupied by the former owner of the apartment, an event she had long awaited. Revitalized, the space, previously blocked by the former tenant, was now freed. Krystyna could start to domesticate and familiarize herself with it, using the possessions she had. She quickly set about furnishing it:

> We arranged ourselves in a clever way because, in fact, there are hardly any furniture pieces, although we have the essentials. Two iron beds make up our bedroom. Instead of bedside tables, I placed two equal boxes covered with small rugs. There is also a three-door wardrobe... I put up curtains, rugs in front of the beds, little Marysia's crib, and Kryśka's crib for now in the pram, and the furnishing is complete. In the room opposite the kitchen, we arranged a dining area for ourselves. There stands a table assembled from two tables: an oval top, visibly once joined in the middle, placed on legs from another table. One must sit carefully at this table because when two people sitting opposite lean on it, the top bends up in the middle, and the tableware ends up on their laps. In this room, I laid down a carpet brought from home and hung up the nicest curtains. In the corner stands my sewing table with a radio on it. I turned the pull-out bed into a small sofa also using a rug. Next to it stands our lamp with a large shade. It looks very pleasant. The third room contains a white wardrobe with a mirror, a sewing machine, and a smaller oval table, visibly very old, as it's already been attacked by woodworm. However, after covering this table with an embroidered doily, as well as the one in the dining room, it's hard to guess that underneath lies an old piece. This is how we have furnished the apartment, and we are very pleased. If Mr. S. were to move out, I won't need anything to be happy. (Krystyna, 1957, p. 9)

The narrator's great joy was evident as she began to familiarize herself with the space, not only changing the function of the rooms but also placing her furniture and other items in them. She tried to conceal or replace the deficiencies and damages in the household items she possessed, using materials she had under control. The missing bed for one of the children became a stroller, and the bedside tables became "two equal boxes covered with small rugs" (Krystyna, 1957, p. 9). She covered the damaged table with a doily, which, as she herself stated, hides an old piece underneath. She hung up curtains, spread out carpets and doilies, creating a space that was acceptable and conducive to living. The only thing missing for her complete happiness was the departure of the last tenant. The apartment became her sanctuary, which she joyfully returned to. She perceived the created space as comfortable, warm, and full of sunlight.

Some items were received from others, or they were borrowed. However, not all of them brought joy and satisfaction to the authors:

> Our household has greatly enriched. I already had several plates, cups, and teaspoons, gifted to me for the new household by the postmaster. In the bedroom, two camp beds were set up. The postmaster loaned us three feather pillows. Of course, without covers. I washed their fillings, sun-dried them. We were disgusted to cover ourselves with them. From the neighbor, a local, I bought two sheets. The bedroom became bright and clean. (Helena, 1957, p. 13)

Helena assumed some of the items as a gift from a friendly Pole. These were positively received by the narrator, who described them as "enriching." However, another category was the borrowed feather pillows. These repulse the narrator's family, despite their prior washing and sun-drying. The strategies previously employed in domestication, such as cleaning and laundering, do not work in relation to the received items. The relationship with them was filled with disgust, which arose in reaction to an object that the person perceives as inherently bad. It is not simply an undesirable object that one does not want or fears to accept, but an object that is considered inherently bad (Ahmed, 2014, pp. 170–173). Sara Ahmed writes: "In the act of disgust, the body 'resists' the closeness experienced as nakedness or exposure on the surface of the skin" (Ahmed, 2014, p. 171). Therefore, the experience of disgust depends on contact, the relationship of touch, and proximity to the object. Contact perceived as unpleasant (Ahmed, 2014, pp. 170–173). Feather duvet, as a type of bedding, are very close to the human body every night. Due to their function, they become reservoirs of biological fragments of their owner, including skin, hair, sweat, or other bodily fluids.

These aspects can evoke disgust in subsequent users. However, in the postwar period, this disgust may have been exacerbated for other reasons. Feather pillows were inhuman witnesses to numerous rapes of women during and after World War II. They were transformed into bolsters. They also became breeding grounds for all kinds of bacteria, lice, bedbugs, and other vermin. Helena describes the condition of the surrounding area where the feather pillows were found in another part of the memoir: "[...] trampled, covered with garbage, feces, buried under furniture, there were still many on the frozen yards, lofts, and cellars" (Helena, 1957, p. 28). They were often torn open, and the feathers inside scattered. Then, dispersed by the wind, spread around, they seemed to encompass the entire space. The author decided to declare war on them.

> It was everywhere. Stuck, driven in, glued, overwhelmed, in corners, on ledges, on windows, on trees, on flowers, in the grass, in the pavement; countless amounts of them were everywhere. The June sun dried them out, while a gentle breeze lifted them, carried them, tossed them, settled them, lifted them again, and hurled them into other, already cleaned up places. Until I clenched my fists when a tiny scrap whirled somewhere nearby. I would look at it no differently than at a typhoid or cholera bacillus. (Helena, 1957, pp. 27–28)

Such an image of ubiquitous feathers lying everywhere could have been the cause of disgust towards specific duvets that Helena herself received, hence her obsessive desire to maintain cleanliness in the house, especially in the bedroom, a space of intimate privacy. Helena, during her further actions, also faced resistance from both things and space. Describing one of the rooms, she pointed out: "There was no space for a dresser or any other larger piece of furniture" (Helena, 1957, p. 19). This space thus forced her to change her previously planned idea, limited possibilities, and influenced the actions taken. The furniture intended for the described room had to be disassembled into smaller parts in order to be brought in, and the oversized table, due to its dimensions, remained: "In the middle of the room stood a gigantic, oval table, probably foldable in place, because there was probably no talk of carrying it out of this room, it was so huge" (Helena, 1957, p. 19). The inability to get rid of the table influenced the decision to accept it in the existing space and incorporate it into the household sphere.

This space was also enriched by salvaging abandoned items. Helena established simple rules for herself while tidying up the second home: "Anything useable or repairable to be gathered in one place. The rest, as fuel material, to be stored in the fuel chamber" (Helena, 1957, p. 19). Together with her family, they sorted, washed, and sorted items. Things were sorted, described, and assigned to new spaces, creating new connections not only with the home space but also with work and future students at the boarding school she also cared for (Helena, 1957, p. 20).

Very interesting in terms of the relationship between things, spaces, and people is the following fragment from Helena's diary:

One day, while clearing a pile of rubbish from the terrace, a worker unearthed a flowerpot with a plant inside. There was a withered stem sticking out, and surprisingly, a tiny leaf. It was the same type of plant I had left behind in distant Ukraine. For the first time, I eagerly reached out for something of former German origin. I replanted the plant in new soil, in a different pot. I watered it. I placed it by a well-lit window. The plant lived. After two weeks, a second leaf appeared. So it lived and will continue to live. It is frail and delicate – but it lives and will live. I smile at it and stroke its rough stem. I still feel that it is us, my family, taking root in this soil and starting anew. This timid leaflet is our symbol. Today, this plant is over a meter and a half tall. It has large, nine-fingered leaves. This is how we, the repatriates, take root here. This is our ancestral home, where our children grow, where we already love every inch of the land into which our sweat soaks our toil takes root. (Helena, 1957, p. 20)

Among the things being cleaned up, the woman finds a plant whose sight evokes memories of her previous home. In this regard, it provides a certain connection to the beloved former place of residence. It anchors a network linking what is now foreign, different, needing to be tamed, with what was familiar, homey. The narrator reaches for this plant. As she emphasizes, it is the first time she does so with such eagerness, indicating that in her understanding, the previous occupation of former German property, both movable and immovable, was not associated with theft or plunder.

The found plant becomes a metaphor for taming the (Ziemie Odzyskane – "RT"). The leaf symbolizes the resettlers, who, battered by the fortunes of war and decisions, initially, like it, were "meager and frail" but quickly grow, develop roots, and subdue space through hard work.

Small gestures also strongly contributed to the process of familiarizing the living space. Helena embellished her home with small things: "In the basement of the house, I found several empty jars. I filled them with roses and placed them in every room. The walls brightened up. The rooms smiled at me. The house reconciled with me. It gave up its old traditions" (Helena, 1957, pp. 20–21).

Items brought from home played a particularly important role in the process of familiarizing the living space – "our things," as Helena called them. According to the author's perception, these items, along with the presence of other Poles, accelerated the process of familiarization, dispelling the sense of foreignness and alienation from the new places: "And the little house became livelier. The atmosphere of foreignness retreated before my attack. Memories of its former inhabitants faded away. I scattered my taste, my flavor, my love of flowers throughout the rooms" (Helena, 1957, p. 20). Helena rid the house of its foreignness through her actions. She swept, scrubbed, and removed memories of the former residents left in the form of existing items, introducing her own order, sense of taste, and flavor.

Krystyna approached her belongings differently. The limited space of the room and the realities of subletting led her to decide not to bring all the previously prepared items during the move. She stated that "this and that might be acquired" on the spot (Krystyna, 1957, p. 5). She made a selection of items, guided by the living space and its surroundings that influenced her. Recognizing the advantages of the allocated garden, she quickly decided to transport the beehives. Among the remaining items, she also took the radio and sewing machine. She was guided by pragmatism in her choices.

By bringing their old belongings into the new space, the women brought with them a part of their former lives along with the relationships and associations linked to them. They brought a semblance of their previous order and life.

FRIENDLY AND TROUBLESOME HOME SPACES

The narrators gradually got to know their new homes and apartments, and the spaces and items found within them evoked both positive and negative feelings in them, becoming either friendly or troublesome elements. Krystyna, describing the reality of her first apartment in a block, was delighted with the central heating: "because it's warm without carrying out ash, bringing in coal, and coaxing the stubborn fire, which so often didn't want to ignite" (Krystyna, 1957, p. 6). On the other hand, she viewed the placement of bathrooms in the basement negatively: "It seems amazing to me that in such undoubtedly nice apartments there are no bathrooms, and you have to go to the basement to the communal bathroom. Especially troublesome when it comes to children" (Krystyna, 1957, pp. 8–9). The presented fragments indicate the relational connections observed by the author between things and spaces, and herself and her family. They allowed her to avoid certain tasks previously performed by her, but they enforced others. Thanks to central heating, the woman no longer had to carry coal into the apartment and remove ash, but the bathroom located in the basement forced her to go downstairs, which became particularly problematic when it came to bathing children. Despite serving such personal functions as washing, the bathrooms, as a communal space, were perceived by the narrators as particularly troublesome. It did not align with her previous, more friendly experiences with the space and functionality of the bathroom.

Another troublesome space for Krystyna was the stairs, which were a shared space with other residents of the apartment block. Like the other areas, this space required periodic cleaning and washing. Due to its shared use with neighbors, the responsibility for this task fell on both sides. Therefore, this space connected not only the author and her family but also neighbors, their domestic help, and the cats that had made the stairs their shelter and resting place. The trouble with this space was associated with the obligation to clean it. The narrator pointed out in her memoirs that her neighbor carefully avoided more intensive cleaning, sending her domestic help to clean two days after she had cleaned them herself. As a result, dirt accumulated again over the next 10 days, and she had to clean the worst dirt again.

Helena also described an unusual and troublesome space in her memoir. It was an Evangelical shrine "leaning," as she claimed, against the north wall of the house. It previously belonged to a German evangelical pastor who ministered to those sentenced in the nearby prison. The shrine was

> [...] dark, gloomy, the stained-glass windows bleeding with vivid red, Saturated with this atmosphere of the interior. What kind of god was worshipped there by his subjects? Some cruel, Mosaic god who established the law: an eye for an eye, a tooth for a tooth. Germanic, Teutonic god. (Helena, 1957, p. 18)

The space of the chapel, in this interpretation, represents a sacred area to which the author referred, portraying it as a place of the cruel, Germanic god who adhered to severity akin to the Code of Hammurabi. The chapel, in the woman's perception, was a gloomy and dark place. She compared the redness of the stained glass to blood, which soaked into the described space of the chapel. For the narrator, this place was profoundly inhospitable and repulsive. In her associations, she linked it to suffering and death, to which, in her perception, Germans had contributed over the centuries. The chapel activated in the woman's perception a reference to the former Germanic nature of the taken-over space, into which the narrator must put even more work, time, and effort to tame.

Changes to Living Spaces

The first homes of the narrators did not become their permanent places of residence. Both of them moved to other locations, although still within the "RT." These changes were associated with various reasons: changing jobs, a desire to improve living conditions, distance from the place of employment. Helena moved once, while Krystyna describes seven relocations in her memoir. The phenomenon of displacement and changing the place of residence in the "RT" was common and characteristic of the situation in these lands. The women did not deviate from other settlers and displaced persons in their actions. During each subsequent move, the authors faced the new challenge of abandoning their old sanctuary and creating a new, familiar place to live.

Helena did not enjoy her first home for long; she had to move to a new one quite quickly due to her and her husband's profession as teachers. She became the headmistress of a boarding school, while her husband taught at the Pedagogical High School. Wanting to be close to their workplaces to have control over everything, they moved to a house located near their educational institutions. Their new home originally belonged to a German pastor, the chaplain of prisoners staying in the nearby prison. Later, it became a warehouse for one of the looters who stored stolen German property there, and after some time, it became the home of the author and her family. As Helena wrote,

> Finally, one day I noticed that the cottage was standing open. I entered. There were a lot of damaged odds and ends, but still useable. I immediately made arrangements for the allocation of this cottage. (Helena, 1957, p. 17)

The stolen German property was removed, leaving only a portion of damaged items behind. The author quickly set to work securing the house and completing administrative tasks.

Describing the new home, the woman devoted a great deal of space and attention to its layout. She conducted a detailed analysis of its appearance, examining the walls, the arrangement of windows and doors, and the surroundings. Interestingly, in her description, she adopted the perspective of someone viewing the living area from all four sides of the world. By including descriptions of elements visible from the windows in this perspective, the perception of the living space is expanded to include broad and rich places such as the courtyard, garden, and lake. The author personified the new residence, referring to it as a "little house," describing it as "maimed" and in need of "healing." Among the areas requiring "treatment" were a trench dug from a field kitchen in the wall, a gap in the terrace floor, and a pile of rubbish in front of it. The woman quickly divided the rooms, assigned them new functions, and got to work. Krystyna, while describing the spaces of successive apartments and houses, focused mainly on their appearance, layout, and furnishings.

> The apartment exceeded all expectations. After a few steps, you enter a glassed-in porch, leading to the hallway. To the left, there's a large room which we turned into a study. From this room, you enter the next, smaller one. Straight ahead, there's a very large, bright kitchen equipped with a huge stove. From the kitchen, there's access to the bathroom and the staircase leading to the first floor where there are two rooms. One is smaller, and the other is enormous, about 7 by 8 meters, which is why Bronek called it the "riding hall." Above all this, there's a spacious attic for drying laundry. The doors to the right of the hallway lead to the five cellars: a laundry room, a cellar with compartments for potatoes, a separate one for coal, another for firewood, and finally, the last one, which houses the smokehouse. (Krystyna, 1957, p. 30)

The narrator and her family moved quite frequently due to issues related to her husband's profession, which had an impact on the quality of their life. Moreover, as they had more children, the challenges increased. After initially starting off well, they found themselves in places with lower standards. Among them were sublet spaces, which led to withdrawal, limitations in their freedom to operate, and a sense of threat, exemplified by living with someone suffering from tuberculosis.

CONCLUSIONS

Women, even before arriving in the "RT", already had certain ideas and associated feelings about the new spaces where they were to live with their families. Among them were curiosity and excitement on the one hand and fear and uncertainty about what they would find there on the other hand. Upon arriving at their new homes, they found them in various conditions. Helena, as a settler from the early postwar years, often encountered extensive damage and garbage. Krystyna, on the other hand, as a later settler, did not perceive such extensive damage in the homes she found. However, she struggled with the problem of the "inhospitality of space" due to the presence of other people – roommates.

Objects in the fragments described by the authors formed various relationships along the human–object–space line. They could be obstacles that needed to be discarded, segregated, or cleaned to give them new life, or a solution for taming and domesticating. Flowers, curtains, carpets, and doilies created a homely atmosphere and covered up what the women wanted to hide. The lack of objects motivated the narrators to seek other creative solutions, such as making furniture from boxes covered with fabric. Objects and spaces resisted not only the narrators but also each other. The space of the room did not allow for the introduction of too large furniture or forced the arrangement of things into smaller elements to carry them out.

Women tamed their new homes in various ways, starting from tidying up, cleaning, assigning them appropriate functions, spatially arranging things, and decorating them. It required hard work, but through it, they created their new world. A world that was revealed from under the pile of garbage, chaos, alienation, and otherness thanks to female orderliness and actions. Creating new relationships and connections through them.

NOTES

1. Piast dynasty – the first Polish dynasty, originating according to legend from Piast Kołodziej, historically ruled in Poland from Prince Mieszko I (approx. 960) until the end of the reign of King Casmir the Great (1370).
2. The etymology of the terms space and thing in Wielki Słownik Języka Polskiego [Great Dictionary of Polish Language] and Słownik Języka Polskiego [Dictionary of Polish Language], e-edition.

REFERENCES

Ahmed, S. (2014). Performatywność obrzydzenia [The performativity of disgust]. *Teksty Drugie, 1*, 170–173.
Bieńkowska, M. (2011). Gender i wielokulturowość [Gender and multiculturality]. *Pogranicze. Studia Społeczne, XVIII*, 26–44.

Bukraba-Rylska, I. (2021–2022). Dokumenty osobiste a doświadczenia migracji. Refleksje metodologiczne [Personal documents and migration experiences. Methodological reflections]. *Archiwum Emigracji. Studia-Szkice-Dokumenty*, *29*, 10–34.

Chrisidu-Budnik, A. (2021). Z problematyki emigracji z Grecji do Polski Ludowej [Issues of emigration from Greece to the Polish People's Republic]. *Studia nad Autorytaryzmem i Totalitaryzmem*, *43*(4), 291–301.

Domańska, E. (2008). Problem rzeczy we współczesnej archeologii [The problem of things in contemporary archeology]. In J. Kowalewski, W. Piasek, & M. Śliwa (Eds.), *Rzeczy i ludzie. Humanistyka wobec materialności* [Things and people. Humanities towards materiality] (pp. 27–59). Instytut Filozofii Uniwersytetu Warmińsko-Mazurskiego.

Domańska, E., & Olsen, B. (2008). Wszyscy jesteśmy konstruktywistami [We are all constructivists]. In J. Kowalewski, W. Piasek, & M. Śliwa (Eds.), *Rzeczy i ludzie. Humanistyka wobec materialności* [Things and people. Humanities towards materiality] (pp. 83–100). Filozofii Uniwersytetu Warmińsko-Mazurskiego.

Fic, M. (2020). Ziemie Zachodnie i Północne w Polsce Ludowej [Western and Northern Territories in People's Poland]. In M. Fic (Ed.), *Powrót do macierzy? Ziemie Zachodnie i Północne w Polsce Ludowej* [Back to the matrix? Western and Northern Territories in People's Poland] (pp. 11–27). Wydawnictwo Uniwersytetu Śląskiego.

Halicka, B. (2022). Kulturowe oswajanie przestrzeni [Cultural familiarization with space]. In E. Opiłowska, E. Opiłowska, M. Dębicki, K. Dolińska, J. Kajta, Z. Kurcz, J. Makaro, & N. Niedźwiedzka-Iwańczak (Eds.), *Studia nad granicami i pograniczami. Leksykon* [Border and borderland studies. Lexicon] (pp. 184–189). Wydawnictwo Naukowe Scholar.

Helling, I. (1990). Metoda badań biograficznych [Biographical research method]. In J. Włodarek & M. Ziółkowski (Eds.), *Metoda biograficzna w socjologii* [Biographical method in sociology] (pp. 13–38). Państwowe Wydawnictwo Naukowe.

Jasiński, J. (2006). Kwestia pojęcia Ziemie Odzyskane [The issue of the concept of the Recovered Territories]. In A. Sakson (Ed.), *Ziemie Odzyskane/Ziemie Zachodnie i Północne 1945-2005. 60 lat w granicach państwa polskiego* [Recovered Territories/Western and Northern Territories 1945-2005. 60 years within the borders of the Polish state] (pp. 15–26). Instytut Zachodni.

Kubera, J. (2015). Powieść autobiograficzna jako dokument osobisty i podobny do pamiętników konkursowych materiał badań socjologicznych [Autobiographical novel as a personal document and sociological research material similar to competition diaries]. *Studia Humanistyczne AGH*, *14*(1), 45–61.

Latour, B. (2009). Dajcie mi laboratorium a poruszę świat [Give me a laboratory and I will move the world]. *Teksty Drugie*, *1–2*, 163–192.

Latour, B. (2010). In A. Derra & K. Arbiszewski (Trans.), *Spajając na nowo to, co społeczne. Wprowadzenie do teorii aktora-sieci* [Reconnecting what is social. Introduction to actor-network theory]. Universitas.

Mazur, Z. (Ed.). (1997). *Wokół niemieckiego dziedzictwa kulturowego na Ziemiach Zachodnich i Północnych.* [Around German cultural heritage in the Western and Northern Territories]. Instytut Zachodni.

Osękowski, C. (1989). Udział kobiet w zasiedlaniu i integracji Ziem Odzyskanych [Women's participation in the settlement and integration of the recovered territories]. *Rocznik Lubuski*, *15*, 111–119.

Osękowski, C. (2006). *Ziemie Odzyskane w latach 1945-2005: społeczeństwo władza i gospodarka* [The recovered territories in the years 1945-2005: Society, power and economy]. Oficyna Wydawnicza Uniwersytetu Zielonogórskiego.

Pałęcka, A. (2014). Teoria aktora sieci jako ontologia dla socjologii wizualnej [Actor network theory as an ontology for visual sociology]. *Przegląd socjologii jakościowej*, *10*(4), 6–17.

Piorunek, M. (2016). Liczby i słowa w badaniach humanistycznych i społecznych. (Nie)dychotomiczność paradygmatów badawczych [Numbers and words in humanities and social studies. (Non)dichotomousness of research paradigms]. In M. Piorunek (Ed.), *Badania biograficzne i narracyjne w perspektywie interdyscyplinarnej* [Biographical and narrative research in an interdisciplinary perspective] (pp. 7–16). Wydawnictwo Naukowe UAM.

Praczyk, M. (2017). Strategie oswajania rzeczy na "Ziemiach Odzyskanych" ze szczególnym uwzględnieniem przestrzeni prywatnej [Strategies for taming things in the "Recovered Territories" with particular emphasis on private space]. *Miscellanea Posttotalitariana Wratislaviensia, 6*, 77–90.

Roeske, M. (2018). *Piwnica bliżej śmierci, strych bliżej nieba. Etnografia ukrytych przestrzeni domowych* [The basement is closer to death, the attic is closer to heaven. Ethnography of hidden domestic spaces]. Polska Akademia Umiejętności.

Serrier, T. (2007). Formen kultureller Aneignung: Städtische Meistererzählungen in Nordosteuropa zwischen Nationalisierung und Pluralisierung [Forms of cultural appropriation: Urban master narratives in Northeastern Europe between nationalization and pluralization]. In T. Serrier (Ed.), *Die Aneignung fremder Vergangenheiten in Nordosteuropa am Beispiel plurikultureller Städte (20. Jahrhundert)* [Appropriation of foreign pasts in Northeastern Europe using the example of multicultural cities] (pp. 15–24). Nordost-Institut.

Skórzyńska, I. (2018). Między etyką troski i sprawiedliwości. Kobiece narracje osobiste wobec polsko-niemieckich/autochtonicznych relacji na Ziemiach Odzyskanych w pierwszym dziesięcioleciu po zakończeniu II wojny światowej [Between the ethics of care and justice. Women's personal narratives towards Polish-German/autochthonous relations in the Recovered Territories in the first decade after the end of World War II]. In E. Kledzik, M. Michalski, & M. Praczyk (Eds.), *"Ziemie Odzyskane" W poszukiwaniu nowych narracji* ["Recovered territories" to search of new narratives] (pp. 355–390). Instytut Historii UAM.

Zborowska, A. (2022). Between hospitality and hostility: The experience of migration through things. *Journal of Intercultural Studies, 43*(5), 573–588.

Zborowska, A. (2023). 'Abandoned' things: Looting German property in post-war Poland. *History and Anthropology, 34*, 578-602.

NETHOGRAPY

Helios, J., & Jedlecka, W. (2018). *Urzeczywistnienie idei feminizmu w ogólnoświatowym dyskursie o kobietach* [Implementation of the idea of feminism in the global discourse about women]. E-Wydawnictwo. Prawnicza i Ekonomiczna Biblioteka Cyfrowa. Wydział Prawa, Administracji i Ekonomii Uniwersytetu Wrocławskiego.

Słownik języka polskiego [Polish Language Dictionary]. https://sjp.pwn.pl. [dostęp 7.12.2022].

Tyszkiewicz, J. (2018). Nazewnictwo terenów przyłączonych do Polski w 1945 r. – zarys problemu [Nomenclature of the areas annexed to Poland in 1945 - outline of the problem]. http://szzip.pl/pl/ziemie-odzyskane-ziemie-zachodnie-i-polnocne/

Wielki Słownik Języka Polskiego [Great Dictionary of the Polish Language]. https://wsjp.pl. [dostęp 7.12.2022].

DIARIES

Helena, B. (1957). Institute for western affairs in Poznań, archives of Polish Western and Northern Territories. *Diaries of the settlers, typescript,* 1–204.

Krystyna, T. (1957). Institute for western affairs in Poznań, archives of Polish Western and Northern Territories. *Diaries of the settlers, typescript,* 1–46.

WOMEN AND "SOLIDARITY": A SKETCH FOR THE UNION BIOGRAPHY OF EWA ZYDOREK

Weronika Halaburda

Adam Mickiewicz University, Poznań, Poland

ABSTRACT

In the article, the author presents the results of biographical research on one of the activists of the Independent Self-Governing Trade Union "Solidarity" during the period of martial law in Poland (1981–1983). The heroine of this story is Ewa Zydorek, one of many women, trade union activities, whose no less than men led to the victory of democratic opposition and sociopolitical transformation in Poland after 1989. At the same time, the roles of women and men in the prodemocratic trade union and political movement in Poland at the end of communism were different. Many women involved in this movement acted as guards and intermediaries for the interned men. When the internees were released, women moved into the background. Only some women, such as Ewa Zydorek, played an increasingly important role in the social and trade union life of independent Poland after 1989.

Keywords: Poland; Independent Self-Governing Trade Union "Solidarity"; martial law; women's of "Solidarity"; biography; Ewa Zydorek

INTRODUCTION

The word *solidarity* has not been used in my article by coincidence. For many Poles, this word has a distinctive meaning due to the nation's historical background, as well as its citizens' memory of the recent events.

Various dictionaries, by explaining the meaning of *solidarity*, redirect their readers to its synonymous expressions such as *proximity*, *intimacy*, *togetherness* or even *teamwork* (*Solidarity*, Dictionary of Polish Language PWN). Dictionary of the Polish Language defines *solidarity* as "[...] sense of community; shared

Scars of War
Research in Political Sociology, Volume 30, 171–183
Copyright © 2025 Weronika Halaburda
Published under exclusive licence by Emerald Publishing Limited
ISSN: 0895-9935/doi:10.1108/S0895-993520250000030012

responsibility which stems from the conformity of beliefs and aspirations" (*Solidarity*, Dictionary of Polish Language PWN). Another definition of this word, presented by the above-mentioned dictionary explains it as a "[...] collective and individual responsibility of a certain group of people for their whole shared commitment" (*Solidarity*, Dictionary of Polish Language PWN).

For Piotr Sztompka, a Polish sociologist, *solidarity* "[...] is a conceptual abbreviation for the entire range of important interpersonal bonds and the values and norms regulated by them. The most important are trust, loyalty, reciprocity, tolerance, readiness to cooperate, responsibility for one's word, and sense of duty towards the community" (Sztompka, 2014, p. 1). Solidarity is therefore "[...] a lasting moral tradition and social convention" (Sztompka, 2014, pp. 1–2); it is the basis of collectively practiced freedom.

Sociohistorical connotations of the word *Solidarity* in Poland, here capitalized, refer to the Independent Self-Governing Trade Union "Solidarity" [Niezależny Samorządny Związek Zawodowy "Solidarność"], which was established in 1980 as a nationwide trade union created in a socialist country. From the beginning, it was an illegal grassroots movement aimed at defending workers' rights. Initially, this movement consisted of numerous strike committees set up in different workplaces under the umbrella of the Inter-Enterprise Strike Committee in Gdańsk, first and most important Committee among all the other strike committees (Skórzyński & Pernal, 2005, pp. 17–19).

Solidarity is also an expression of the alliance of the Polish intelligentsia and workers, after the former established the Workers' Defense Committee [Komitet Obrony Robotników] in 1976 in connection with the strikes in Radom in the same year. The communist authorities punished then the workers and their families using various repressions. The Workers' Defense Committee provided legal and economic assistance to the victims of the regime. Members of the Workers' Defense Committee also publicized a case of abuse of power against striking workers and then everyone who called for the democratization of life in socialist Poland. In 1981, when "Solidarity" was registered as a legal nationwide trade union, members of the Workers' Defense Committee who participated in process of legalization of it, decided to dissolve themselves in order to cooperate with workers, uniting prodemocratic citizen movement in Poland (Lipski, 2022).

In the late 1970s and early 1980s, Poles were protesting as a result of constant worsening of their country's economic situation, which could be seen in the increase of prices within a centrally controlled market, as well as in the limited possibilities for private initiatives in this field (Kamiński, 2013, no pagination).

In 1980, when the food prices were raised once again, even though there had already been a shortage of food products, people decided to take matters into their own hands. In different parts of the country, new enterprises from various regions started entering the initiated strikes. Poland's entire attention was centered on the union members of the Gdańsk Shipyard. In August 1980, strike postulates were formulated as part of the union's preparation for negotiations with the government.[1] These *21 Postulates* had not only mentioned the economic and stock matters but also the bigger issue – the country's political situation and the changes that the strikers anticipated in this sphere. Among others, these postulates were as follows:

1. Accepting free trade unions, unrelated to both the party and employers, resulting from the Convention No. 87 of the International Labor freedoms. [...];
3. Respecting freedom of speech, press and publication granted by the Constitution of the Polish People's Republic and, at the same time, nonrepression of independent publishing houses, as well as opening mass media to the representatives of all faiths. [...]; and
6. Taking viable measures aimed at leading the country out of crisis by (a) not withdrawing any information about the country's socioeconomic state from the public.[2]

In total, 21 postulates were presented to the authorities. These days, the original document can be found in the European Solidarity Center located within the area of the Gdańsk Shipyard.

Among the employees' demands were the right to create their individual representation, as well as freedom to establish independent trade unions. According to the government, some of them undermined the existing system and, above all, the affairs of the Polish United Workers' Party [Polska Zjednoczona Partia Robotnicza], which was dependent on principals in Moscow (Skórzyński & Pernal, 2005, pp. 19–21). The range of their protests was so wide that the authorities decided to withdraw from using force even though they had done it before (1956, 1970, 1976). Therefore, negotiations began, which then led to signing the so called Gdańsk Agreement [Porozumienie Gdańskie] (Skórzyński & Pernal, 2005, pp. 19–21).

Women played a special role at that time as Solidarity activists. Among them was Henryka Krzywonos, a tram driver at the Municipal Tram Transport in Gdańsk (Strycharski, 2019), Alina Pieńkowska, since 1974 employed by the Gdańsk Shipyard, the member of the Free Trade Unions of the Coast, and editorial team of the *Coastal Worker* ["Robotnik Wybrzeża"] – newspaper created by the above-mentioned organization (Łątkowska & Borowski, 2023), and Anna Walentynowicz, an oppositional activist strictly associated with the Independent Self-Governing Trade Union "Solidarity," worker of the Gdańsk Shipyard and co-founder of Free Trade Unions of the Coast. Her dismissal from the Gdańsk Shipyard in August 1980 just before retirement was one of the reasons for initiating and continuing strikes there (Cenckiewicz, 2010).

These and other women, who got involved in the "Solidarity" movement, directly contributed to the establishment of the Independent Self-Governing Trade Union, which in the 1980s, was the biggest trade union in Poland and expressed not only of workers' opposition to the economic crisis in Poland but also of civil opposition to the regime's violations of human rights. In addition to women known for their activities in the nationwide "Solidarity" movement, there were those who were active in the regions. Ewa Zydorek was one of them. They played a special role during martial law (1981–1983).

WOMEN AND "SOLIDARITY"

The martial law was imposed on the December 13, 1981, right before Christmas. In legal terms, this was a state of emergency imposed in violation of the Constitution in force at that time, which was officially supposed to stabilize the country. In reality, however, the state of emergency was introduced to pacify the workers and Polish intelligentsia, both of whom demanded freedom and sustenance. During martial law, almost 10,200 members of the Independent Self-Governing Trade Union were interned in order to weaken and, finally, destroy the union. Among the interned more than 10,000 trade union activists, the majority were men, although there were also 1,008 women. In 1982, the regime authorities in Poland began to release women to their homes and families, while men were still imprisoned. Therefore, it was women who took on a huge part of the responsibility for "Solidarity," while also taking care of the internees (Marcinkiewicz, 2021, pp. 1–4).

What is surprising though, women's involvement in the so called "Solidarity underground" was till recently inversely proportional to the role and place that was assigned to them in history and historiography of "Solidarity." In the monograph *From Solidarity to Freedom* by Jan Skórzyński, the author listed the main "faces" of Solidarity including Lech Wałęsa, Adam Michnik, Bogdan Borusewicz, Zbigniew Bujak, Władysław Frasyniuk, and Jacek Kuroń as well, but there are almost no women on this list (Skórzyński, 2005). The other publication *They Created Solidarity. Region of Greater Poland* containing the biographical notes of 37 union activists are only three women: Bolesława Borowska, Aleksandra Karska-Zagórska and Irena Kolińska, (Kaźmierczak et al., 2010).

Because of the lack of female representation in history, authors such as Shana Penn (Penn, 2014) and Ewa Kondratowicz (Kondratowicz, 2001, 2013) decided to properly portray women's involvement in "Solidarity." Thanks to them, among others, the contribution of Polish women to the oppositional structure had been well documented and accurately described on a national scale. And more, along with research on gender history, numerous biographies and autobiographies of female "Solidarity" activists entered the publishing market. It is significant that in 2016, Polish film director and writer Marta Dzido published the book *Women of Solidarity* (Dzido & Śliwowski, 2014) and created the documentary *Solidarity According to Women* reaching also local women – activists of the union.

However, the female representation is still not well documented and portrayed on a regional and local scale. Among them is Ewa Zydorek, whose story is the primary focus of my article.

FROM THE UNION BIOGRAPHY OF EWA ZYDOREK

While I was collecting various materials for my article (2021–2022), Ewa Zydorek served as the secretary of the National Commission of the Independent Self-Governing Trade Union [Komisja Krajowa NSZZ "Solidarność"].[3] She joined "Solidarity" in 1981 as a staff of the District Film Distribution Company [Okręgowe Przedsiębiorstwo Rozpowszechniania Filmów]. In 1984 she started operating in the

Cross Company Council of "Solidarity" [Międzyzakładowa Rada Solidarności] in Poznań. In 1988, she moved to the Regional Consulting and Information Center of Greater Poland [Regionalny Ośrodek Konsultacyjno-Informacyjny Solidarności w Regionie Wielkopolskim]. Since 1989, she was responsible for coordinating the work in the department of Free Speech Association [Stowarzyszenie Wolnego Słowa] at the Temporary Regional Board in Greater Poland [Tymczasowy Zarząd Regionu w Wielkopolsce]. At the same time, as a teacher, she represented the "Solidarity" of the Primary School No. 80 in Poznań during the Assembly of Delegates of Educational Workers in the Region. Additionally, she was a chairwoman of the Founding Committee of Educational Workers [Komitet Założycielski Pracowników Oświaty i Wychowania] and continued her work for the organization as the vice president in the following years. In 1990, on behalf of "Solidarity," Ewa Zydorek became a member of both the bureau of the National Section of Education [Krajowa Sekcja Oświaty i Wychowania] and the Education Committee of the Poznań City Council [Komisja Oświaty Rady Miasta Poznania]. Simultaneously, she was a union teacher and member of the "Education for Democracy" Foundation [Fundacja "Edukacja dla Demokracji"]. In the same year, she joined the Regional Management of Greater Poland [Zarząd Regionu w Wielkopolsce]. Three years later, she became the sec- retary of this organization, and in 1992, she was appointed delegate to the National Delegate Convention [Krajowy Zjazd Delegatów]. In 1995, she joined the Statutory Committee of the Convetion [Komisja Statutowa Zjazdu], 15 years later, she became a Vice President of this Committee. Since 1999, she was a member of the National Commission of "Solidarity" [Komisja Krajowa] serving as its secretary since 2010. On top of that, in 1999, on the recommendation of the Solidarity Electoral Action [Akcja Wyborcza "Solidarność"], she entered the Advisory Board [Rada Pro- gramowa] for the Poznań department of Polish Television. Since 2003, Ewa Zydorek served as member of the Advisory Board for a weekly magazine "Solidarity" ["Solidarność"]. Seven years later, she was appointed chairwoman of this board. In 2011, she became: a chairwoman of the Council of the Economic Foundation [Rada Fundacji Gospodarczej] in Gdynia, vice-president of the Solidarity Center Foun- dation [Fundacja Centrum Solidarności] and member of the Council of the Euro- pean Solidarity Center [Rada Europejskiego Centrum Solidarności]. Since 2013, she served as chairwoman of the National Electoral Commission of Solidarity [Krajowa Komisja Wyborcza "Solidarności"]. In 2016, she became a vice president of the Company Supervisory Board [Rada Nadzorcza Spółki] for Tysol, an enterprise which was a publisher of the weekly magazine "Solidarity" mentioned before. Undoubtedly, Ewa Zydorek was, and still is, a woman of "Solidarity." She can even be called one of the most important figures of this union.

EWA ZYDOREK: (AUTO)BIOGRAPHICALLY ABOUT "SOLIDARITY" DURING MARTIAL LAW

In order to expand my research on Ewa Zydorek's union biography, I have conducted more interviews with her. Thanks to these interviews, we were once again able to travel back in time to her life as a member of the Independent

Self-Governing Trade Union. This was during martial law, at the time when the Union was being created and the government authorities were trying to pacify this process.

During our conversations, Ewa Zydorek admitted that martial law put her back on track. For her, this was a moment of mobilization in which she understood that she could no longer be just an observer.

> [...] And, actually, Solidarity woke me up, put me back on track. By this I mean, to be honest, Poland under martial law. I felt that I needed to do something. [...] My turning point was, I believe, the year 1981. [...] This was when I became really active! (Zydorek, 2022)

> [...] I felt as if this had passed me by, that I did not do anything about this matter. I felt somehow[...] empty inside. Damn it, why?! Martial law pushed me into taking some actions. (Zydorek, 2022)

Ewa felt as if an important part of history was slipping through her fingers. She was under the impression that she was missing out on something, she felt some kind of a void. On the other hand, signing the Gdańsk Agreement in 1980 and then the year 1981 when she joined the Union were the years of her awakening. Her political awareness was born:

> I remember sitting in front of the television, crying helplessly. Probably I was beginning to understand what this is about. [...] That something important happened, these are big historical events. History is being made in front of us, but this breakthrough[...] I think it got to me what this system that is holding us here really is. (Zydorek, 2022)

Ewa Zydorek took the actual actions to support "Solidarity" before introducing martial law. Among others, she participated in the action "We will get off the walls once we find our way to the radio and television." By this, the activists aimed to gain access to the mass media. They were painting and writing on the walls, hanging up posters, distributing leaflets. Moreover, the strikers recorded a short video for the purpose of this action, which was then broadcast before film shows in cinemas. Daily, Ewa Zydorek kept minutes of the meetings of the "Solidarity" Trade Union Committee [Komisja Zakładowa NSZZ, "Solidarność"]. She was in charge of providing information, including rewriting and distributing announcements of the Regional Board [Zarząd Regionu]. As Ewa mentioned, she did not know what to do and how to behave after introducing martial law in Poland. At first, as a sign of her disapproval of the oppressive government at that time, she was drawing pictures of snails on fogged-up tram windowpanes. This was a call for keeping it slow at your workplace. In the meantime, Ewa, together with her later husband Julian Zydorek, who was "Solidarity" activist, member of the editorial board of an informative and journalistic magazine "Rezonans" and member of Greater Poland's Defence Committee for citizens imprisoned for their beliefs started carrying out opposition activities (Zwiernik, 2023; Łuczak, 2023, no pagination). These activities involved printing, publishing and distributing opposition magazines such as the "Rezonans." She claimed that at that time, every opportunity was good enough to get under the government's skin. For instance, in the 1980s, Ewa came inside one of the grocery stores in her neighborhood and spotted a number of one-sided credit card-sized calendars. Since there was plenty of room to note something down on the reverse, she decided to buy them all.[4]

[...] While still living in Winogrady [a district in the city of Poznań], I was wandering [...] near the former dorms of the School of Agriculture [Szkoła Rolnicza]. There was some kind of a stationery store. I do not remember why I came inside, but I did. I noticed tiny calendars of the National Publishing Agency [Krajowa Agencja Wydawnicza] which on one side [...] had a calendar but on the other side were empty. My goodness[...] I bought them all. [...] Wojtek Wołyński drew an image of Lech Wałęsa making the so called "Kozakiewicz" gesture. And there we were, in Julian's basement, printing the calendars [...]. (Zydorek, 2022)

Despite the differences in the importance of various opposition activities, many of them could not escape from repression. Julian, Ewa Zydorek's later husband, was interned on the first day of martial law. Since then, he was transported from one place to another multiple times. First, they imprisoned him in Gębarzewo. Then, he was put in custody in Ostrów Wielkopolski and Kwidzyń. He also spent some time at a hospital in Gniezno. Julian's absence caused Ewa to become more active, thanks to which she met almost the whole elite of the Independent Self-Governing Trade Union in Greater Poland. Whenever visitors came to the solitary facilities, all conversations were basically only about what was happening on the outside. People were thinking through new plans for future actions. Women, who were frequently visiting the places of retreat, as well as keeping in touch with the people kept there, were those who shared information about what was happening in the real world, in the Union and with the other internees prisoned in other parts of country. Additionally, women were also communicating with the outside world. They shared verbal information and the internees' messages. Moreover, they were disclosing what was happening in the places of retreat. Ewa Zydorek keeps up until this day the message her later husband wrote by him when he was interned in such a place of retreat (Zydorek, 2022).

Visiting the internees was not safe and practically impossible for bystanders. Ewa, when meeting with Julian, had to pretend to be his sister as the couple was still to be married at that time. To avoid arising suspicion from the authorities, she learned by heart all of his sister's personal details. This was also how she met her later husband's family (Zydorek, 2022).

After Julian came back from the place of retreat (on the 4th of December 1982), the help for those who remained there grew even more. The couple kept their house open to those associated with the underground. Additionally, Ewa was taking care of distributing protective clothing and food stamps as part of her work at the supply department of the economic section of the District Film Distribution Company in Poznań (Zydorek, 2007 in Olaszek, 2007).

Women were extremely helpful to each other. In addition to sharing information about the country's political situation, they also brought news from the internees to their families and vice versa. Since daily contact with the internees was not possible, food parcels were often passed between the visitors and then delivered to the interned. Alcohol, then seen as a symbol of freedom, was also being smuggled. Contact with the internees' families was maintained and women played one of the most important roles in this. Henryka Krzywonos was one of the women who helped in this way. Grażyna Kuroń, who was an oppositional activist actively supported the actions of the Workers' Defence Committee, because her husband, Jacek Kuroń, was interned in Gołdap and Darłówko. She had been an internee herself but was released due to illness and, drawing from her own experiences, she was teaching other women how to take care of the internees. This included showing them how to write appeals, how to send parcels and letters as well as advising on which regulations to learn and highlighting the ones that were particularly important (Skrzydłowska-Kalukin, 2011).

Even though this mutual assistance may sound like a carefree, solidary cooperation, there were some tragic moments as well. Women had to support each other during these difficult times. Internees were beaten in the places of retreat. These beatings also happened when Julian was kept in one of them. One time, when Ewa was visiting him there, the Motorized Reserves of the Citizens' Militia (ZOMO)[5] [Zmotoryzowane Oddziały Milicji Obywatelskiej], together with their dogs, were surrounding the prison yard. They were accompanied by a large number of crying, devastated women who had been waiting there since the previous day, just to see their family members. One of Ewa's friends from the opposition told her that the day before, there were ambulances leaving the building one after another. Had it not been for Ewa's strong personality, she would not have been able to see Julian that day. She was allowed to enter the place of retreat only after getting into a terrible fight with one of the commandants.

Daily life under martial law was also about women using their work connections in order to help. For around four years, from 1982 to 1986, Ewa Zydorek was working as a medical assistant in the Institute of Orthopedics and Rehabilitation of the Medical Academy [Instytut Ortopedii i Rehabilitacji Akademii Medycznej] in Poznań. During that time, Franciszek Kuźma, one of her interned friends, was sent to the Institute and, thanks to Ewa, was able to escape from the hospital. She could have lost her job but still decided to help – aware of how important this is for the Union activists and their families. Ewa was wondering for a long time why this situation had never come to light. Only after some time, she learned that the person held accountable for her actions was the director of the ward where Kuźma was hospitalized (Fabiańska & Szwochert, 2022; Zydorek, 2007 in Olaszek, 2007; Zydorek, 2022).

As I have mentioned before, Ewa and Julian allowed people involved with the underground to stay at their place. In the interviews, they used to call their apartment at that time an "open house." Back then, they used to work for the Union during late evenings and nights, as they still had to find time for ordinary work and daily life. There was a reason why Ewa mentioned that while others were busy with setting up their lives, they were fighting communism (Zydorek, 2007 in Olaszek, 2007). Other women and families intertwined with "Solidarity" shared the same experience. For instance, Gaja Kuroń whose husband put the *revolution of freedom* before her and their son (Skrzydłow-Kalukin, 2011, pp. 12–13). What is more, home was not always a safe haven. Searches conducted by security forces [Służby Bezpieczeństwa], surveillance and spying on the homeowners were all very common.[6] Ewa Zydorek mentioned how scared she was back then. She admitted that she was suffering from anxiety and mental exhaustion. This whole invigilation happened despite the fact that Julian did teach her how to avoid the security officers. Over the years, while going through documents stored in the Institute of National Remembrance [Instytut Pamięci Narodowej], she learned that there were security officers conducted at their apartment when they were not there as well as that a wiretap had been planted inside their house.

> It hit me. It really hit me! Not even because of the wiretap, but because of the searches. For me it was unbelievable. This was such an awful thing, being aware of the fact that, without my supervision, some strangers were walking around my apartment and going through my stuff, underwear and God knows what else[...] it's hard to imagine how humiliating it was. (Zydorek, 2022)

Once, Ewa let the so called *sad men*[7] into her house voluntarily. It was very early, around six a.m., and Ewa was still drowsy. She glanced through a peephole and assumed that one of the men was her brother-in-law. Only after she opened the door did she realize that this was not him. It was already too late though. More security officers came out of hiding. During the interview, she explained the situation:

> [...] I remember the time when my home was being searched. Unfortunately, I let the *sad men* into my house. How did they behave? Really well. But still, they were checking out every corner. Every single thing was taken out and thoroughly examined. Just horrible. (Zydorek, 2022)

Apparently, they found many things which proved Ewa and Julian's involvement in illegal activities. Ewa could not forgive herself:

> How come [...] Julian had trained me so well! They will not force the door. You are not home. You do not answer the door, just like that. [...] That is why we have doors – to keep them closed. (Zydorek, 2022)

Unlike other women of "Solidarity," Ewa had never been questioned. Henryka Krzywonos, for example, had been so badly beaten during the questioning that her health considerably worsened. Plus, she suffers from the effects of these beatings up until today. Her husband, Krzysztof Strycharski, wrote about this in his book devoted to his wife's opposition activities (Strycharski, 2019, pp. 49–51). Additionally, the publication mentions that after the hearings, Henryka was banned from working in the Republic of Poland and forced to leave Gdańsk, the city in which she lived at that time (Strycharski, 2019, pp. 49–51).

After Julian Zydorek left the next place of retreat that he had been sent to earlier, the publishing process of an underground monthly magazine "Rezonans" began. Julian was the publisher of this magazine and, what is more, a co-creator of "Awers" publishing house. However, he could not have done this alone. Again, Ewa was there to help. She used to type the articles that were later published in the magazine. She made important publishing decisions. She was describing individual demonstrations, adding some things, searching for quotes, creating descriptions and coming up with jokes. All of these actions were supposed to encourage people to keep buying the magazine. Her work was priceless and greatly influenced the whole magazine. As a part of the magazine, Ewa and Julian created a series of stories with a funny title *How to Push a Trooper to Make a Blooper* ["Jak z łupka zrobić głupka"]. The main idea of the series was to teach its readers how to behave during questioning (Zydorek, 2007).

Ewa was also taking care of distributing the magazine. While she was collecting the copies, she also received clear, ready to use instructions on which taxi to take and where to go next in order to distribute the copies among the union activists. Ewa mentioned that this task often evoked many emotions. She remembers that one day, an FSO Polonez cut the taxi driver's way. This car model was the most popular among the *sad men*. It turned out to be a sheer coincidence but still caused Ewa a lot of distress (Zydorek, 2007 in Olaszek, 2007). However, she had never been caught distributing the magazine.

Julian kept preparing Ewa for the possibility of even more security officers. She had the texts ready and knew exactly what to do in order to keep the magazine running. When men were being interned, women had to know what to do next. This was all based on knowledge and cooperation but also on the women's self-reliance.

During the interview, Ewa Zydorek mentioned her sister G., who was a mother of three at that time. Even though she could not engage in the opposition activities fully due to maternity, she tried to help as much as possible. For example, she participated passively in different kinds of demonstrations against the authorities. She did it as a sign of protest, as well as to show her solidarity with the people who were active protesters. Additionally, her apartment was open to Ewa, so that she could rewrite articles for the underground magazine there. Moreover, Ewa kept additional copies of the magazine in the apartment (Zydorek, 2023). R., her sister's husband, knew how to make tightly sealed foil packaging. He used an iron for this. Sealed packages were then hidden on a special shelf inside the furnace. The shelf was high enough to keep the packages away from fire. They used this place for storing things from Ewa's office that had to be hidden at the news of a threat of martial law. Back then, Ewa came into her own house and felt helpless. She knew that the only people she could turn to were G. and R. (Zydorek, 2023). When talking about her sister's involvement, Ewa mentioned also that she "[...] carried some leaflets, as it usually was [...] in a stroller" (Zydorek, 2023). Therefore, even though Ewa's sister had children whom she always put first, there was no doubt whether or not she should be getting involved in the country's political affairs.

In an interview, Ewa a particular number of female voters were needed for the city council elections in Poznań in 1989. Maciej Frankiewicz, oppositional activist a co-organizer of strikes involving higher education institution and co-founder of the oppositional printing houses (Fabiańska, 2022), later elected vice president of the Poznań, asked G., Ewa's sister, to sign the list. Ewa could not explain why he chose her sister over her, as she was definitely better known by the opposition than G. She told me that Frankiewicz "met my sister through me so he had to have some trust in her. Maybe they were doing something there [...]. It never occurred to me to ask" (Zydorek, 2023).

CONCLUSIONS

The women of "Solidarity" were undoubtedly part of the avant-garde of the Union movement, which led to them leaving a lasting mark on the organization's history. However, neither historians nor the women themselves had noticed the importance of their involvement in overthrowing communism in Poland. They marginalized their role in this process. Ewa Zydorek explained that she does not regret any of her actions in the 1980s. What she does regret, however, is not doing more, not giving more of herself. Throughout her whole life, she believed, just like her mother, that our life's purpose is to serve others and that it is worth helping even one person. Ewa said that "[...] my mom made me serve the world, she used to say that we live mostly for others, not for ourselves" (Zydorek, 2022). It was also her mother who pushed her to get involved with the Union. Even though, Ewa still thinks that Julian was the star. She was just standing by his side – as a devoted wife, his right hand, his help and support during the Union activities. Is it a bad thing, though? Is it really important who initiated the actions and who was co-implementing them? It seems much more important, for cognitive reasons as well, who actually talks about the actions. Do women of "Solidarity" use their own voice, or are they represented by someone? If so, is this representation their own choice or the choice made by bystanders, chroniclers and "Solidarity" historians – who are unwilling to allow women to share their common heritage which, undoubtedly, "Solidarity" still is in Poland. It is not a coincidence that other women, like previously mentioned Shana Penn, Ewa Kondratowicz or Katarzyna Skrzydłowska-Kalukin and, lately, Marta Dzido were the first to fight for the women of "Solidarity." For the same reason, my article was created as kind of tribute to women of "Solidarity," especially during the martial law when the fate of "Solidarity" was at stake and when women's solidarity prevented a catastrophe.

NOTES

1. 21 postulatów z 17 sierpnia 1980 roku, [21 postulates of the 17th August 1980], [https://www.solidarnosc.org.pl/21-postulatow].

2. In total, 21 postulates were presented to the authorities. These days, the original document can be found in the European Solidarity Center located within the area of the Gdańsk Shipyard.

3. Information regarding Ewa Zydorek comes from three interviews conducted by the author of this article. The interviews occurred on: the 28th of July 2022, 26th of January and 31st of January 2023. Ewa Zydorek gave full permission to quote interviews for scientific purposes. The narrator's consent to the scientific use of fragments or the entire interview is held by the author of the text.

4. In the People's Republic of Poland, paper was rationed and publications censored. That's why it was so difficult to publish materials in the second circulation. Small calendars, where the reverse was not printed, were used to print prodemocracy slogans outside state control.

5. Formed in 1956, after the 1956 Poznań protests. Their main role was to keep order, which meant using violence to suppress any public gatherings, e.g. strikes against the government. ZOMO was a strictly anti-oppositional institution.

6. Security forces (Polish: "Służby Bezpieczeństwa") served as a strictly oppositional security system in the Polish People's Republic. This system was created in the year 1956.

The forces' main role was to keep citizens under surveillance, both in the country and outside of Poland.

7. A colloquial joke about the secret officers.

REFERENCES

Cenckiewicz, S. (2010). *Anna Solidarność. Życie i działalność Anny Walentynowicz na tle epoki (1929-2010)* [Anna andsolidarity. The life and actions of Anna Walentynowicz in the years 1929-2010]. Zyska i S-ka Wydawnictwo.

Dzido, M. (2016). *Kobiety Solidarności* [Women of Solidarity]. Świat Książki [World Book].

Kaźmierczak, K. M., Kmiecik, S., Kretkowska, K., & Talaga, P. (2010). *Oni tworzyli "Solidarność". Region Wielkopolska* [Theycreated solidarity. Region of Greater Poland]. Polskapresse.

Kondratowicz, E. (2001). *Szminka na sztandarze. Kobiety Solidarności 1980-1989. Rozmowy* [Lipstick on a banner. Women of solidarity in the years 1980-1989. conversations]. Wydawnictwo Sic! [Sic! Publishing House].

Kondratowicz, E. (2013). *Być jak narodowy sztandar. Kobiety i Solidarność 1980-1989* [Being like a national banner. Womenand solidarity inthe years of 1980-1989]. Wydawnictwo Naukowe Scholar [Scientific Publishing House Scholar].

Lipski, J. J. (2022). *KOR: A history of the workers' defense committee in Poland 1976-1981*. Aneks Publishers.

Penn, S. (2014). In M. Antosiewicz (trans.), *Sekret "Solidarności". Kobiety, które pokonały komunizm w Polsce* [Solidarity'ssecret: Thewomen who defeated communismin Poland]. Grupa Wydawnicza Foksal [Foksal Publishing Group].

Skórzyński, J. (2005). *Od Solidarności do Wolności* [From solidarity to freedom]. Wydawnictwo Trio [Trio Publishing House].

Skórzyński, J., & Pernal, M. (2005). *Gdy niemożliwe stało się możliwe. Kalendarium Solidarności 1980-1989* [When impossible became possible. The calendar of Solidarity in the years 1980-1989]. Bertelsmann Media.

Skrzydłowa-Kalukin, K. (2011). *Gajka i Jacek Kuroniowie* [Gajka and Jacek Kuroń]. Wydawnictwo Czerwone i Czarne [Red and Black Publishing House].

Strycharski, K. (2019). *Warsaw. Moja żona tramwajarka. Opowieść o Henryce Krzywonos-Strycharskiej* [My wife the tram driver. The story of Henryka Krzywonos-Strycharska]. Wydawnictwo Książkowe [Book Publishing House].

Sztompka, P. (2014). Wolność i solidarność [Freedom and solidarity]. *Kultura Liberalna, 269/36*, 1-6. Fundacja Kultura Liberalna [Liberal Culture Foundation].

NETOGRAPHY

21 postulatów z 17 sierpnia 1980 roku [21 postulates of August 17th 1980]. https://www.solidarnosc.org.pl/21-postulatow

Fabiańska, B. (2022). Frankiewicz Maciej Krzysztof. https://encysol.pl/es/encyklopedia/biogramy/15827,Frankiewicz-Maciej-Krzysztof.html

Fabiańska, B., & Szwochert, P. (2022). *Kuźma Franciszek*. https://encysol.pl/es/encyklopedia/biogramy/17173,Kuzma-Franciszek.html

Kamiński, Ł. (2013). *Sierpień '80* [August '80]. https://polskiemiesiace.ipn.gov.pl/mie/wszystkie-wydarzenia/sierpien-1980/historia/115528,Sierpien-80.html

Łątkowska, M., & Borowski, A. (2023). *Pieńkowska Alina*. https://encysol.pl/es/encyklopedia/biogramy/18114,Pienkowska-Alina.html

Łuczak, A. (2023). *Wielkopolski Komitet Obrony Więzionych za Przekonania* [Greater Poland's Defence Committee for citizens imprisoned for their beliefs]. https://encysol.pl/es/encyklopedia/hasla-rzeczowe/14712,Wielkopolski-Komitet-Obrony-Wiezionych-za-Przekonania.html.

Marcinkiewicz, M. (2021). *Internowanie kobiet w stanie wojennym* [Internment of women during martial law]. https://ipn.gov.pl/pl/historia-z-ipn/155840,Marta-Marcinkiewicz-Internowanie-kobiet-w-stanie-wojennym.html

NSZZ "S" [NSZZ "S"]. https://www.solidarnosc.org.pl/o-nszz-solidarnosc/o-nszz-solidarnosc/kim-jestesmy

"Solidarność" Encyclopedia PWN. https://encyklopedia.pwn.pl/haslo/solidarnosc;3977446.html

"Solidarność" The dictionary of Polish language PWN. https://sjp.pwn.pl/sjp/solidarnosc;2575796.html

"Solidarność": synonym. https://synonim.net/synonim/solidarno%C5%9B%C4%87

Zwiernik, P. (2023). Rezonans Poznań. https://encysol.pl/es/encyklopedia/hasla-rzeczowe/23900,Rezonans-Poznan.html

INTERVIEWS

Zydorek, E. (2007, 13 May/10 August). Interview by J. Olaszek Archiwum domu Spotkań z historią. Ośrodek KARTA. Archives of the History Meeting House, KARTA Center, Warsaw.

Zydorek, E. (2022, 28 July). Interview by W. Halaburda. Halaburda W., private archive.

Zydorek, E. (2023, 31 January). Interview by W. Halaburda. Halaburda W., private archive.

DOCUMENTARY

Dzido, M., & Śliwowski, P. (dir.). (2014). *Solidarity according to women.* The Adam Mickiewicz Institute and Silesia Film.

Printed and bound by CPI Group (UK) Ltd, Croydon, CR0 4YY

25/03/2025

14647588-0002